Modern
DRAMA

FROM IBSEN TO FUGARD

TERRY HODGSON

Modern
DRAMA

FROM IBSEN TO FUGARD

B. T. Batsford·London

© Terry Hodgson 1992
First published 1992

Typeset by J&L Composition Ltd, Filey, North Yorkshire
and printed by Dotesios Ltd, Trowbridge, Wilts

Published by B. T. Batsford Ltd
4 Fitzhardinge Street
London W1H 0AH

A CIP catalogue record for this book is available from the British Library

ISBN 0 7134 6243 4

Contents

The theatre has been created to teach us that the sky can fall on our heads.

Antonin Artaud

We are in the grip of forces . . . (Character in *The Silence*.)

Ingmar Bergman

When a family is ruined I don't seek the reason in an inexorable fate, in hereditary weakness or special characteristics, but try to establish how it could have been avoided by human action.

Bertolt Brecht

. . . the dizziness of freedom when freedom looks down into its own possibilities . . .
Every tension can have two different effects. It can reveal the strain that it creates, but it can also do the opposite; it can conceal the strain, and not only conceal it, but constantly transform it, change and transfigure it into lightness. Thus the lightness is invisibly grounded in the strain produced by the tension, but this strain is neither seen nor suspected; only the lightness is revealed . . .

Soren Kierkegaard

What an imposition! Hundreds must hold their breath just to hear one egocentric actor air his soul!

Erwin Piscator

Acting is like holding a bird in the hand: if you close your hand too tightly, the bird will be killed; if you open it too much, the bird will fly away.

Michel Saint-Denis

Here is a circle [running a finger round the edge of a glass]. In the centre is a superobjective. It is the circle of your life – the role. Life begins here, and death . . .

Konstantin Stanislavski

Although it might be possible to regard other people as wholly causally determined, it would be very difficult to see oneself in the same light.

Mary Warnock

Determinism is one of the great alibis pleaded by those who cannot or do not want to face the facts of human responsibility, the existence of a limited but nevertheless real area of human freedom, either because they have been too deeply wounded or frightened to wish to return to the traffic of normal life, or because they are filled with moral indignation against the false values and the, to them, abhorrent moral codes of their own society, or class, or profession and take up arms against all ethical codes as such, as a dignified means of casting off a morality which is to them, perhaps justifiably, repulsive.

Isaiah Berlin

There is a real barrier in the mind which at times it seems almost impossible to break down: a refusal to accept the creative capacities of life; a determination to limit and restrict the channels of growth; a habit of thinking indeed that the future has to be determined by some ordinance in our own minds.

Raymond Williams

External freedom is worth nothing without inner freedom.

Erich Fromm

To genuine tragic action it is essential that the principle of individual freedom and independence, or at least that of self-determination, the will to find in the self the free cause and source of the personal act, and its consequences, shall already have been aroused.

Hegel

To think of representation is to think of tragedy, not as a representation of fate but as the fate of representation.

Jacques Derrida

Acknowledgements

Acknowledgements are due to my family and to generous friends and colleagues, actors, publishers and teachers, who read sections of the manuscript, gave advice and lent support. They include Tony Seward, Bernard Gallagher, Tony Inglis, Michael Jamieson, Gough Quinn, Richard Reynolds, Martin Ryle, Cliff and Joan Skeet, Silvia Vickers, Cedric Watts and Carole and David Walton. The burden of errors that remain is mine.

This book is dedicated to my mother and Anne, Claire, Tess and Stephanie.

The four plates illustrate something of the transition from the spectacular theatre of the nineteenth century, with its emphasis on heavy scenery, to the new, intimate fourth wall theatres of Antoine and Strindberg, to the variety of staging whereby twentieth-century theatre has sought to establish new (and recover old) actor/audience relations.

Behind the scenes during a play. Note the method of lashing the wing-pieces to the masts rising through the floor-grooves. [From Laumann's *La Machinerie au Théâtre.*]

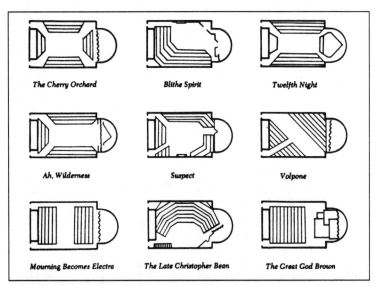

The Cherry Orchard   *Blithe Spirit*   *Twelfth Night*

Ah, Wilderness   *Suspect*   *Volpone*

Mourning Becomes Electra   *The Late Christopher Bean*   *The Great God Brown*

Preface

This book has a number of aims. It seeks for the benefit of all who care for the theatre, whether their aim is to watch, perform in, teach or write about it, to trace and define the different twentieth-century dramatic forms up to the explosion of 'fringe' drama in 1968. Post 1968 theatre and drama is referred to but detailed discussion will be reserved for a forthcoming full volume on the contemporary scene.

The book pays attention to performance as well as to selected forms and themes, hoping in the process to close the still regrettable gap between those who work in the theatre and those outside who teach and study it. The plays and authors discussed have been chosen for several reasons: they throw light on the evolution of modern forms of theatre; they are for the most part still performed; and they retain their interest for different kinds of theatre student, from sixth formers and graduates to drama school students and experienced theatre-goers. A theory of drama underlies the discussion of these plays but care has been taken to avoid falling into abstraction or treating the plays as dead relics. Plays of value have a living form and the book attempts to do some justice to this.

The book takes modern terms such as: 'naturalist', 'expressionist', 'epic', 'absurdist', 'theatre of cruelty', as well as the more general categories of farce, melodrama, tragedy, comedy and tragi-comedy, applying them to styles within a single play, or to different plays in parallel or subsequent theatre movements. The discussion of naturalism is especially important

1

since it is the dramatic movement against which other forms rebel.

A central theme of the book is freedom. It holds together the various and necessarily condensed discussions of individual plays and genres. Every emergent dramatic form seeks to free itself, for aesthetic, psychological, political or other reasons, from the dominant forms of the time. Since tensions between freedom and restraint also exist *within* dramatic forms as within the historical process from which they emerge, within the author who selects the form, between the characters who inhabit those forms and within the spectators who respond to the characters' predicaments, the theme is central. Indexes of critical books surprisingly make little mention of it, perhaps because its obviousness tempts the critic into platitudes. This danger, I hope, has been avoided by combining discussion of theme and form, relating it to questions of 'play', imagination and creativity.

It was originally intended to limit the book to a discussion of post-war British drama, but the latter is hard to discuss without defining important theoretical developments earlier in the century. Inclusion in the first half of the book of continental as well as British material seemed more important than an attempt to deal in detail and in too short a space with the proliferation of drama in the post-1968 period (since European movements early in the century form a basis for recent drama also).

Throughout I have tried to enliven the survey material with selective description and analysis, concentrating on a number of important plays and placing them within a chronological framework which shows them both reacting against and moving in parallel with one another. The selection of plays may be seen as obvious, or idiosyncratic, or both. Yet one cannot ignore well-known plays which have helped to form the modern theatre. I hope they receive some freshness of treatment and that any personal choices help to enliven what could become, in the restricted space, too abstract, too simple or too solemn an account.

The book aims to convey some of the rich simultaneity of dramatic performance. It constantly assumes that a script may be illuminated by voice and dramatic style, gesture, movement, use of colour and setting, the handling of props and costume and other theatrical signs. The choice of these in mutual interaction is a source of energy and enjoyment. Theatre should never be solemn, says Peter Brook, and critical accounts must try to be serious without forgetting that theatre is a species of 'free' play, and all accounts of it personal.

If this book defines some of the complex interplay occurring during writing, rehearsal and performance, its canvas is too broad to attempt any full definition of interchanges between the dramatist, theatre architect, media engineers, social administrators, institutional structures, public legislators and theatre public. This interplay of power is important but I have been able to make only occasional sallies into such territory. There has in any case been much recent critical emphasis on the theatre's relation to social and political power. I felt it important to retain a sense of this whilst emphasizing that a play is a creative game played by characters who may or may not speak, who give meaning to each other's speech and predicament by the way they move, grimace, stand, dress, and gesture. Too much academic writing about theatre still treats it as literature. It remains important to focus on the creative theatrical process whilst remembering its embodiment of serious human concerns.

The book derives from experience of running drama classes and workshops, from experience of acting, writing and directing, as well as from university seminar teaching. If such experience shows that creativity and intellectual analysis do not always run together, it also reveals how stimulating and valuable it is to attempt both. Each form of consciousness has its own validity. The processes meet in the head of the director and if both actor and student can reconcile them so much the better.

Those who work in the theatre may not analyse their functions, or the political and dramatic structures they work within, in the same way as students and academics. They are right to be cautious of academic analysis for it can dissipate creative energy. In rehearsal, individual presence and personal relations are crucial. Whilst masks are being adjusted performers are particularly vulnerable and the moment to ask 'why?' must be carefully chosen. Intellectual analysis can devastate. It can also be seized on as a defence and inhibit creativity.

This is not to say that a developed theory of the function of theatre cannot also energize, as was the case with Brecht. But even Brecht's analytical theatre depends on actors who must learn to forget as well as remember how their story ends. The self which knows the play's future must in performance (at times) be set aside. And for the spectator an absorption in the present moment precedes the retrospective 'why?' Critics in their studies tend to ignore what Keats said about 'negative capability'. In a crowded room (or auditorium) the mind can be invaded by personalities other than one's own. The active analytical will is part of a broader imaginative process which it can sometimes undermine. It is this broader process the book assumes and argues for.

Authors struggle to reconcile form and content just as directors and actors struggle to control material which threatens to get out of hand. Authors must offer their material a certain freedom from their will. Actors need freedom as well as direction, and they must take care not to 'direct' too strictly the characters they perform. The processes of dramatic production reveal the tensions between control and free expression which inform a dramatic structure and a social process in which the self should not become too central. How this relates to questions of form and performance, the reader is invited to judge from the chapters which follow. I have been seeking a way of reconciling more recent kinds of academic work on the theatre with older, more ingenuous approaches, using a language which excludes no one who cares for the theatre, either within it or outside.

The New Naturalism and Popular Forms

Melodrama, farce and costume drama

The corner-stone of twentieth-century drama is the naturalist movement represented by the work of Ibsen, Chekhov, Hauptmann, Becque, Strindberg and others. Ibsen was the great forerunner and it is clear that productions of his plays by the early directors in the 1890s, André Antoine in Paris, Otto Brahm in Berlin and J. T. Grein in London, radically changed the course of English and European drama. The movement is so important that the forms of drama against which Ibsen was rebelling, farce, melodrama and the historical costume dramas which formed the staple theatre diet of the rapidly expanding Victorian entertainment industry, are given scant attention in surveys of modern drama. These forms, however, are worth discussion. They lived on to entertain the twentieth century and formed a basis on which both the naturalists and those in reaction against them could build their new and more complex forms of theatre.

Melodrama had grown up in the eighteenth and nineteenth centuries to provide popular entertainment for the urban poor. Its ancestors include Goethe's early plays, Schiller's *Die Räuber*, the Gothic novel, Jacobean blood and thunder and Shakespeare's *Macbeth*. But the melodrama simplified its major antecedents for a mainly illiterate urban population which needed immediately identifiable heroes, villains, heroines and comic men. This audience did not seek the moral and psychological subtlety of a Macbeth. They expected and were given a clear morality play opposition between good and evil. The audience for melodrama did not want any invitation to sympathize with the abyss, or scrutinize its own simple moral responses. It wanted stereotypes which it could laugh or hiss at. Its moral sympathies needed to be simple.

The novels of Dickens and Mrs Henry Wood provided plots. So did local hospitals and madhouses, law courts and places of execution, local crimes and the daily news-sheet. But whereas such sources might supply a Dostoievski with material for close psychological and social analysis, the hack writer of melodrama, working fast, badly paid and without copyright, appealed directly to raw emotion, without irony or food for thought. The early naive and highly responsive audiences wanted to know where they stood. Hissing Bill Sykes as he pulled Nancy by the hair, or booing the aristocratic, corked-up villain, with his basso profundo voice and countenance steeped in gloom, was an essential part of the pleasure.

It is worth remembering that such pleasure is fundamental to drama. Hatred and fear, together with extreme pathos, were the principal effects which melodrama achieved, and such an audience reaction recalls Aristotle's view that tragedy, through pity and terror, effected 'the purgation or catharsis of the emotions'. Melodrama and tragedy are closely allied.

In the tradition of Shakespeare rather than classical tragedy, melodrama contained in its list of characters a Comic Man, clever but low in the social order, who provided relief and a sympathetic viewpoint for the popular audiences in the fit-up[1] theatres. Despite this complication, however, the plays remained naive. Unlike tragedy in which the heroes were generally destroyed, or comedy in which the villains were often cured, melodrama held to a simple moralism, ending happily for the good and disastrously for the wicked.

Melodrama was not for the sophisticated but, as the London theatre business expanded in the later nineteenth century, it encountered West End audiences who mocked its general serious-ness and curious innocence. The stupidity of a hero who needed the Comic Man to help him forestall the mustachio-curling villain or the raven-haired, bejewelled, huge-hatted villainess; the ever-suffering heroine, fleet of foot in her pursuit of purity and flight from Sir Jasper; these provoked laughter when the audience knew more subtle forms of theatre and did not share the class sym-pathies of the urban poor. Actors and writers began to parody this moralistic naivety wherever it was found. The innocent governess Miss Prism in Wilde's *The Importance of Being Earnest*, expresses a preference for melodrama: 'The good ended happily and the bad unhappily. That is what fiction means'. In this way melodrama became a component of more complex drama. As a simple form it died in the theatre with *grand guignol* soon after World War I. It lived on, however, in the early silent cinema, along with farce, and costume drama. The popular nineteenth-century theatrical forms provided the basis of the new film medium.

Melodrama was given to violent on-stage action which the cine-camera could capture more convincingly than the most advanced stage machinery. But nineteenth-century naturalism had already shown a preference for a return to older ways of handling violent action – by narrating it as an off-stage event. Ever since Aeschylus, dramatists have chosen to narrate certain events instead of enacting them on stage. It is simpler; it saves dramatic time; it avoids violent shock and focuses attention on motivation and effect. In the new naturalism, following the Greek example, action was relegated to the wings. Chekhov moved melodrama off-stage where it was sudden and occasional, as when Tuzenbach is killed in the duel in *The Three Sisters*. Deaths and drownings, such as that of Grisha in *The Cherry Orchard*, difficult or impossible to enact on stage, occur before the plays begin and form an object of discussion or of hesitant reference. Ibsen brings such events nearer. They happen, like Hedvig's suicide in *The Wild Duck*, only just off-stage or, like the fall of the Master Builder from his tower, are even meant to be seen in the distance. His dramatic structures are closer to melodrama than Chekhov's in that they build to climaxes, present more passionate relations and often end in death and suicide.

In Ibsen, however, the moral patterns are not simple. His plays puzzled the sophisticated as well as the innocent. His characters, half-villains, half-heroes, not only disconcerted audiences but also dismayed the stock-company actors who worked within the old conventions. The new drama required actors who could portray characters neither hero nor villain, attracting sympathy and yet half-repellent. Ibsen and Chekhov rounded the stock heroes, villains and comic types, deepening the drama and giving it what Dostoievski had given the popular novel. The new naturalist plays employed the popular forms as Shakespeare had used the naive and popular morality play in *Macbeth*. They were palimpsests.

The older forms showed through and lent dramatic power. The violent activity of the melodrama (and farce), set in the background, provided an ironic reminder of what lies beneath the conventional surfaces of life. At the same time the subtler dialogue revealed the limitations of the more innocent characters, who looked at life in simple terms. The plays indeed analysed the way people melodramatized their lives. Melodrama becomes an ironically distanced component of the drama itself (much as Hamlet examines with distaste this tendency in himself). In this new drama the apparently immoral are part excused and the simple moralizers part-condemned. The whole process of full identification or full disapproval is itself attacked.

The same, of course, can be seen happening in the English novel of the period. Hardy's *Tess of the D'Urbervilles* (1890) has the melodramatic pattern of a 'pure' heroine caught between a machiavellian villain and a man she makes a hero of, both of a higher class than she. The hero is even called 'Angel' and plays a harp. Hardy, too, much influenced by the drama of his time, wrote palimpsests, imposing psychological subtleties on a cruder base. Melodrama, in Hardy and Ibsen, as in *Hamlet* before them, is held up to scrutiny as a suspect psychological state. In this way it becomes an ironic component of the work which supersedes it.

The same is true of farce. Just as Shakespeare incorporated farce in his comedies, in the Pyramus and Thisbe episodes in *A Midsummer Night's Dream* or the Sir Topas episode or duel in *Twelfth Night*, so Chekhov, in his tragi-comedies, uses the farce material abundant in his early plays. The techniques of farce; its pratfalls and accidents; its obsessive eating and drinking; its country cousins and parvenus behaving clumsily in polite society; its attack on dominant social codes; its Italian straw hats (the props which take on a life of their own); its deep sense of approaching chaos – are adapted and naturalized by Chekhov in various ways. He makes Trofimov, for example, at a dramatic point in *The Cherry Orchard*, exit with dignity, then fall downstairs. But the fall happens off-stage, effects a change of mood and subtly alters our view of him. The physical knock-about of customary farce, whose accelerating mechanism only stops when the characters stand exhausted at the final curtain, is transformed by Chekhov into a new form of wryly sad and decelerating naturalism which ends, as he said, 'against all the rules, pianissimo'.[2]

Farce has been the most permanent of European theatre forms. From the Greek *phlyax* and Roman Atellan farce, through the *Commedia dell'Arte* to Feydeau and Ayckbourn, it retains a fundamental appeal. The modern West End diet of farce finds its origin far back in the long history of dramatic entertainment. Perhaps because farce, like the pratfalls of the circus clown, conjures away the hurts and humiliations of life,[3] it has remained immensely popular. Twentieth-century writers from Chekhov to Brecht, from Stoppard to Dario Fo, have, like Shakespeare, used it for their own purposes. The laughter which it evokes is deeply intriguing and we could do worse than remember Nahum Tate's words in 1693: 'I know not by what Fate it (farce) happens (in common notion) to be the most contemptible sort of Drama.'

In 1900, Bergson's *Le Rire* scrutinized the long tradition of French 'new comedy' and farce from the importation of the *Commedia dell'Arte*, through Molière to Scribe, Sardou, Labiche and Feydeau. These plays generally concern love, money and power relationships, in which the older generation block the aspirations of the young. In the defeat of the old the plays celebrate the overcoming of property and ownership barriers. They mock the hypocrisy of conventional facades, hinting, to an audience paying lip-service to those conventions, at their fragility and at hidden truths behind the facades. It is not surprising that more overtly political and social plays have seen new uses for the methods of farce. Chekhov thus appropriates the freeze, the sudden tableau which cuts across the movement of a play and foregrounds a set of relationships, or underlines a situation, often just before a curtain. The freeze is a technique which, of all dramatic techniques, fulfils Bergson's definition of comedy as 'the mechanical encrusted upon the living'.[4] Chekhov adapts it, making his Three Sisters 'freeze' for a posed photograph. We watch indulgently until the young soldier photographer tells the sisters 'You can move now'. Then the old technique acquires a new poignancy. The sisters can move physically, but are they mentally frozen? It is by no means easy for these characters to move on or out. In this way the play presents a subtle psychological mirror to the semi-paralysed gentility of Chekhov's time.

Farce arguably presents the hilarious manoeuvres of low characters who are trapped by chance and fate. Beneath the hilarity and without the happy ending its vision is sombre. The laughter, indeed, signals awareness of this. From such early farces as *The Bear* to the final *Cherry Orchard*, Chekhov is concerned with the traps people choose or fall into. The laughter he provokes alleviates but recognizes a threatening situation.

Chekhov's comedy, however, did not encourage acceptance of a rigid fate and an unchangeable social frame. He saw the world was moving and felt that people must establish social and personal control. He therefore brings the suffering of the characters closer to his audience and cuts down the laughter. His characters no longer have the fixity of farce. If they appear trapped, the plays ask how far the responsibility lies with the characters themselves.

In another sense his characters were freer. Unlike the startled ingenuous heroes of farce they smiled; unlike the neighing villains they wept. This gave them a human dimension, a character of freedom in an often confining situation. Their laughter and tears suggested not only a momentary freeing of the mind but the possibility of choice and control. Their apparent independence, even of the author, suggested the possibility of change. In this way the later plays, though often played for tragedy, are paradoxically, if not in tone at least by implication, less sombre than farce. 'How should I not believe in freedom?' said Chekhov, knowing of his own emancipation from a family descended from serfs. And though the Three Sisters may seem trapped, the play is full of questions about the need to take responsibility and work for a better future.

Although farce may be seen as no more than a public safety-valve, acting in the interests of a rigid power structure, and though it often appeals to racial and sexual prejudice, Chekhov uses farce as a component of his drama because it invites recognition of the dangers of human rigidity. It mocks the inflexible. Its repetitions of phrase and situation, its reduction of character to stereotype, calls forth a distancing response. According to Hegel, the capacity to laugh is a form of freedom from an imprisoning mentality. It may at times express a contempt for others but it may also reveal a healthy self-recognition: 'The blessed ease of a subjectivity which, as it is sure of itself, can bear the dissolution of its own ends and means'.[5]

All the main theories of comedy and laughter are theories of freedom of different kinds: freedom from the thralldom of others;

freedom to participate in the saying of the socially unsayable; freedom to recognize personal limitations; and freedom to mock rational chains of cause and effect. Laughter derides rules and conventions. The theories of Bergson, Freud and Kant[6] all stress the way laughter beguiles and mocks social, racial, sexual and rational controls. It is not surprising that it has been associated with secular and popular drama, expressing the needs of groups who wish to be free. The point where the subjective 'I' refuses to remain in subjection marks where comedy seeks to beguile the power relation (a point which Trevor Griffiths makes in his powerful *Comedians* (1975)). Some forms of comedy share equal importance with tragedy, even if its operation is ambiguous and even though, in its cruder forms, the tensions it dissolves and the attitudes it encourages may act in the interests not of freedom but of power.

The historical costume play is another popular form which has been assimilated into twentieth-century practice. Like farce and melodrama, it was eagerly appropriated by the new cinema. It led directly to D. W. Griffiths and his *The Birth of a Nation* (1915). A sub-type, the Roman costume drama, or 'toga plays', lay behind the epic film *Ben Hur*.[7] The taste for historical plays in the nineteenth century celebrated a growing sense of national identity, and to this end it often took as model the historical plays of Shakespeare and the German *Sturm und Drang*. The Germanic tradition was strong in Scandinavia and northern Europe. In England almost all the well-known romantic poets had tried their hands at historical drama, although mainly for the reader and with less success than the early Ibsen and Strindberg.

As the twentieth century developed, the form would be re-worked. Shaw presented his own realistic interpretation of the life of St Joan, and Brecht set plays in a historical past to serve as parables for the present. The early seventeenth century, with its conflict between monolithic authority and a new individualistic mercantilism, seemed particularly relevant. In writing of Galileo or of the Peasants' War in *Mother Courage*, Brecht founded a new form of realism, rewriting history as allegory, and appealing to an audience's free judgement. Galileo succumbed to authority, and Brecht hung a mushroom cloud as backdrop to his actions. Brecht's audience was to compare Galileo's situation with that of modern scientists who split the atom. Did they owe responsibility to themselves, to their country, to science or to the future? Mother

Courage, too, struggles through the Thirty Years War, perhaps learning nothing, as Brecht wished to emphasize in his notes on production, but asking questions of the audience about the competing virtues of survival and self-sacrifice in modern warfare.

In this way Brecht adapted the traditional chronicle form which lay behind the nineteenth-century costume drama. Like melodrama and farce, it was a form on which other drama could be built. More easily adaptable than the complex drama of Shakespeare (though he was also adapted in a variety of ways in later forms of drama, film and television), the cruder, more popular and superficial nineteenth-century forms richly fed the twentieth century.

Ibsen

Naturalism, fate and freedom

By 1890 the English theatre had become respectable. In mid-decade Henry Irving was knighted, after having turned down a knighthood in 1883.[1] State or municipal funding was non-existent and training schools scanty, but the numbers of actors and actresses had increased fivefold. In London there were now 50 theatres, 200 in England as a whole. An increasingly well-educated audience attended a variety of plays: musical comedy at the Savoy, sensation melodrama at the Princess, classical tragedy at the Lyceum. Audiences brought new expectations and an air of gentility. Clad in evening dress they flocked to see long-running popular hits. The old stock repertory companies faded away and a new exclusivity reigned.

Upon this flourishing commercial scene Henrik Ibsen entered with as explosive an effect as any author in theatre history. Ibsen was the new man who, according to Emile Zola in his articles for the press between 1875–9, was desperately needed 'to scour the debased boards and bring about a rebirth in an art degraded by its practitioners to the simple minded requirements of the crowd ...'. This man would 'finally install the real human drama in place of the ridiculous untruths that are on display today.' He would build in the middle of 'this desert of mediocrity' and prove 'that there is more poetry in the little apartment of a bourgeois than in all the empty worm-eaten palaces of history.'[2]

Zola's articles coincided with the writing of Ibsen's first two naturalist plays: *Pillars of the Community* (1877) and *A Doll's House* (1879). Ibsen had previously experimented, mainly in

13

verse, with standard forms of theatre, especially comedy and national historical plays. His compromises with public taste and the techniques of Scribe, the master of French farce, are less interesting than his exploration of historical subjects ranging from the early *Catiline* (1848) to *The Pretenders* in 1863. The latter was a play about different ways of holding social power. It brought him recognition and a travel award which sent him out of Norway to write the crucially important verse dramas *Brand* (1866) and *Peer Gynt* (1867). He then wrote a big ten-act play, *Emperor and Galilean*, which took as subject the last pagan Roman emperor. These plays are at the centre of Ibsen's development, for they explore issues which lie behind the tightly-patterned naturalist plays which follow. The latter are very different, set as they are in middle-class apartments, with their carefully constructed climaxes; timed entrances and curtains; their rounded ordinary citizens; and their venial sins and Victorian waistcoats. Yet these plays inherit the tensions of *Emperor and Galilean* between Christian belief and pagan veneration for a sun god, and the psychological opposition in *Brand* and *Peer Gynt* between spiritual law and anarchic free choice. Questions of faith and emancipation, both social and personal, were central:

> 'Everything I have written has the closest possible connection with what I have lived through, even if it has not been my personal experience: in every new poem or play I have aimed at my own spiritual emancipation and purification, for a man shares the guilt of the society to which he belongs.'[3]

Ibsen's drama shows characters struggling to develop, struggling to be themselves and thus struggling to be free. The struggle, however, was complex, since there are different ways of being oneself. Independence can be achieved by the acceptance of a rigorous code. It can also take the form of a relaxation of standards – the satisfaction of a will to joy or pleasure. The Thin Man in *Peer Gynt* states it thus:

> There are two ways of being yourself. . . .
> You can either show the straightforward picture
> Or else what is called the negative.

Brand and Peer Gynt demonstrate these two ways. The stern uncompromising steely-willed prophet Brand is set against the self-indulgent, irresponsible, and chameleonic Peer. Brand is Peer's *modsaetning* (antithesis) said Ibsen in a letter to Edmund Gosse in 1872. These two states of mind, one morally committed, the other wayward and self-seeking, emerge in different forms as an ideological conflict both within and between characters in the new naturalism.

This new drama, the counterpart in the theatre to what Balzac and Zola had achieved in fiction, emerged in the strongly Germanic cultures of Scandinavia. In it, the old forms of melodrama, farce, 'well-made play', picaresque and romantic verse drama, intermingle with a fuller psychological realism and gain strength from Ibsen's deep personal concern with the physical, economic, social and psychological constraints on individual freedom. This new drama became the corner-stone of twentieth-century naturalism, leading into the work of Strindberg, Hauptmann, Chekhov and Stanislavski.

It also led, through Strindberg, into the subjective dreams of the expressionist drama which rebelled, in its turn, against naturalism. Ibsen was a poet and his concern with social freedom, in the first naturalistic prose plays, *Pillars of the Community* and *A Doll's House*, led naturally to the analysis of constraints on the creative individual. He began to examine characters whose creativity was threatened by social conventions which operated both outside them and from within their own psyches: Allmers in *Little Eyolf*, John Gabriel Borkman, the masterbuilder Solness, Rubek in *When We Dead Awaken*, the writers, architects, sculptors and philosophers who people the later plays.

To express the thoughts of his dreamers and men of vision he experimented with a new symbolic language. The deeper study of psychic reality carried Ibsen into areas of the mind which prose dialogue has difficulty in conveying. At the edge of dream Ibsen encountered the limitations of the new realism, with its emphasis on social surfaces, its accurate costuming and period furniture.

At the same time the realist framework of Ibsen's prose drama provided a much-needed ironic commentary on the more escapist and egotistical forms of romantic dream. It was radical in attitude and form. It attacked the sentimentality of the old melodrama and bombastic costume drama and it freed the European stage of its conventional formal shackles.

Ghosts, written in 1881, but reaching Berlin in 1887, Paris in 1890 and London in 1891, was the play which contributed most to this effect. Its early reception in Scandinavia roused Ibsen to anger: 'The so-called liberal press . . . those leaders who talk and write of freedom and progress and at the same time let themselves be the slaves of the supposed opinions of their subscribers . . .' he wrote to Brandes. Then, again, in a letter to Frederik Hegel in March 1882: 'All these decrepit and fading figures who have spat upon this work will one day bring upon their heads the crushing judgement of future literary historians . . . My book contains the future.' George Bernard Shaw, in his articles for *The Saturday Review* (1895–8) (later collected as *Our Theatre in the Nineties*), corroborated this judgement: 'If Mr Grein had not taken the dramatic critics of London and put them in a row before *Ghosts* and *The Wild Duck*, with a certain small but inquisitive body of enthusiasts behind them, we should be far less advanced than we are today.'

It is interesting how often the idea of freedom is associated with Ibsen at this time. Max Devrient, for example, in Vienna in 1892, greeted Ibsen as the writer who had given man an 'inner freedom, banished ghosts, and had the courage to admit daylight to dark corners.'[4] The known response of London newspaper critics to Jacob Grein's production – they called the play variously 'foul', 'loathsome', 'fetid', 'disgusting', 'an open drain', 'a lazar house' – illustrated the need to illuminate dark corners. Ibsen had the courage to speak of subjects such as syphilis, paving the way for Shaw to write of Mrs Warren's profession and other unpalatable social problems.

The social questions were linked with questions of personal responsibility and creativity. In *Ghosts* the theme of creative freedom is expressed through the artist Oswald, who scathingly contrasted the claustrophobic and morally hidebound minds of the Scandinavian bourgeoisie with 'the glorious free life in the south'. Tragically, Oswald's creative capacity is destroyed by the irresponsibility of his father and the failure of his mother to take control of her own life. Oswald inherits his illness as a result of a double failure – that of a blinkered society and the irresponsibility it provokes. The irresponsibility seals Oswald's fate but Ibsen does not merely visit the sins of one generation upon another. He raises the question of the obligation of the older generation to the younger. Destructive forms of living have more than personal consequences. Fate is not mechanical. It results from choices.

Ghosts is a play in which the younger generation are freer, and have wider perspectives than the old. This is true not only of the artist Oswald but also of the young servant Regina, who fights against the future which Engstrand, her father, prepares for her. She does not wish to serve in his home for sailors, which will probably be little better than a brothel: 'There's got to be some women around, that's for sure . . .' To achieve his end her father manipulates the convention-ridden Pastor Manders so that he will bring pressure on Regina. Children, he cunningly argues, should love their parents and owe them a duty. The Christian doctrine of love in this way becomes an instrument of power. But the young have a duty to themselves, an area of personal freedom where the writ of social codes does not run. The conventional moral attitudes subserve the interests of the old.

Regina's fight for her own future parallels the desire of Oswald to pursue his own life. Unfortunately 'ghosts' in the form of obligations and duties, family ties, inherited attitudes and, in a more sinister way, inherited disease, limit the choices. The young, and one member of the older generation, attempt to lay the ghosts: 'I'm not putting up with all these duties and obligations any longer . . . I must somehow free myself, says Mrs Alving, 'I was too much of a coward'.

But it is not enough to wish for freedom. The constraints of ignorance and custom, old habits of reliance, undermine the desire. Old beliefs may be set aside, but a clear sight of the motivations of others, of such as the secretive and manipulative Engstrand, are also necessary. For Engstrand the way of freedom resides in lying to those who have more power than he. Such minds as Engstrand's and Pastor Manders's combat the emancipation of others, blurring their recognition of the right path until the future is no longer controllable.

This happens to Mrs Alving who seeks her freedom by devoting her marriage settlement to building a memorial to her husband. This, she believes, will lay the ghosts which whisper against his reputation. The initial crime, however, against herself, compounded by her returning to Captain Alving, have created other ghosts. Her plan to free her son of all taint of her husband's money comes to nought when Oswald is found to be tainted by his disease.

Ghosts is a sombre play. Characters are deceived in their aspirations after freedom and audiences are deceived in their hopes for the characters. Ibsen, critics still protest, imposes, like Hardy, his bleak vision upon his play and mocks his audience's need to hope. More important in retrospect is Ibsen's emphasis on the need to take responsibility for one's own life. The consequences of not doing so, for oneself and others, may be dire. The play which followed *Ghosts* in 1882 was less pessimistic. This was *An Enemy of the People*. It begins with an uncomfortable meeting between two members of the press and the local mayor. It takes place in the living room of the mayor's brother, a doctor in charge of the spa which promises to improve the fortunes of the town. The spa brings invalids, employment, fame, and raises the value of property and land. The community develops and thrives. Unfortunately the spa is a fraud. To save money the builders have economized on the water installations which are now contaminated. A complete re-laying of the system over a period of several years is required and this will be too heavy a financial burden for the town to carry. Accordingly, the citizens question the validity of the evidence laid before them. Concern for their pockets robs them of clear sight. Thus, as in *Ghosts*, the characters collaborate in a lie. Their reason acts in the defence of self-interest. Citizens conspire to keep silent about the smell of the drains. Only one family stands out against this conspiracy of silence. This is the family of Dr Thomas Stockmann, the man who has written the document setting out what should be done to contain the contamination.

To the doctor's surprise the townsfolk do not believe in the purity of his motives. They assume he has written out of self-interest, in order to gain power, to revenge himself on the mayor, his brother, or to bring down the price of shares so that he can buy when the price falls. People see in Dr Stockmann a reflection of their own motives. No one believes in altruism. Stockmann will buy up the shares, give the spa a clean bill of health, then make a killing on the stock exchange. When Stockmann refuses to respond in a way they understand the townsfolk turn nasty. He is threatened with violence and poverty. His job is taken. His eldest daughter is dismissed from her job; his younger children are attacked. The community of kind people, the landlord and the school headmistress, are pressed to evict this family which does not live by common standards of self-interest. The 'kind' turn out to be weak and succumb to group pressures. The play builds to a climax, leaving the family isolated in a house with broken windows, bravely but foolishly declaring they will stay on in the town. Their escape route to America, which involves the help of a friendly sea captain, comes to nothing when the captain, as a result of his friendship for the family, is relieved of his command. However, the wife is not sure she wishes to go to America. What if America is like here? Not large and broad-minded, but narrow. It would be a pity to travel a third the way around the globe to find they had arrived in the same place.

This suggestion that America, despite romantic propaganda, might not be the land of the free, is picked up by Arthur Miller in his acclaimed production of the play, performed at the Young Vic and Playhouse in 1988. Miller's version defined with absolute clarity the nature of an unfree community – the 'liberal' newspapermen, tied by the need for popular support, the holders of power who do not understand generosity of spirit or naive but honourable declarations that a spade is a spade when it would be wiser to conceal it.

The situation is familiar. It recalls the anti-semitism of Nazi Germany, Miller's refusal to capitulate before the witch-hunting of the McCarthy era, and other instances of scapegoating which salve national pride or cover up fear. The passion behind it is obvious. Ibsen hated the narrow moralizing of an unfree community. The mentality of a Pastor Manders infects a whole town. The town then uses the machinery of democracy to manipulate votes and prevent free speech.

The play has the misgivings of Plato about the rule of the *demos*. Majority rule has limitations: the frequent incapacity of the many to recognize the talents of the few; the ease with which group egoism can be manipulated. Informed individuals can be right when the majority are wrong. And they can speak against both self and group in the interests of a truth which the many will not recognize. It takes courage to contradict the many to their faces rather than collude in received truths. Stockmann has that courage and speaks a truth which, in the long run, is in the interests of the community. A short-sighted township does not agree. Only an attack of typhoid will clear its mind.

Interestingly Thomas Mann treats of a similar conspiracy in *Death in Venice* (1912) and the suppression of truth in the interests of profit has not been restricted to pages of fiction. Actual attempts to hush up, for short-term gain, contamination of the water supply, or the failure of a public service, underline Ibsen's realism. His play belongs to a long tradition of political drama. From Sophocles's *Antigone* through Shakespeare's *Julius Caesar* to the plays of Brecht, ideas of freedom and the problems of rule have been central. Ignorant and insensitive misuse of power, whether it is within the family, municipality, or state, tempts its victims to verbal and even physical violence. The institution then cites this violence to justify itself in its opposition to change. The group shown in this play, headed by the mayor, acts slowly, ruins a scheme by its own parsimony, and when the scheme threatens failure it blames others and tries to muzzle those who disagree.

Ibsen is writing a public play about the old problem of might and right. 'What is the use of right if you haven't got might?', says the Doctor's wife, Katrina, echoing Pascal's *Pensées*: 'Instead of making right mighty we have made might right'. Parallels to the basic dramatic situation of *An Enemy of the People* have recurred since the age of Sophocles. Plays continue to ask what one should do when the state suppresses individual freedom. 'When my sons grow up to be men', Stockman decides, 'I want the right to look them in the face.'

Stockman, honourably, will not compromise in his own vested interest. And he is imprudent enough to tell his fellow citizens to their faces that they are wrong. He does not play games to protect his own liberty of action. He acts in the open, at which point the community will use any weapon against him. Even his own hospitality is an excuse to call him a drunk. An unfree society, and the press which panders to its customs, destroys individuals who proclaim the values by which it ought to live. This play is not local. Its power derives from the paradox that truth and freedom operate not only as a value but a threat to a community. The play is not a closed tragedy. Like Brecht, Ibsen asks the audience how it wants the world to be run.

In his next play, *The Wild Duck* (1884), Ibsen again takes up the theme of liberation. But if *An Enemy of the People* presents one individual standing against an unfree society, the next play shows how a man who stands alone fools himself in thinking he is free. In *The Wild Duck* it is the older generation holding social power that proves itself less bound by convention, the past, or neurosis. The figure of the older Werle, and the woman he wishes to marry, Mrs Sørby, have more dignity and a greater aware- ness of reality than any of the characters around them. In this play it is not the community which is condemned but the deluded individuals who believe that all people desire to be free.

Ibsen said in preliminary jottings for the play: 'Liberation consists in securing for individuals the right to free themselves, each according to his own particular need.' In this play the younger generation, and the father of Hjalmar Ekdal too, do not want their freedom. They live within four walls, and their favourite room is a dark attic in which they play out compensatory dreams. The domesticated wild duck which they play with is an image of themselves, a damaged creature, unable to return to its natural habitat. Like them, the creature has forgotten what it is to be free:

'How can a man like you – a man who loves the open air – live in the middle of a stuffy city, shut in here . . .', says Gregers. But Old Ekdal no longer wants the 'free life of forest and heath'. Nor does his son feel 'the pull of a free open life'. When Gregers endeavours to bring the Ekdal family into the open air, like the clever dog which brought up the wild duck from the bottom of the sea, he makes the same mess of their lives as he has made of his room when he puts out the fire in his stove. The truths he tells are destructive truths. Gregers is not used to living with others, nor is he sensitive to the demands it makes. His recipe for freedom – a complete revelation of past illusions and confession of past lies – proves not to be the recipe which frees the men of the Ekdal family. The elder is imbued with shame and fear and the son is unable to feel anything for anyone but himself. The two men retreat into their attic whenever the cold wind of reality begins to blow.

The women on the other hand, free of the illusions of the menfolk, aware that the games in the attic are unreal – though the girl Hedvig, still plays – indulge the men as if they were children. Only when the men are happy can the women find some freedom. And so they tolerate their dreams.

Of course, the women are imprisoned also. Gina, the wife, is tied down by marriage to Hjalmar, which is the price she pays for conceiving an illegitimate child. She accepts her domestic situation, however, and does not consider it limiting since she has a higher station and greater freedom than her social position would at one time have permitted. Hedvig is imprisoned in a childish adoration of her father which eventually brings about her death.

The people in the play who are most free are the ostensible villains: erstwhile seducer and his mistress. The former has fobbed off his child on the unsuspecting Hjalmar. Ibsen, however, varies the stereotypes of melodrama and shapes them newly. Old Werle, seducer of Gina, is able to feel consideration and, it seems, a concealed tenderness for his daughter. Despite his social standing he is able to understand his son's dislike of himself without being enraged. Again, although he is going blind, he suffers no self-pity, indulges in no romanticizing of his own position. He speaks quietly of it and is making clear and responsible arrangements for the running of his business before departing for life up in the forest at the Høidal works.

The forest is in one sense a symbol of freedom. It is here that the older Ekdal has been a great hunter in his youth. But ironically Old Werle's partner has not known where his own lands ended and other men's began. He cuts down trees which are not his. The forest, as he is fond of saying, avenges itself and society sends him to gaol.

Gregers also lives up at the Høidal works, on the edge of the forest, but he too has not known freedom for his time has been misused. He has done nothing, made no friends, and though time seemed to pass slowly, 'now, looking back, I hardly know how time went.' The forest is thus not the image of freedom it at first appeared to be. Gregers has 'buried himself' up at the works. And this too is the place to which, bravely, Old Werle, in his growing blindness, will retire. The free open life is delusive.

Life, this play seems to say, is down where we have responsibilities, in the town. When Gregers is offered work in his father's firm, he prefers the lone task of 'saving' a family which would much rather not be saved. It is an ideal mission tainted by feelings of revenge. Gregers is not man enough to assume real responsibilities. He prefers instead to implicate others in his dream. A man who does that is not in command of his own destiny.

This lack of mental freedom is revealed in the way characters talk. When Gregers darkly says his destiny is to be thirteen at table, the play has already mocked the tendency of the neurotic and self-absorbed to melodramatize their own condition. Poetry based on self-absorption is not a language of free expression; the joking of the sensible Mrs Sørby as she keeps her former suitors and potential scandalmongers admiringly at bay is preferable. Her ability to jest and her capacity to be serious, her sympathy for Old

Ekdal and her concern for Hedvig, her recognition of the qualities the cynical, intelligent Dr Relling has damaged in himself, all these things give her a broader consciousness than anyone else in the play. Only Old Werle rivals her. In making this couple his moral centre Ibsen offers his audience the freedom and discomfort of seeing in unconventional ways.

A final word about Ibsen's next play *Hedda Gabler* (1886): it was performed at the Olivier Theatre in 1989 in a highly praised production by Howard Davies with Juliet Stevenson as Hedda and Norman Rodway as Judge Brack. Ibsen's naturalistic plays were written for the proscenium arch and not for an open auditorium like the Olivier. The decision, however, to stage it there, and possibly the insufficiency of earlier stagings in this theatre, such as the *Wild Duck* production in 1979, led to a grandiose circular set which filled the huge stage with high glass-fronted bookcases, mounted on a railed gallery. Stage-left a high glass wall gave onto the main vestibule. Small trees grew on either side of the circular stage and dead centre a stove sent up its pipe right up to the roof. From this, puffs of smoke emerged when Hedda burned Eilert Løvberg's papers far below.

This kind of set might be thought inappropriate for Ibsen's naturalist plays which derive their atmosphere from a claustrophobic room, in which the characters are trapped and from which the stronger spirits struggle to escape. Even if they do escape, the Norwegian landscape, glimpsed through a window in one of the stage-flats or in occasional verbal reference, often remains oppressive. In *Hedda Gabler*, however, the mansion-like setting and greater sense of freedom seem appropriate. The young married couple, Jørgen Tesman and Hedda, his wife, have just returned from abroad. The house suits the aristocratic Hedda, but will be too large for the owner's purse if he does not succeed in increasing his income. The husband, a scholar and putative professor, is therefore anxious to secure a professional post. This will give him a space he can happily live within. Hedda, however, needs more space. Her husband inhibits her freedom, and it is soon revealed that she married him in the expectation of relative plenty. The confinement of her husband's mind, moreover, is beginning to threaten her sanity, an effect intensified by others: the aunt with her desire to dedicate herself to a cause; the local judge who seeks sexual power over her; the husband who has no sense of her needs; the pretty Mrs Elvsted who arouses jealousy through her connection with a former suitor Eilert Løvborg; even the maid who falls below her standards. Above all, Løvborg himself signals her loss of control, since he has half-escaped her influence. Hedda is losing a position of power as the general's daughter who has been a beautiful and flirtatious hostess. Now, without affection, and lacking the capacity to dedicate herself either to the service of others, she is empty. She fills the emptiness with hatred and contempt, threatening to destroy with her pistols whoever places limits upon her.

In the Olivier production Juliet Stevenson pointed the pistols at each character in turn[5] before finally turning them upon herself when her control failed. Excluded by her husband, threatened by Judge Brack, unable to destroy Eilert Løvborg, unable even to ensure that the book she burns will not be reconstituted, Hedda finally kills herself. Unable to give, unable to escape social convention, she fills her emptiness with games, dangerous games played with people who do not acknowledge them as play. When she loses the power to play and to hurt others, set apart from the centre of her world, she cannot bear existence and cancels her own.

Who is responsible is an important question. Was it the father whose portrait normally dominates the stage, who brought her up as an only child to whom he left no economic sufficiency? Is it the men who treat her as a doll as soon as marriage has entrapped her? Is it her own incapacity to take stock of her selfishness and to repudiate it in the light of some code of moral values? There is no full explanation. We have a play full of small people in which Hedda's suppressed anger, hatred and rage emerges as the central source of energy. She longs for a fuller freedom than it is possible to embrace.

Just as in *Ghosts* Oswald longs for the sun and cannot embrace it; just as Thomas Stockmann in *An Enemy of the People*, Gregers Werle in *The Wild Duck*, Solness, the Master Builder, and John Gabriel Borkman all have dreams which bring them low, so Hedda's dream destroys her. The dreams vary in quality. Hedda's is worth less than Stockmann's because it is more egotistical, but selfish or altruistic these dreams are dangerous.

Ibsen does not treat dreams of freedom in an entirely satirical manner: he is a tragi-comedian interrogating the imaginations of those who would create a freer world for themselves. The drama

24

of Ibsen explores the desire for freedom, then sardonically questions the possibility of its full attainment. He mocks the way the mind enchains itself with routine, governed by fear, narrow hopes and compensating visions. If freedom exists, it resides in the audience's and author's shared recognition of the reasons why individuals go under.

Hedda Gabler, like Strindberg's *Miss Julie*, is a powerful case study of a woman who goes under, whose exits are blocked. The games she plays, in an attempt to find room for herself, destroy the gifted Løvborg and lead to what Camus once called the final assertion of freedom – suicide. But the play encourages no confidence in such an act. Only the submissive giving of Miss Tesman, Mrs Elvsted and Jørgen Tesman at the end can be placed against the major egoism of Brack, Løvborg even, and Hedda herself. The play's ironies seem to imply that blessed are the meek, who find their freedom without aspiring to it. The characters capable of the same sardonic irony as their creator find no release in life. For them the large aristocratic room within which the play was performed at the Olivier provided only an illusion of freedom.

The subject continued to obsess Ibsen in his late plays about wounded artists and a further comment on Ibsen's last play *When We Dead Awaken* will be found in the chapter on symbolic drama. Meanwhile the theme of freedom became the concern of a different form of naturalism in a Russia which had only in 1861 emancipated its serfs.

Stanislavski, Chekhov and creative freedom

The impact of Ibsen on stage performance was immense: in the main this was due to his capacity to render a fuller and more complex version of humanity than earlier romantic, melodramatic and farce forms had allowed. He echewed the stereotyping of character, mingled the single categories of good and evil, and took an ironic view of the workings of the human imagination. Precedents could be found in the work of Shakespeare, and in the nineteenth-century Russian, French or English novel. The romantic imagination, the human tendency to long for other worlds, or to see the self as a participant in a drama containing angels and devils, was not for Ibsen a life-enhancing faculty.

The imaginative faculty continued to have its defenders. The emphasis that Coleridge had placed on 'primary imagination' as 'an echo in the finite mind of the Infinite I am'[1] was carried forward by later writers like Gerard Manley Hopkins and D. H. Lawrence, who invented the terms 'inscape' and 'otherness' to define a special consciousness of the world's pattern or mystery. Dickens, too, in his emphasis on the world of childhood, was a romantic as well as a social novelist. But the imaginative faculty also became subject to sceptical scrutiny. The dangers of a self-focused romantic imagination were sufficiently evident in George Eliot's *Middlemarch*, in Hardy's *Jude the Obscure* or Joseph Conrad's *Lord Jim*. Moments of vision and faith energize but may delude. The psychology which mythologized in simple characters Love, Beauty, Goodness or Evil came to seem unreal, whether it was expressed in Victorian poetry or popular melodrama. Such

26

categories might frame the novels of a Dickens and at times a Dostoievski, yet a richer, more complex and mocking vision was available in both. Ibsen similarly turned a mocking eye on a romantic ideal.

In familiar ways late romanticism was giving way to a new 'modernism'. After Darwin and the German philologists had thrown doubt on the fundamental God-given truth of the Bible and Marx had spoken of religion as the opium of the people, the structures of society and the processes of language, faith and art itself were suspect. Moral categories overlapped and Satan played many good tunes. It was a complexity which developed first in fiction. In romantic and historical costume plays, in melodrama and farce, the stereotypes were still rampant – perhaps because, in the absence of copyright laws, the theatre had not offered a reasonable living to gifted writers. Zola's 'new man'[2] was needed to bring the drama into line with the times. Ibsen made his entrance and broke the stereotypes of popular drama.

One effect of this was to demonstrate the limitations of current acting styles. Ibsen's plays puzzled conventional actors who were constantly attempting to reduce his characters to the stage types with whom, as Shaw said, they were familiar:

'The more experienced he (the actor) is, the more certain is he to de-Ibsenize the play into a melodrama or farcical comedy of the common sort . . . the whole point of an Ibsen play lies in the exposure of the very conventions upon which are based those by which the actor is ridden.'[3]

Ibsen built in the middle of the 'desert of mediocrity' through which Zola asserted the theatre was passing, and he revealed the need for a new dramaturgy and new methods of actor training. Two men who responded to this need were Antoine in Paris, and Stanislavski in Russia.

André Antoine (1858–1943) came to Paris and became a paid claqueur at the Comédie Française. He studied, staged student productions and, after military service, returned to found in 1887 the celebrated Théâtre Libre. In a small theatre in Montparnasse he established a new style of production. Much influenced by the Meininger[4] troupe, he worked to eliminate declamatory styles and exaggerated gesture. He opposed the star system and the imposition of the actor's personality upon the role, seeking to hide the actor both within the role and within the movements of the group or crowd. He opposed the painted sets and the highly artificial plotting of Scribe's[5] elaborate games. Now that not only the novel, but painting and photography were depicting a new realism, the theatre had to take up the challenge. Accordingly the stage environment had to be as convincingly real as possible. The elimination of footlights (which heightened shadow on actors' faces and was conducive to the presentation of black and white stereotypes); the abandonment of rich wigs and superfluous make-up; the addition of convincing sound effects; the use of electric light from a source appropriate to the action (to create, say, the effect of a sun rising or an up-stage table lamp); the use of realistic furnishings and real props such as sides of beef for a play set in a butcher's shop – these all enhanced the new style of naturalistic acting. In a tiny auditorium, realistic costuming, quiet voices, natural expression, unobtrusive stage movement and gesture, even backs turned on the audience, sought to create the illusion of a 'slice of life'.

The illusion, of course, was highly restrictive. A box-set on a small stage could more convincingly and less expensively represent a room than it could a public space, such as a market place or railway station. Accordingly there was a disproportionate emphasis on the room as a dramatic setting. There were many other realities than middle-class drawing-rooms and the representation of the single room soon proved a new convention and an arbitrary limitation. It was a limitation which Strindberg was to transcend in his late expressionist work by making his rooms metaphors of the psyche, a symbolic function soon to be explored in German expressionism, Kafka and surrealism as later in the absurdist sets of Beckett, Ionesco and Pinter. In the early days, however, the emphasis was on the rendering of outer appearances: costume, voice, accent, language, lighting, accessories. The naturalist theatre aimed to represent 'real' people living in a particular place at a particular time. Ibsen was the dramatist who first demonstrated the power of the new style; Antoine was the first to establish a new theatre; Stanislavski was the first to develop an appropriate theory of acting.

Stanislavski (1863–1938) was a young producer and actor when Ibsen's *The Wild Duck* was being written. Brought up with the older acting styles, he was well-established as an actor by the age of 35. He had performed Ibsen character parts, notably that of Dr Thomas Stockmann in *An Enemy of the People*. He had played Shakespeare and had begun to develop methods whereby

28

the actor could achieve a fuller representation of character on stage. In particular he sought means to prevent the actor becoming stale and automatic in his playing.

This interrogation was to last 40 years. The results became known through the European tours of the Moscow Arts Theatre, and more specifically through Stanislavski's later publications, *My Life in Art* (1922), and *An Actor Prepares* (1937). Later posthumous publications in English, especially *Building a Character* (1949), extended his influence, and companies such as the New York Actors' Studio applied his principles systematically, extending Stanislavski's influence to the post-World War II realism of Marlon Brando's acting and the films of Elia Kazan.

Stanislavski analysed the psychological and technical demands of a role, bringing together the actor's physical and mental preparation. He sought, he declared in his books, to connect the actor's 'inner and outer work on himself' with 'his inner and outer work on the text'. He worked for total relaxation and concentration, for a state of mind which brought the actor to 'love the part in himself, rather than himself in the part'. Through the elimination of self-consciousness, protected by the mask of character, actors could give fully of themselves. In this way Stanislavski avoided the old stale clichés used by actors who 'exchange art for business' and exhibit 'rubber-stamp' stereotypes to the spectator. Stanislavski's 'psycho-technique' liberated the actor. If the training worked, all the improvisation, self-analysis, observation, examination of the text, and exercise of the body, would contribute to those moments of creative release which actors speak of as a gift for which they are grateful, a recompense for the difficulties and risks of their profession.

Stanislavski's 'system' underpinned the new naturalism and has been absorbed piecemeal into the methods of British acting schools. It continues to aid actors in their creative preparation despite the fact that other theories, notably that of Brecht, and other traditions of acting, for example, mime, have returned to favour, and we find a theatre today in which naturalism is one of a number of theatrical styles. In the western world, however, it is still the most important.

In 1898 Stanislavski along with Nemirovitch Danchenko, had founded the Moscow Arts Theatre. Its curtain carried a picture of Chekhov's Seagull as a tribute to the play and author whose plays had capped the enterprise.

'What is so wonderful about Chekhov's plays', said Stanislavski, 'is not what is transmitted by the words, but what is hidden under them, in the pauses, in the glance of the actors, in the emanation of their innermost feelings'.[7]

Chekhov provided Stanislavski with hints which led the actor to build rich personal worlds around his chosen role. His plays gave actors freedom, encouraging them to discover and develop elements left implicit. Comments such as: 'Uncle Vanya is crying but Astrov whistles', or, of Trigorin in *The Seagull*: 'It was wonderful. Only you need torn shoes and check trousers',[8] fell on fertile ground. Stanislavski had played Trigorin in spotless and very elegant white clothes. Chekhov's hints suggested a 'sub-text', the layers beneath the play which Stanislavski had not perceived. Here was a life worked out by the author but not fully explicit on the play's surface. Unconscious give-aways, Astrov's whistle or Trigorin's torn shoes, revealed unspoken thoughts and suggested hidden experience. What is Astrov thinking? Why is Trigorin careless of his dress? Chekhov characteristically leaves Stanislavski, and the audience, to find an answer. His drama was a composite structure of roles whose dialogue, movement, costume, posture and facial expression developed the plot and hinted at the story. They created a past life, a potential future life, and life off-stage behind the scenes. These characters were full of silence and in their silences lay a fullness. The actor had to discover, and possibly create an off-stage existence which could be brought into the action. The people were little people, but their lives and dreams extended in time and space in a way which made the two-hour traffic of the stage a momentary glimpse of a broad historical flow.

The Seagull may, or may not have been written before Chekhov's remake of *The Wood Demon*, *Uncle Vanya*. But it is usually taken to be the play in which, after assimilating the work of the new naturalists including Ibsen, Strindberg and Hauptmann, Chekhov achieved his new style. It was a less dynamic dramatic form than Ibsen's, using a larger cast, and covering a longer time span with time gaps between the acts. In addition the characters were quieter, more reflective than passionate, and less threatened by emotional breakdown than Ibsen's.

The plays, however, like his predecessor's, are concerned with personal and social freedom and are pervaded by a sense of longing for personal and social change. As a doctor, Chekhov had a strong commitment to the improvement of Russian life. But he was no revolutionary. The changes were coming and he hoped the sensitive, the educated and committed, the doctors and teachers would play some part in them. Their role, he hoped, would lie in shaping personal and social relations, not in the transformation, infiltration or destruction of political institutions. His plays ask personal questions. To his friend Gorki they said: 'You live badly, my friends. It is shameful to live like that.'⁹

In *The Seagull* the emphasis is mainly on personal creativity. The characters' self-realization is very important, not surprisingly since they include two actresses and two writers, at different stages in their careers. The older actress is established, indeed famous. The younger seeks to climb the ladder. Similarly the older writer is highly respected; the younger badly needs forms of approval. The young envy or admire those whose artistic success has brought recognition and satisfaction.

As in Ibsen's later plays, the artist/protagonists seek to acquire, maintain or recover a state of personal liberty. But Chekhov does not identify this liberty with success. Success brings its own bondage. For the successful Trigorin an artistic vocation is still a kind of slavery, which the envying young fail to appreciate. Success is at the expense of something else, usually of people — children, lovers and friends — who interfere with, or may even be exploited in the exercise of a vocation. In order to live creatively, Chekhov's successful writers and actors need but resent their human ties. They may seem to have mastered the material conditions which enchain the less productive, even semi-comic characters around them, but Konstantin's actress mother, Arkadina, chafes at the demands of her son and Trigorin chafes at the demands of authorship. He has lost spontaneous response to the world. He sees everything in the light of material to be used. Thus he uses Nina as material for his art and in so doing uses up his own attachment to her. He is tied not to Nina but to his writing. His is a form of freedom which can singe those who come too close to its flame. Paradoxically, the tie in both cases subserves creativity. But Nina remains tied whilst Trigorin's creative use of her dissolves his feelings. The knot of a human relationship can be creative or destructive, or both at once.

Enchainment is certainly an image in the play. Characteristically, Chekhov represents it by a sound effect, as well as verbally and visually. A chained dog howls all night. The brother of Arkadina, Sorin, has no rich life to remember. Old and tied by sickness in a desultory, self-mocking regret, he seems, in his complaining, to resemble the dog. Unlike the dog, however, perhaps because he is insufficiently haunted by his failure, he does not stay awake at night. It is another character, Sorin's bailiff's wife, tied by a hopeless affection for the doctor, who resembles the dog in this. Chekhov, perhaps more subtly than Ibsen, employs stage symbolism to reflect the situations of different characters in turn. The stronger characters break some of their chains. The young Nina, who longs to be an actress, is tied to the house where her father and stepmother have other ambitions for her. They do not encourage her relation with Konstantin since he as yet lacks money and prestige. Both Nina and Konstantin fight to free themselves from family and economic restraints. The method Konstantin adopts is to write an avant-garde play which his mother cannot understand, which she believes is decadent nonsense, and would certainly not act in. The established theatre and theatre audience will not allow Konstantin an economic independence if he works in this vein. The actress in the play, Nina, knows this and wishes to find her way in the commercial world with which Konstantin does not wish to compromise.

Chekhov asks how far an artist should compromise his integrity to gain recognition and a measure of freedom. Konstantin must change his style. Possibly, however, if he can sense a fuller human reality, he can enter the commercial world, as Chekhov did, without self-compromise. His play is haunting and shows talent, but its character is thin and its subject is death. Liberation for Konstantin needs to come from within. If he can create real living human beings he may win through. But his relations with Nina and his mother are crucial, and the prospects are not promising since each rejects him in the interests of her own career and self-realization. The achievement of a sense of human wholeness, which Chekhov feels essential to dramatic expression, lies in the gift of others, and perhaps of chance. The writer himself is not fully responsible for this enlargement of his talent.

In Act II characters try to take their freedom. The melancholy Masha determines to shake off her mood. Ironically, her means of doing so – marriage to a poor schoolmaster obsessed with money – only enchains her further. Nina, too, makes her bid to be free. As the act begins, her father and stepmother have gone away for three days, leaving her a freedom which leads into her affair with, and subsequent abandonment by, Trigorin, from which she cannot free herself. Konstantin achieves a measure of success in his vocation, as does Nina in hers. But his love for Nina, like Nina's for Trigorin and Trigorin's for Arkadina, cannot be shaken off. Life enhancing, yet potentially destructive, love becomes a necessary chain. Trigorin writes out of his feelings for Nina and at the same time dismisses these feelings. Then he falls back on the original tie with Arkadina. This tie, and the call of his vocation seem indissoluble. To escape both Trigorin goes fishing on the lake. At first, the lake is a symbol of hope. Konstantin spends whole days on the lake, references to which hint at states of freedom and creativity. Arkadina, for example, is reading Maupassant's *Sur l'Eau*, a book about his escape from the travails of his later years aboard a yacht in the Mediterranean. Water is the element that attracts the creative spirits. Above the water flies the seagull of the title, 'happy and free'. Unfortunately a lake is more closed in than the sea and the seagull is wantonly killed. Like Ibsen's wild duck on which the play is in part based, the seagull and the lake, like the chained dog, reflect on the double-edged nature of the search for freedom.

The creative characters are freer than those without a vocation on which they can fall back: Sorin or the snuff-taking Masha, or the desperate, love-lorn Polina, yet they too are tied and by more than love. Sorin longs to be elsewhere but must stay in a place he dislikes. Unlike Sorin, the ambitious and talented move away, on or up. Moving on, however, may solve nothing. Happiness, says William James,[10] can be calculated as a ratio of achievements measured against goals. The ambitious are liable to discontent: low achievements and high goals are a disastrous combination. Thus, even the successful Arkadina is not happy and free. She knows there are greater actresses and is jealous of the renowned Eleonora Duse. Similarly Trigorin knows his limitations. He is not Turgenev. Meanwhile Konstantin is not Trigorin and Nina is not Arkadina. If one has never been a minor writer, says Sorin, it would be pleasant to become one. But the successful writers long for something else. Chekhov gently mocks the longing for greener pastures to which the imaginative seem especially prone.

In his even-handed way, Chekhov tempers sentimental and naive respect for the famous. Of course, the conditions of their craft and talent are not easy. In Trigorin's case they amount to painful obsession. He is under the compulsion of haunting ideas 'which compel a man to go on night and day thinking, for instance, of the moon'. This enslavement to one's own talent and nature is shared by the others. The lake, indeed, which seemed at first an image of freedom and happiness, also represents a prison. It entraps Nina, who is obsessed by the image of a gull on the lake. Yet her life is of higher value and in this sense freer than the half-drugged lives of the snuff-takers and drinkers in the play. Chekhov presents the audience with contrasting images of courage and weakness. Whereas Nina courageously attempts to live, Sorin never struggles and Konstantin chooses suicide. The women seem the freer spirits. Dr Dorn, though wise, has accepted the advance of age. The younger men, enchained in different ways, are less able than the women to take what vividness life offers or to combat the painful obstructions their gifts encounter and part create.

The theme of freedom continues through Chekhov's work to *The Cherry Orchard* (1904) performed in the last year of his life. Although written in the knowledge that sickness would soon terminate his talent, Chekhov's tone is not one of unrelieved tragedy, even though the play ends with a powerful spectacle of human unconcern, as the aged Feers sits alone, abandoned and unreproachful in an empty house. Something snaps at the end, as his life draws to a close, embodied in the mysterious sound effect which has been heard before in Act II.

The play emphasizes youth as well as age. The negative vision has a positive, as the positive has a negative side. The cherry orchard which is beautiful, no longer yields a crop. Like its owners it lacks a function. Entwined as it is in their emotional lives, its chopping down destroys a part of them. At the same time, for the young, as Trofimov says, all Russia is their orchard. The encumbering past is behind them, and the destruction of the orchard is a release. So too, for the energetic Lopakhin. His dream may be suburban, while he aspires to the status of gentility, but at least something is moving. The characters, even the older ones, are starting anew, and the sadness of the final departure is tempered with hope. Like the lake in *The Seagull* the cherry orchard is ambivalent. It represents both value and loss, but less sardonically than Ibsen's wild duck. The characters may be tied to the estate and its orchard but their love for it, and the way it is held in memory, suggest not only a form of emotional paralysis but also a form of liberation.

A further and different point can be made about the use of a central symbol in these plays. The different kinds of naturalism, with their common emphasis on the surfaces of life, impose limits on a writer wishing to render such realities as will and desire, or dream and hope. Images of past and future are as real in their influence on human conduct as the images of the present which naturalist drama presents to an audience. A playwright doing justice to this fuller reality must find a means, a poetic means, to render the inside of the head. The titles of these plays, metaphors inscribed in the landscape rather than names of houses or people, announce (as do parallel changes in the titles of novels) a movement towards expression of an inner world. A new form, as the old forms restrict them, is to emerge from the writers' search to render and extend their representation of 'reality'.

Pirandello

Creativity, pessimism and the limits of naturalism

Naturalism, in its attempt to present a full realism, leads from an examination of human and social surfaces into the exploration of what lies hidden behind. In the cases of both Ibsen and Chekhov it led them to examine the nature of creativity and social and personal freedom. It seems appropriate next, therefore, to discuss an author whose most famous work was both a critique of naturalist theatre, and an analysis of the creative process.

The Paris and London productions of Pirandello's *Six Characters in Search of an Author* (1921) made a powerful impact on European theatre and helped found the French theatrical tradition represented by names such as Cocteau, Giraudoux, Anouilh, Beckett and Genet, all of whom were concerned with the processes of theatre and its relation to the 'real world'. Of English contemporary dramatists, Stoppard is closest to this tradition.

In his 1921 production, Georges Pitoëff, the Russian actor who had established an important theatre company in Paris after World War I, built into his stage-set an ancient lift in which the Six Characters descended to make their entrance. This strange and memorable effect caught the imagination of playgoers as powerfully as the stage images of Samuel Beckett's *Waiting for Godot* 30 years later. Pirandello's play, Pitoëff later said, was like 'a window suddenly opened' and it fertilized the minds of a generation of dramatists. According to T. S. Eliot, a perhaps unexpected source of tribute, Pirandello was 'a dramatist to whom all serious dramatists of my generation and the next must owe a debt of gratitude . . . He has had the courage and imagination which have made it possible to penetrate 'realism' and arrive at reality.'

For Eliot, Pirandello was a serious dramatist because his concern with the real led him to interrogate the limits of the dramatic medium. Only by adapting existing forms, and by calling attention to their inadequacy, could Pirandello communicate what he felt about the world. Eliot approved his sense of levels existing beneath the shallow surfaces of life. It was a feeling very similar to the sense of 'sub-text' imparted by Chekhov's drama and explored by Stanislavski's system. But Pirandello, far more pessimistically than Chekhov, mounts a radical attack on the conventions of naturalism and projects human relations as states of mutual incomprehension.

Pirandello's sombre ideology is often taken as the full 'meaning' of his work. Meaning, however, lies also in the vibrant response his plays arouse. The vitality of the imagination which selects the methods whereby the pessimism is mediated plays as large a part in this as the sombre pessimism itself. As with Beckett, the apparent intention and the general response are at odds with one another. The pessimism exists alongside a sympathy and creative excitement generated in both author and spectator by the discovery of new forms and the recognition of human experience.

In *Six Characters* there is a Father who seeks recognition and does not receive it from the other Characters. Yet the spectator responds. His situation is painful and though the Characters may not sympathize – indeed they exist in a state of mutual bafflement – the same condition does not prevail between author, Character and audience. In acknowledging the Father's need for recognition, an audience responds to that need.

The situation is familiar in tragedy generally, where the negative statement is only a component of the total effect. When, at the climax of Shakespeare's *King Lear*, Kent demands recognition of the master he has served in disguise, and fails to receive it, the audience acknowledges and sympathizes, even while the king is too blind and old to know him. The presentation of a failure of communication expresses the human need to communicate. The effect, at its height, is to overcome the sense of separateness existing between members of the audience, as also between an audience and a particular character.

This can be true even where an audience recognizes the essential otherness of the suffering presented. Between ourselves and the suffering of Gloucester and even more of King Lear, there may be a barrier. The suffering may be too extreme, or even too foolish, to share in. But by introducing spectators on stage as the audience's representatives, or by using echo figures, who normalize the extremes so that we can make the connection, we may be brought to participate. Edgar, Kent and Cordelia fulfil this function, bridging the gap between ourselves and the protagonist. Edgar feels pity for Gloucester, whilst remaining separate, inviting audience sympathy for the man who feels pity, sympathy too for his isolated situation. It is the kind of effect which Nietzsche defined in *The Birth of Tragedy*. There is a wall but also a bridge between spectators and stage action. The audience can enter the cell of dramatic characters in solitary confinement.

A sombre play may well seem more pessimistic in the study than in the theatre where audiences recognize the confinement together and where multiple forms of communication, operating simultaneously, create an excitement that the reading cannot match. A reader is alone as a member of an audience is not, although both may be made to feel the nature of aloneness. At the same time the direct operation of theatre upon the retina and ear-drum create a more intense and immediate effect than language sifted through the mind.

The point is worth making at some length because the charge of pessimism about human relations is levelled not only at Pirandello but at Chekhov and the absurdist writers who follow. But the excitement they generate makes the criticism seem inadequate. To take an example from absurdist theatre: Ionesco used to speak with delight about his favourite production of *The Chairs* (1952). In the play two lonely characters fill the stage with empty chairs to receive imagined guests who are to hear a message of great import. Speaking in 1961 to a group of French students, Ionesco described the production: not only was the stage full of empty chairs, the auditorium was also empty except for two spectators huddled at the back. The spectacle of extreme isolation drove the couple together. *Ca se prolongeait dans la salle* said Ionesco amid laughter.

The laughter was intriguing. It presumably arose at the idea of two pairs of isolated people, each desiring to remain separate within the stage conventions, yet brought painfully into contact by the sharing of a similar situation. When Ionesco talked about it from a distance his listening students could laugh. The theatre audience was presumably too close to laugh.

Each response involves forms of sharing within, across or beyond the fourth wall and recognition of suffering and isolation is present in both. The comic response acknowledges the existence of a play world. We play together a game which is not for real, although we recognize a relevance to the real. Tragedy on the other hand, involves us more deeply in performance. Both responses are forms of communication. Academic discussions which restrict a play's meaning to the thematic content too easily forget the emotional and physical response.

The theatrical game, then, may be positive even when 'messages' are negative. Ionesco makes this point in parody. At the end of *The Chairs*, the audience, together with the two old people on stage, wait in trepidation for a message to be brought. A stagy mountebank enters and writes on a blackboard a final incomprehensible word: ANGELBREAD. If it is a message, the truth it contains lies in the realm of metaphor and imagination, not the logic of prose. If the word means nothing, the powerful climax announces a meaning which lies beyond verbal categories.

This brief excursus readily refers us back to Pirandello's concern with the processes of language and play. How can drama, he asks, and how can words allow us to escape from isolation and misunderstanding? *Six Characters* begins with the form of free experimentation known as a play rehearsal. Within the framework of an earlier Pirandello play, entitled appropriately *The Rules of the Game*, actors and director improvise. Trapped within the script, they explore the limited freedom it offers and attempt to bring it to life. They make choices about how and whether to follow the author's precise stage directions, whether to wear such and such a costume, where to enter, where to stand, when to move, how to interpret the lines, in short, all the problems which lend excitement to the openness of rehearsal before the performances are fixed.

The individual Actors begin by competing with one another. Soon they compete with the Characters and with the author himself in their determination to be themselves and not puppets of the script or of another's will. The competition leads to compromise, to an acknowledgement of common purpose (though still, as in life, not equally shared. Bottom cannot play all the parts, and actors do not all accept this with equal grace).

Strong personalities seeking freedom are held in check by the requirements of text, or stage space, or audience expectation, or by other actors. This play, which shows us a play in the making, presents us with a model of social communication, as well as with a model of transactions purely dramatic.

The transactions take the form of a competition between liberties, and posit the need to recognize common concerns. However, this is rudely interrupted by another kind of transaction. Six Characters enter, and ask for their own play to be performed. They seem to have come from nowhere, making demands to which the Actors and Director submit. It seems they represent material the author has not succeeded in making into a play but which insists on breaking into the normal procedures of theatre. It is as if Pirandello the writer is competing with Pirandello the director. The writer wins, for Director and Actors break off rehearsals to improvise the new material. In place of the play in rehearsal (material on which the author has written his name), the Characters attempt to substitute material which is spoken inside his head, but which he has not fully made his own.

The Characters bring a free process with them, challenge the Directors and Actors, as they challenge the author, to make something out of them. The process seems akin to what Keats described as 'negative capability'.[1] Other personalities obliterate the personality of the creative writer, so that he is 'written through' by inner voices which choose to speak through him. Thus Pirandello allegorizes a creative process in the mind as different characters make different claims upon his attention.

The Director in the play is placed in the position of author. The Father and the Stepdaughter speak to him of a situation each explains in different ways. Their clamant voices conflict, the Father protesting his case but rational and apologetic, the Stepdaughter contemptuous and melodramatic in her denial of the Father's version of reality. The author gives them freedom to speak, but their opposition seems to admit of no resolution. For some reason these Characters cannot change.

It seems the Characters are fixed by events which have already occurred, but we only discover at the end that the death of a little girl and the suicide of her brother have enchained the older surviving characters in various ways. The Mother is tied by sorrow and possesses no capacity to understand and distance her loss. The Son distances events by denying involvement and responsibility, a denial which limits his human potential. He has no direction to work in, nothing to give, no one he wishes to give to. On another level, of course, he is no more than a talking image inside the author's head. Without the chain of events he, like the other Characters, does not exist.

The Daughter seeks to impose the mask of villainy upon the Father. She writes melodrama. Out of love of others whom she considers he has harmed, out of her hatred, comes a denial of his complexity.

Only the Father, in his claim for indulgence, in his recognition of another's need to see him in simple terms, appeals to the more complex judgement of the freer spectator. He does not achieve recognition from his fellow 'Characters' or the Actor who attempts to play his role. Yet he communicates beyond the proscenium arch. What he demands is the satisfaction of full representation, a satisfaction he does not get in the play within the play. The Actor who attempts to represent him, unlike the actor who plays him, cannot sense his fullness. He has the limitations of the actor used to playing stereotypes in farce and melodrama or romantic costume plays. When playing the Father he cannot render his character's desire to be free.

The play is about self-expression, self-identity, creativity and the nature of drama. Creativity depends on an understanding of the medium it works in and the conventions which inform it. But to understand does not mean fully to accept. Full acceptance of convention is slavish. The possibility of breaking the Rules of the Game, as Pirandello breaks the rules of the fourth-wall theatre of illusion, opens the chosen form to possibilities previously denied.

Pirandello in 1921, with the Pitoëff production of *Six Characters*, did just this. He made an appeal which changed the recognition of the possibilities of theatre, extending Chekhov's and Stanislavski's stress on rounded character by placing the rehearsal process within the play frame so that the characters can comment on the way the actors play them. This was not without precedent: *Hamlet* and *The Seagull* also place the theatre within the play frame. The 'play within the play' is an old device. But Pirandello uses the rehearsal to introduce discussion of the nature of play and 'reality' and goes beyond naturalism in dramatizing the process of making a play 'natural'. The Characters are creatures of art, and some of them, for reasons Pirandello defines, are harder to naturalize than others.

It is important to recognize that Pirandello's Characters plague the author with an impossible demand. They may be vividly alive in his head and demand to be written into a play, but their story is unsuitable for containment within conventional dramatic rules. It is too long and sprawling a story; it contains problems of ageing; it has too many outdoor locations for a box-set illusionist theatre; it contains young children with untrained, weak voices; it has one obstinately silent and another inarticulate character, both 'undramatic' in the sense that good dialogue cannot come out of them. Another character, the brothel-keeper, can only whisper her secrets, and what use is that if the audience cannot hear? Also, scenes in brothels can offend dramatic and social proprieties. This is a story which the dominant contemporary conventions cannot easily handle.

What does Pirandello do? He has the articulate Characters tell their history in fragments, whilst arguing over the truth of it. The audience is thus drawn creatively into the recreation of past events, and the play tells not only the story, it illustrates the creative process, the shortcomings of the naturalist theatre, and the need for an author to overcome these shortcomings. In doing this, Pirandello acted on creative minds in the next generation. Serious dramatists had, as Eliot said, a great deal to thank him for.

Pirandello in part justifies recent 'post-structural' theory in its challenge to the autonomy of the author, in its emphasis on the disparateness of the 'subject' and doubts about the indivisibility of the 'individual'. Certainly Pirandello is aware of the various voices which speak through a writer. Indeed he claims that plays should not appear to have been written by one person. The writer should be a collection of voices, not far from schizophrenia in this regard, and lacking in central identity.

Actors have similarly been described, and at times Pirandello appears in sympathy with suggestions that actors wish to act in plays in order to acquire an identity of their own. 'At least,' one recalls Fenella Fielding saying, 'when you are playing a part you know who you are supposed to be.' One may turn, however, to Pirandello's comments on the great actress Eleonora Duse. He suggests she became a greater actress as she developed her own personality. It made acting more difficult but gave it depth and power.

For Pirandello the subjective identity could be both integrated and scattered. A man with a life-time experience of acting and writing could speak with some authority. What he demonstrated was the need for control of the voices within him which clamoured for freedom to speak. If those voices were violently hostile to himself, and details of his biography persuade us that such accusatory voices must have lived in his memory, the need to retain identity in the face of accusation must have played a large part in the process. When the Father says of the Stepdaughter: 'She is here in order to fix me' it is not surprising he endeavours to retain his freedom in the face of her scorn.

Pirandello is concerned not only with individuals fixing categories on others but with the way situations impose or cause a mask to be assumed. Tragedies can fix a life in Sorrow (the Mother) or Shame and Revenge (the Stepdaughter) or Indifference (the Son) or Pity (the Father). If laughter cannot relieve one of such 'fixities', at least a kind of freedom can be found in surveying them, releasing the self by setting the voices and images free on stage. The author, like his Characters, like his Actors, seeks to be free in order to be whole.

Symbolist Drama

Maeterlinck, late Ibsen and Strindberg

Whilst Ibsen was writing his later plays, a Swiss student of music, Adolphe Appia (1862–1928), was developing an anti-naturalist theory of drama which owed much to his study of Wagnerian opera. *Music and Theatrical Production*, published in German in 1899, and *The Work of Living Art* (1921) contain his central ideas. The first advocated a new stagecraft, which eliminated two-dimensional scene painting and substituted a kind of sculptural movement, a musical control of the actor's body in space, and fused the whole through use of light. The rhythms of stage movement were to express a platonic reality, a beauty behind appearances. Appia believed in the reality of 'inner being', the expression of which was the function of art. Since this inner being had a different rhythm and time duration from that of our ordinary selves (and consequently from the outer life which naturalism sought to represent) the dramatic art he advocated was stylized and more akin to the Greek chorus (or to the neo-platonic Renaissance court ballet) than to the contemporary naturalism of Ibsen. 'Actualism in dramatic art ... is a coarse negation of musical life,' he said. The actor's gestures and movements were akin to dance. The body spatialized the time units of music under a play of light and colour, a synaesthesia expressing some essence of beauty and perfection.

Appia had much in common with the neo-platonic symbolist movement which arose out of nineteenth-century romanticism. His later theories brought into relation the eurythmics of Dalcroze and the ideas of Schopenhauer: 'Music never expresses the phenomenon, but only the inner essence of the phenomenon'. Walt Whitman, not surprisingly, appears alongside Dalcroze in the dedication of *The Work of Living Art*. Appia remains an important and influential figure for he reminds us that music and spectacle are as much in the mainstream of theatre history as the emphatically speech-centred drama of contemporary naturalism.

One should also, at this point, mention Edward Gordon Craig (1872–1966), son of Ellen Terry. He was a European stage designer; lover and companion of Isadora Duncan; editor, founder of a school of acting, and an important dramatic theorist. (See in particular *On the Art of the Theatre* (1911) and *The Marionette* (1918).) Craig and Appia developed in parallel and their ideas closely correspond. Apart from Appia's preference for a hierarchy of the arts, and Craig's more democratic view that the value of each form of art will vary with the artist's needs; apart also from a greater emphasis in Appia on the moving human body rather than Craig's tendency to see the actor as an element in the total scene, they agreed that suggestion and symbolic presentation were superior to realism, and each worked for a harmony of the various theatre languages.

Appia and Craig carried on an old tradition. The contemporary dramatist with whom they shared most was the Belgian symbolist, Maurice Maeterlinck (1862–1949). Maeterlinck, educated by the Jesuits, wrote poetry and took a deep interest in mystical writings from Plato to Novalis and Plotinus to Emerson. Behind him, too, were the powerful poetic and pictorial traditions of romanticism: the symbolic universe of William Blake; Doré's illustrations of 'The Ancient Mariner'; Samuel Palmer's 'Magic Apple Tree'; Edward Calvert's 'Primitive City'. The sense that nature was but an imperfect reflection of some divine ideal fed into Pre-Raphaelite painting and poetry and nourished symbolic drama. Maeterlinck surrounded himself at home with paintings by Redon[1] and Burne-Jones, producing plays full of a nostalgia for a world beyond the time-ridden present, such as suffuses the early poetry and drama of W. B. Yeats. His one-act drama *L'Intruse* (producd 1891) caused a sensation. The Flemish clock in one corner of the stage announced that 'Time is the moving shadow of eternity.' There is an old blind grandfather of whom it is remarked: 'Not to know where one is, not to know whence one comes, not to know whither one is going, no longer to distinguish midday from midnight, summer from winter . . . and always these shadows . . . these shadows.'

Drama of such a kind runs an obvious danger. Its solemnity does not easily subjugate the satirical spirit and it ran counter to the new abrasive emphasis which Ibsen placed on the short-comings of contemporary society. If careful lighting effects go wrong, and lamps brighten when they should dim, or dim uncontrollably when they should brighten, as happened during one performance of *L'Intruse*, the spectacle of man's solemnity at the mercy of machines provokes hilarity. Worse, it leads to ruffled dignities and even physical exchanges. The leading lady, it is said, suffered on this occasion an accidental blow, aimed by the stage manager at the director, Lugné-Poë,[2] who ducked. . . .

Although Ibsen's naturalism encouraged criticism of this late romantic drama, Ibsen himself moved towards symbolic expression in his later works, without, however, losing his tough, ironic, prose framework. Meanwhile, Maeterlinck produced some fine and imaginative works including the sombre *Pelléas and Mélisande* (1893), an atmospheric, fairy tale allegory in which Love combats Death and loses. The scenes exist to present symbols as much as to develop the simple plot. Thresholds, gates, fountains, cellars, forest, sea, lamp, tower, castle, all communicate, even in the reading, a powerful sense of mystery. Performance requires absolute professionalism. In the original Paris production a bare stage, grey overhead lighting, slight shadows, Pre-Raphaelite costuming and a gauze to separate audience and action made a powerful appeal. The opera Debussy created out of it in 1902 asserted the continuing power of the musical and scenic non-naturalist tradition.

Maeterlinck's most famous drama, *The Bluebird* (1909) was less melancholy in its nostalgia and has obvious connections with fantasy plays for children, such as Barrie's *Peter Pan in Kensington Gardens* (1906) or *Where the Rainbow Ends*, and such cinematic progeny as *The Wizard of Oz* (1939). *The Bluebird*, indeed, was written for a newspaper editor who requested a Christmas story. In it the spirit of pantomime is strong; its vivacity and lightness make it hard to sustain the common accusation of portentousness. W. B. Yeats, however, now in strong reaction against his own earlier poetic style, was not impressed: 'Possibly another of the gasping things, Maeterlinck, struggling well beyond his nature, does to please his wife, who was there last night in a red turban, looking like Messalina.'[3] For Yeats, Maeterlinck was like 'a little boy who has jumped up behind a taxi-cab and can't get off'.[4] Artists should appeal to free and adult spirits. The writer should not be subjugated by current fashion or anyone else's will. Maeterlinck had lowered his sights to please a non-adult audience. Symbolism had become fantasy and the serious concerns of the symbolist movement lost sight of.

Such a shift towards fantasy, however, is not surprising. An appeal to children (as in the later prose allegories of C. S. Lewis, for example) has its own power. By abandoning the solemnity of symbolism, fantasy frees the writer from the strictures of the critical and the satirical mind, making its appeal to a common, if occasional, adult need to return to the world of childhood. It does not run the risk of losing audience sympathy by trying to impose a portentous vision. It implies a free spectator, able to return at will to a childhood world which the spectator has both left behind and carries still within. To be too dismissive of this kind of appeal is to forget that drama is always a type of game.

Naturalism, it has already been remarked, does not ignore the operation of fantasy. It analyses the workings of fantasy, dream and imagination within a realist framework. If characters longed for worlds beyond the box-set, methods had to be found to render such dreams, albeit ironically. The 'real' was not only the outside world. It was what people made of the world inside their heads. Reality consisted of mental images of past and future, as well as images of the contemporary scene. Accordingly, Chekhov and Ibsen found a symbolic method to communicate and comment on the dreams of their characters. The difference between the naturalists and Maeterlinck lay in the importance which the former ascribed to everyday social activity, and the irony which arose from the counterpointing of actuality and dream.

Where this irony wavered, as especially in Ibsen's last play, *When We Dead Awaken* (1899) a resemblance to the work of the symbolists grew strong. Symbolic writing, of course, was fundamental to Ibsen's earlier poetic plays, *Brand* and *Peer Gynt*, which pointed in other directions than the ironies of prose naturalism. Chekhov, it is rumoured, was planning a symbolic drama with a shipwreck when he died and the later work of Strindberg went beyond Ibsen into the realms of dream and metaphysics. The expressionist drama, however, which emerged from the explorations of these writers, employs elements of symbolism with an energy and violence very different from the nostalgic fantasies of Maeterlinck.

When We Dead Awaken is shorter and has less emphasis on plot than Ibsen's preceding plays. The sets are symbolic; there are vivid, often black and white, visual effects; frequent reference is made to the Lohengrin legend, popularized by Wagner, in which the son of the pure knight Parsifal comes to the rescue of Elsa in a boat pulled by a swan. The play uses heightened speech which a semi-insane character, Irene, speaks without irony, since her mind functions symbolically and not logically. The earlier naturalist plays satirize dreamers like Gregers Werle and emphasize the dangers of symbolic thinking. The late plays, and especially the last, are less certain in their attitudes than The Wild Duck and the irony is less controlled. At times the symbolism makes a strong dramatic point. The supernatural Lohengrin, for example, disappears at a point when Elsa's thirst for knowledge becomes too great. Irene's symbolizing, too, appears related to her desire to know and to possess, yet here the process is held at an ironic distance. On the other hand, Ibsen's ending, in which Irene and Rubek go hand in hand up the mountain to certain death sounds a great deal closer to Maeterlinck's romanticism than the painful double suicide at the end of Rosmersholm.

When in 1903 the play was performed in London in Archer's translation, Shaw and Joyce spoke highly of it. According to the former, 'It showed no decay in Ibsen's highest qualities'. And the young Joyce ranked it with 'the greatest of the author's work – if indeed it be not the greatest'. For Ibsen the play formed an 'epilogue to the series of plays which began with A Doll's House . . . If I write anything more, it will be in quite another context; perhaps, too, in another form . . . if I return I shall come forward with new weapons and with new equipment.'

Like The Master Builder (1892), When We Dead Awaken is a play about fears of failing powers, and about the link between love and creativity. Rubek, a restless sculptor, 'feels in his heart of hearts nowhere truly at home'. The feeling of a claustrophobic homeland and the longing to renew creative freedom through love, have an autobiographical ring. In 1898, Ibsen watched a performance of Brand, a play he claims not to have thought about for 30 years. It may have awakened in him a fresh desire to begin again in a new style. Brand, he had once observed, could as well have been a sculptor, or politician, as a priest. In *When We Dead Awaken* the sculptor Rubek seeks a final freedom amid the alternating phobias of the Norwegian landscape. If mountains and heights were dangerous (Brand had died in an avalanche and the Master Builder fell from a tower) the claustrophobia of the fjords and provincial towns constituted just as great a threat to the autonomy of the artist. The glaciers might be cold, but at least the sun shone there. Rubek and Irene climb upwards at the end of the play, while Maja and her new love seek security down below.

If we forget the final irony of a Maja on her journey downwards proclaiming she is free whilst her husband and Irene die in their search for the sun, the treatment of Rubek and Irene lacks the earlier tragic and ironic tone with which, in *Rosmersholm* (1886), the deaths of Rosmer and Rebecca were treated. The earlier drama sees the deaths as atonement for guilt. The later play, in its vision of a possible freedom in death, seems about to lose that awareness of limits which paradoxically extends our freedom in life.

When We Dead Awaken also suffers from the insufficiency of the naturalist means to support the symbolic effect. To take an example: sunlight figures strongly in the lighting plot. Sunrise and sunset may poignantly suggest the rising and setting of the artist's life and talent. The attempt, however, to create powerful poetic effects of light on mountain scenery may be less than poignant within the limits of the box-set. Even more difficult, of course, is the final avalanche when Rubek and Irene are seen momentarily, before being buried in the snow.

The superiority of the cinema in the achievement of such effects was soon to become evident. The coming of film would throw the theatre back on its own resources, on the actor's invitation to an audience to create the scene around him. Naturalism might at first have seemed a liberating medium for it created a full world in which an audience could lose itself. When the cinema came, however, the theatre could not compete with the size and realism of its studio sets or the extreme vividness with which the camera could capture a scene. The cinema would force the theatre to advance from inside the proscenium arch to per- form on open stages where actors would create settings in the audience's imagination. This technology would also encourage the development of a new form, radio drama, in which the absence of everything except voice and sound effect would allow a listener even greater freedom to create his or her own independent world. This was not, however, the immediate direction taken.

When We Dead Awaken employs very ambitious scenic effects together with dialogue which borders on melodrama. There are moments in the play, especially when Rubek and Irene move into moments of shared vision and double madness, which have a heightened prose difficult for actors to sustain within a naturalist setting. In 1900 the play failed everywhere. It had only 11 performances in Christiania. According to Brandes: 'The play is good enough, big enough. The actors were too small.' Perhaps it was rather that Ibsen had fallen back on the bigger rhetorical style of traditional poetic drama or opera and had not managed to reconcile it with the new naturalism. Prose was not adequate to express areas of experience which music expresses more naturally, and the heightened tone of the final scene needs music. At the same time, Ibsen's intention remains uncertain, for the irony is still present. As Rubek and Irene are whirled away to their deaths, after having declared their intention of seeking the sun and freedom, if only for an hour, the sound of Rubek's wife is heard in the valley:

'I am free! I am free! I am free!
My imprisonment is past! . . . .'

The two unresolved visions of freedom make us wonder what direction Ibsen would have taken next.

In this discussion of irony and symbolism it is relevant to mention Chekhov. If from the Russian dramatist's social and psychological concerns we separate questions of technique: his use of light, sound, verbal suggestion, atmosphere, fragmented structure and pervasive stage symbol, it is tempting to assign Chekhov to the symbolist school. This would be a mistake, however. Chekhov's techniques are closer to impressionism, an artistic movement based on close observation, whose principal concern was with the outer world and the play of light across its surfaces. Although the artist's subjectivity inevitably colours the world presented, he retains critical detachment. Thus Chekhov, even when presenting his character's dreams and self-absorption, distances the audience. The tone of Chekhov's unbalanced Nina:

'I'm a seagull . . .' does not draw us fully in. The words are contained within a 'natural' dialogue which is not struggling to move into poetic tragedy. We see Nina within the world, not the world wholly absorbed within Nina. In the semiotic terms of C. S. Pearce, Chekhov's symbols are contained within a pattern of iconic and indexical signs. This is helped by Chekhov's use of Konstantin's symbolist play in Act I. This play within the play has something haunting about it, yet Nina dislikes the lack of living characters. Its stage author, Konstantin, has not yet achieved the fullness of which the theatre is capable. His play needs Chekhov's ironic naturalist framework. In Roman Jacobsen's terminology, *The Seagull* presents a metaphor held within a metonymic structure.[5] Chekhov's naturalism contains the symbolic drama. It is not superseded by it.

Returning to Ibsen, one wonders whether, if he had not suffered in old age a series of strokes, we would have witnessed a last experimental period mixing fairy tale and realism in a form analogous to the final work of Shakespeare. Such an impression is given in Michael Meyer's full biography (*Ibsen*, 1967) when he recalls Henry Moore's observations about the way late works of great artists 'become simplified and fragmentary, become imperfect and unfinished. These artists cease to care about beauty and such things and yet their works get greater'.

The naturalist dramatist, like Konstantin in *The Seagull*, began to seek new forms. The cinema appropriated naturalism, extending its visual realism and enabling rapid changes of location. In the theatre, the late plays of August Strindberg (1849–1912) announced a new direction. These, as Ibsen knew, for he had read the first part of *Road to Damascus* (1898–1901) before embarking on his final play, were to carry the drama in a direction Chekhov, Ibsen himself and the earlier Strindberg had not taken. These would travel beyond Maeterlinck's imaginative fantasies, towards a greater astringency and power.

In 1900 Freud's work on *The Interpretation of Dreams* was published, elevating dream to its high status as the 'royal highroad to the unconscious', thereby conferring a stamp of authenticity on symbolist and romantic preoccupations. Shakespeare, long ago in *A Midsummer Night's Dream* had integrated states of realism and fantasy within a structure which ends with the supernatural Puck sealing the sleep of mortals who have just watched a play. Its farcical treatment prevents them from seeing how it speaks of dangers experienced by them in earlier waking states. The characters shift in levels of consciousness which vary between waking and sleep, dream and nightmare, and states of mind induced by art.

In Ibsen's plays, a few characters, such as the witch-like Hilde in *The Master Builder*, or the 'Lady from the Sea' come disturbingly close to the supernatural and threaten the audience's sense of reality. Yet in most of his plays, Ibsen keeps the threat at a distance since characters dream, or day-dream, within a recognizably real context. After Freud, however, the growing prestige of dreams as sources of truth encouraged a generation of writers to shape whole plays as fragmentary dream structures, characterized by dislocated settings; sudden unaccountable and capricious shifts of narrative; grotesque exaggeration; splitting and fusion of identity; evaporation and scattering of characters – all accepted by the dreamer and his characters with astonishing lack of surprise. A structure was sought which placed consciousness within dream, rather than dream within consciousness. The novels of Franz Kafka were not far off. The hallucinatory chapters of Dostoievski, albeit within a wider social and historical realism, had already shown the way.

This new dramatic structure, therefore, was a representation not of external action, the mimesis of a mythos, but of the inside of the head. Just as Edouard Dujardin's[6] *Les Lauriers sont Coupés* (1887) had suggested to James Joyce a new narrative technique (which Dujardin later described as one of direct access to the unconscious before logical organization) so the late drama of Strindberg anticipated interior monologue and the 'rag-bag', as the infuriated C. E. M. Joad called it, of Joyce's *Ulysses* (1921) as well as the fragmented organization of T. S. Eliot's *The Waste Land* (1922) and Joyce's *Finnegan's Wake* (1939).

In the earlier naturalist plays of Strindberg, from *Miss Julie* (1888) to *Easter* (1900), dreams played an important part in the action. In the last decade of his life, Strindberg found a new direction, one which Dostoievski had already partly travelled. It lay in what Erich Auerbach had defined as 'the essential characteristic of the inner movement documented in Russian realism . . . the unqualified, unlimited, and passionate intensity of experience in the characters portrayed'. The characters, he says, especially of Dostoievski, have something monstrous in them, 'in the change from love to hatred, from humble devotion to animal brutality, from pious simplicity to the most cruel cynicism. Such changes often occur in one person – almost without transition – in tremendous and unpredictable oscillations.'[7] Dostoievski explored the realm of dream, madness, hallucination and phantasmagoria as had few before him. Other precedents can be found, in Shakespeare's *King Lear*, in Blake, in Emily Brontë's Heathcliff, in Melville's Captain Ahab, of extreme states which threaten the stability of the narrative structure and challenge the sanity of reader or narrator. In fiction, the insanity was usually contained within a kind of normality: a placid narrator, or a world of recognizable causation. With Strindberg, whose nature had always run to extremes, the play structure itself took on the looser patterns of poetry and the guise of dream or madness. Causality was what the spectator searched for, not what the play offered.

In *A Dream Play* (1902) and *The Ghost Sonata* (1907) Strindberg fractured the drama, attempting to represent the inner world of characters and at the same time to suggest a realm beyond the visible world. He combined the aims of Ibsen and Chekhov on the one hand and the symbolists on the other.

The Ghost Sonata, said Strindberg, is 'like life, when the scales fall from the eyes, and one sees *Das Ding an Sich*'. He added, 'What has kept my soul from plunging into darkness during my work is my religion, the hope of something better, and the firm conviction that we live in a world of illusion and folly from which we must free ourselves.'[8] The play is, on one level, an ironic psychological allegory about secrets to be found in every home. It was written for Strindberg's own Intimate Theatre and abandons naturalistic characterization. The characters are symbolic, representative of different stages of life and of different attitudes to it. The action is dream-like. Characters who can be seen by one are invisible to others. The central character, who is a 'Sunday child' with special vision to whom the dead appear, is the Student. His name is Arkenholtz, suggestive of the ark saved from the flood. He is a rescuer, an idealist, an artist admiring beauty, a knight on a quest, who happens upon an ordeal in a 'Hyacinth Room' which he discovers is not the world of his ideal imaginings. The young lady who lives in the room withers away and dies. She seems to be a product of the Student's romantic vision. If this is true, the play makes a comment on its own origins – in the conflict within Strindberg between the real and the ideal.

The aspects of the Student reminiscent of Strindberg himself encourage this view: a prophetic didacticism reigns and a detached self-analysis. The irony is guarded, less direct than in Ibsen, more astringent than Maeterlinck. The Student is in danger of being poisoned by the flowers. He absorbs the poison and seems to become, like the Old Man in the play with whom he has an affinity, a poisoner: 'Your flowers have poisoned me and now I am squirting their poison back at you.'

The Student is an allegory of parasitic creativity, living on others, especially women, as others live on him. Thus he enters a symbolic house with various symbolic rooms, seeking beauty and finding a knowledge he did not expect: the house contains time and ageing as well as beauty. But if one passes through this room, the play seems to say, the walls will disappear and the Great Liberator will come. At this final point the play moves out of psychological allegory, using music and prayer, into the realm of theology:

> You wise and gentle Buddha, sitting there waiting for a heaven
> to spring from the earth, grant us patience in our ordeal and purity of will, so that this hope may not be confounded.

The strings of a harp hum softly and a white light fills the room:

> I saw the sun. To me it seemed
> That I beheld the hidden . . . . .

The play ends with music 'soft, sweet and melancholy'.

Strindberg has dropped the irony which qualified Ibsen's climactic deaths in *When We Dead Awaken*. He has moved from the realm of tragedy into a church. For those who believe the church encompasses the drama, this is an advance. If drama encompasses the church (and originally moved out of the church to recover irony and humour and a secular spirit) then Strindberg's play is not an advance but a return.

Such a movement was bound to call forth a further reaction. It was clear that this psychological allegory which lapses, or climbs, into theology, would soon invite an answer from a new secular spirit. Before that occurred, however, there was a brief and intense flowering of a drama too little known in Britain. This was German expressionism.

German Expressionism

Its methods and effects

The late plays of Strindberg, written in the first decade of the twentieth century, together with elements in *Brand* and *Peer Gynt* which lie beneath Ibsen's naturalistic drama, lead into German expressionism. This movement in its turn gave rise to epic drama and heralded the most influential playwright of the century – Bertolt Brecht (1898–1956).

The expressionist movement within the theatre parallels a similar shift in the visual arts. Edvard Munch (1863–1944) the Norwegian painter, like his fellow Scandinavian writers, spent much time in Germany, influencing the work of Ernst Kirchner (1880–1938), Emil Nolde (1867–1956), Karl Schmidt-Rottluff (1884–1976) and the Austrian Oscar Kokoschka (1886–1980). This expressionist art movement had a strong influence on theatre design.

The term 'expressionist' applies to other artists: to the composers Alban Berg (1885–1935) and Arnold Schoenberg (1874–1951), to the film director Robert Wiene (1881–1938) who made *The Cabinet of Dr Caligari* (1919), to the war poets Georg Trakl (1887–1914) and Franz Werfel (1890–1945), the architect Erich Mendelsohn (1887–1953) and the novelists Alfred Döblin (1878–1957) and Franz Kafka (1883–1924). Such obvious variety of reference does not encourage a precise use of the term. However, there remains fairly common agreement about its meaning: a general movement in the arts during and just after World War I which expresses extreme feelings of personal, familial and general social breakdown. 'Apocalyptic' is the adjective frequently used of this highly subjective movement in which artists figure frequently as protagonists projecting their sufferings over a fractured world.

Apart from Munch, the prophets of the movement are, in the visual arts, El Greco, Grünewald, Goya and van Gogh. The literature of the movement, preoccupied with the agonies of war, finds its ancestry in the insights of the *Sturm und Drang* movement, in Schiller, Schopenhauer, Nietzsche, Dostoievski, Freud and Wedekind. Strindberg is only the latest of a succession of writers examining the depths of the psyche under extreme conditions. Thus the dream structure, disjointed, concentrated, caricatural, questing, strange, is the dominant form of expressionism. The characteristic setting has clusters of powerful primary colours, with heavy flickering shadows and strong lighting. The platonic visions of Adolphe Appia have been transformed into nightmare.

The fundamental drive behind expressionism is, as usual with new movements, a drive towards freedom. It saw naturalism as a restrictive, determinist, positivist, materialist and reactionary programme, which took people to be products of the environment. In its place it posited freedom from all constraint and an embracing of all mankind. Its politics were anarchic. It believed in love, the renewal of the individual and the achievement of brotherhood. In particular the creative artist brought mankind the chance of redemption. Unfortunately it was a chance mankind did not always appreciate.

In Georg Kaiser's *From Morning to Midnight* (1916), one of the crucial plays of the movement, a bank cashier revolts against the world. An idealist searching for the absolute, he repudiates society, embezzles money and flees into a symbolic snowfield where he has a conversation with Death. He plunges on, offering high prizes to winners of a six-day bicycle race, but the people are too tame for his vision. He continues to travel, seeking his brothers in a Salvation Army hall. Here he finds people confessing their sins. He confesses himself, and throws his money into the hall in an ecstasy of abnegation. The 'saved' throw themselves on the money. Understandably the cashier loses faith. He can now trust only one person, a girl, but she calls the police and he shoots himself. *From Morning to Midnight* is a vivid episodic play embodying a vision of the collapse of modern industrial civilization. In its episodic structure it looks forward to Brecht and back to *Peer Gynt* and *Brand*.

Walter Hasenclever (1890–1940) was a writer whose *The Son* (1914) is considered the first representative expressionist play. Hasenclever used the word himself to describe this ecstatic drama, brilliantly interpreted by the young Ernst Deutsch as the Son who desires freedom from a domineering burgher Father. The father-dominated central European world of Freud and Kafka was brought very close. Hasenclever was nevertheless dissatisfied with the stage realism of the first Prague production. He preferred Richard Weichert's later rendering in January 1918, which, against a hauntingly unreal set, presented the Son isolated within a cone of light.

Reinhard Sorge (1892–1916) was another who protested against the dominance of the family. This time, in *The Beggar*, produced posthumously in 1917, it is a mother who obsessively loves her son. The father has a mad obsession with the planet Mars. The son poisons both his parents in an act of symbolic liberation. He is then wedded to a new person, a 'vital force', and reaches out towards her. In this play the people have no names. An adolescent idealism makes its demands on behalf of the oppressed. The language runs to rhetoric, turning to song and verse as the play, in a series of short scenes, leads towards cataclysm.

A writer who precedes all these is Oscar Kokoschka, a Viennese more famous as a painter. Such a picture as 'The Tragedy of Man' (1908) is clearly expressionist. In it, one sinister, agonized figure holds up another in a grotesque parody of the deposition of Christ from the cross. The primary colours are red and black, and a symbolic sun and moon preside over the scene. The tense brush strokes and thickly applied colour recall Munch and Van Gogh, and the picture clearly defines the emotional characteristics of the drama it depicts: Kokoschka's one-act play, *Murder, Hope of Women* which was performed as early as 1909 amid noisy scenes at the Vienna *Kunstschau*.

In England the movement made itself felt, over a period of time, within the work of individual and very different artists, especially those of European stature. One can cite D. H. Lawrence whose paintings and prose fiction clearly reflect expressionist influence. In his novels, after the autobiographical naturalism of *Sons and Lovers* (1913), there is a strong movement towards the exploration of extreme states. 'I will never write in that way again' he said, in a letter to Edward Garnett, and determined to explore the deeper, rawer realms of the psyche, the common areas beneath the apparent 'psychological' differences on the surface.

Lawrence married a German woman and knew German culture well. The new expressionistic vitalism was reflected in *Women in Love* (1920), where the landscapes, without losing their naturalism, reflect the intense psychological states of his characters. But Lawrence, expressionist in his painting, and to a degree in his fiction, never became an expressionist in his drama. His plays belong to the earlier naturalistic phase of his career, and it was not until the late 1960s, nearly 40 years after his death, that his potential as a dramatist was recognized. The plays, especially the fine *Daughter in Law* (1911), will be discussed in a later chapter on the resurgence of working class naturalism.

The second British dramatist one might include is W. B. Yeats (1865–1939). Certainly the shift in his poetic techniques between 1917 and 1921 suggests a movement towards apocalypse and breakdown. The approach of a nightmare world is prophesied, for example, in a famous post-war poem 'The Second Coming' (1921). His drama, however, lies a long way away from continental expressionism. Other influences, oriental in particular, were to be seen in such symbolic plays as *At the Hawk's Well* (1917). In the later *Purgatory* (1938), however, the heightened use of lighting, the symbolic set, and the violent relation between father and son is suggestive of the German movement. But Yeats's later drama, like Lawrence's early work, did not carry into the public domain. Expressionism never became a group movement in Britain. It only influenced a number of very different individuals.

One of these was T. S. Eliot (1888–1965) whose long poem *The Waste Land* (1921) employed fragmented semi-dramatic techniques to convey states of personal and social breakdown. Eliot, however, specifically denied that the purpose of his art was expressionist. Art, he said, was not an expression of personality but an escape from it. Nevertheless his early attempt at drama: *Sweeney Agonistes: A Fragment of an Agon*, shared with his early poems (which are often fragmented dramatic monologues, even radio plays for voices) an expressionistic grotesqueness, a preoccupation with murder and violence, and typological characterization. It was a style which is still faintly recognizable in the sombre, family-centred drama which he wrote for the public stage: *The Family Reunion* (1938).

In Weimar Germany during the 1920s expressionism was much more than a private influence. It flourished as a real theatre movement through the brilliant generation of directors and designers who impressed their imaginations upon the whole decade. Leopold Jessner's production of Schiller's *William Tell* in 1919, using the designs of Emil Pirchan, was an expressionist revival of a play which seems at first an oddly romantic choice for the period. However, a Germany in crisis after the abortive revolution at the end of the war welcomed the production. Schiller had written the play in 1804 when Europe was under the threat of Napoleonic domination. It calls for freedom, the unification of a people, and ends with a baron freeing his serfs. The plea of a rich aristocrat for acceptance by the Swiss Confederation as 'your citizen' could be taken as a parallel to the situation in Weimar Germany. With a public which feared extremism, yet aspired to liberty and justice, the production was highly popular.

Arguably, however, expressionism was already in decline. Jessner was more a bourgeois liberal than a revolutionary. His public longed for security as much as freedom. Expressionism was to be seen more in the theatrical style than the play's statement. Jessner eliminated Schiller's scene-painting. The play's pictorial stage directions were ignored. Geometrical silhouettes, characteristic of the expressionist painters, replaced the pastoral lakeland scene of mountains and green meadows. In place of scenery, Jessner used actors on varying levels. The use of light, colour, gesture, and words, however, revealed Jessner's debt to Adolphe Appia as much as to the agonized highlighting of earlier expressionist productions. The theatre, despite the heightened emotional tone and the cry for liberation, was moving back towards classical balance. In fact, the production imposed an intellectual precision upon the emotional core. The simplified scene, with pillars for trees, details eliminated, windows stylized – the whole dominated by a naked and monumental staircase – had a strong architectural emphasis. Jessner used its levels to allegorize the theme of repression and placed the different social strata at different heights on the set, the instruments of repression above and the citizens below. Such a set seems to have caused problems for Albert Bassermann, the actor who played William Tell and whose training was naturalist, but not for Fritz Kortner, a more stylized actor who played Gessler with an incisive diction and economy of movement in keeping with the visual presentation of the play. This famous production, with its growing objectivity, its non-naturalism, its social protest and use of a kind of epic allegory, anticipates the work of Brecht. It also reasserts, especially through Pirchan's designs, the terracing of the set, and the strict economy of means, the theatre of Appia and Craig.

Ludwig Sievert (1887–1966) was more representative of the expressionist movement, at least in that phase of his long career between 1918–26 when (for example in Hasenclever's *The Son*), he employed brilliant cones of light falling from above to illuminate and isolate character within a disintegrating box-set, or, as in a production of Strindberg's *The Great Highway* (1923), he used as backdrop the long perspective of a street leaning towards collapse around a central vanishing point. Otto Reigbert, too, (1890–1957), with his sharp contrasts and distorted sets revealed the characteristic violence of artists marked by war. Both these artists anticipated later developments: Sievert in the symmetry of his designs, and Reigbert in the exposure of the industrial city which enclosed the sufferings within the fragmenting room. Brecht's plays in the 1920s, from the expressionist *Drums in the Night* (1922) to *The Mother* (1932), do not fill the stage space with the naturalist room but reduce its size so as to represent the urban and factory scenes outside.

In the mid-1920s the theatre moved away from an emphasis on violence and suffering towards a more balanced social realism which was termed the 'new objectivity' or *neue Sachlichkeit*. As memories of war and private anguish retreated, the social concerns of expressionism came to the fore.

If we except the movement's predecessors, August Strindberg and Frank Wedekind (1864–1918), Ernst Toller (1893–1939) is probably its most important exponent. A Jew from a wealthy background, he joined up as a nationalist in 1914 to become a pacifist, socialist and utopian revolutionary. The freedom he sought was not that of the individual within the family but of the oppressed classes in society. When the Bavarian revolution failed he was jailed as head of the Workers and Soldiers Council and spent five years in prison writing plays. His first play *The Conversion* (1917–8) was finished at the beginning of his gaol sentence. It depicts the 'Struggle of a Man', the play's subtitle. The Man undergoes suffering in factory and prison before a personal transfiguration compels him to publish his manifesto on behalf of fraternity and humanity. Toller's later works turn towards realism and pessimism. *The Machine Wreckers* (1922) is a historical parable about the Luddites and attacks the processes of capitalism. It has an optimistic element and foresees the possibility of a united body of workers. With the growth of fascism Toller's vision moved towards tragedy. His work reveals the contradictions which give the expressionist movement its power. The longing for a just society is less clear-headed than the steady rejection of despair in the work of Brecht. A desperate and remorseless fatalism develops in *Hoppla Wir Leben* (1927) carrying an early prediction of Toller's suicide in the year which saw the Stalin-Hitler pact announce a new World War.

Between the wars German expressionism affected British and American public theatre mainly through the work of W. H. Auden (1907–72), Sean O'Casey (1880–1964) and Eugene O'Neill (1888–1953). Auden collaborated with Christopher Isherwood on three plays: *The Dog Beneath the Skin* (1936), *The Ascent of F6* (1937) and *On the Frontier* (1939). The second is an allegorical drama in which an individual embarks on a quest for a mother figure and seeks in the process to liberate both himself and society. Such a plot invites the term 'expressionist' but Auden was coming to intellectual maturity as Brecht's astringent operatic burlesques, *Mahagonny* (1930) and *The Threepenny Opera* (1928) caught public interest. Auden's verse drama mixes expressionism with satirical opera, musical comedy, the still recognizable rhythms of Eliot's burlesque prose and the 1930s cult of the athletic mountain climber.

Sean O'Casey is also said to develop from naturalistic techniques towards expressionism, especially in the second act of the play about World War I, *The Silver Tassie*, which Yeats refused to put on at the Abbey Theatre in 1928. Yeats had also excluded the poetry of war poets, such as Wilfred Owen, from his *Oxford Book of English Verse* on the principle that readers were likely to enjoy it for the wrong reasons. War and suffering he felt were not appropriate subjects for art, and this may be why O'Casey was sent into the wilderness. Yeats's judgement was a great loss for Irish drama. Others could have learned from the powerful expressionism of *The Silver Tassie* whose subject permitted less use of the brilliant O'Casey stock-in-trade of comic Irish speech. If such a talent sometimes undercuts our sympathy with his lower-class characters, this play runs no risk of that. In the second act of *The Silver Tassie*, O'Casey creates the atmosphere of the battlefield. He uses song and choral chanting, stylized and repetitive dialogue, vivid sound and lighting effects on a lacerated landscape. A sick soldier, named the Croucher, acts as prologue. He intones the prophetic biblical vision of an army which becomes a valley of dry bones. The soldiers engage in half-line exchanges. A visitor inspects the men, then hurries off after the men have prevented him striking a match on the crucifix. The scene ends as a ritual act of worship of the gun as the enemy approaches. Then the men fire the gun soundlessly in rhythmical movements.

In the 1930s there was little room for expressionist theatre, indeed, this movement was little known in England. O'Casey himself scarcely mentions it in his letters, Toller is the writer he most admired and even so came to him late:

> England will be standing nearer to a finer drama when Toller has his London season. That dawn seems a long way off, for as I write in London, and probably all over England, of all the plays presented there are but three or four that can be said to come within the circle of drama, and of these one was written by an Irishman and the other two were written hundreds of years ago.

O'Casey wrote this in *The New Statesman* in February 1935. The British theatre was not able to take the experimentation either of O'Casey or of the German dramatists with whom, almost accidentally, he found something in common.

American drama was more open. The Theatre Guild was putting on expressionist German plays very early. Kaiser's *From Morning to Midnight* and *Gas* (1926) together with Toller's *Man and Masses* (1924) and *Machine Breakers* (1927) were among these. Kenneth Macgowan called attention to the Freudian and psychoanalytical side of the German movement in his book *Continental Stagecraft* and such dramatists as Elmer Rice and John Lawson experimented with the style. Eugene O'Neill, however, anticipated these events. He was using innovative methods from 1920, when *The Emperor Jones* was staged. This play is about the flight of its eponymous hero through the forest. Abandoned by his subjects in the first scene, he falls a prey to visions which are presented through the use of vivid colour, light, music and movement. On his journey Jones sinks into his own psyche, moving from sense impressions through personal memory towards the non-personal archetypes of Jung. Death and solitude are the fundamental concerns, and the freedom Jones seeks is similar to that of Strindberg's Stranger in *Road to Damascus* which had been staged in New York in 1914–15. In that play the Stranger states: 'The idea that I am master of my fate gives me a sense of unbelievable power'. Jones, who carries around a silver bullet for final use on himself, has a similar sense. If Strindberg's Stranger declares he is more afraid of solitude than death: 'for in solitude you can always meet somebody', this, too, reminds us of Jones.

It seems that O'Neill's expressionist techniques, which he was prone to deny, came from the study of Strindberg. His breaking away from the dominant naturalism of the American theatre is clear from the next play, *The Hairy Ape* (1921). O'Neill shows the social and physical disparity between the stoker Yank, who works in a sombre and violent stokehold in the bowels of a ship until he wakes up to consciousness of himself when a top-deck passenger, Mildred, faints at the sight of him. Seeking freedom, he goes on a similar journey to Kaiser's Cashier, but is hemmed in by iron bars wherever he is, whether in the stokehold, in prison, or in the zoo where he dies. Yank cannot find a language to convince others of his pain, unlike his author who embarked on a more successful voyage towards self-expression.

O'Neill disliked the 'expressionist' tag. He felt the writers it described spoke too subjectively, restricting the freedom of their characters. Perhaps this is true. O'Neill's drama is still performed because his characters possess a vivid independence beyond the flat anonymity of many expressionist plays, now relegated to theatrical archives.

Expressionism had its moment, when the agonies of war distorted human vision into hallucination and nightmare. In the recovery from such visions the pendulum swung again towards realism. Marxist critics argued that such states of mind were not universal visions but products of a particular period of history. The work of Erwin Piscator and Bertolt Brecht became less extreme, saner, and more objective and analytical in the middle and later years of the Weimar Republic, before the Nazi curtain came down on the German theatre. The *neue Sachlichkeit* and the epic theatre established a new critical realism. Meanwhile O'Neill would develop the intense poetic naturalism which was to carry through to the work of Tennessee Williams after World War II.

Irish Drama

Comic subversion in Wilde;
nationalism and naturalism in Yeats

At the beginning of the twentieth century a growing Irish nationalism led in 1904 to the foundation of an indigenous Irish drama at the Abbey Theatre, Dublin, where W. B. Yeats, John Millington Synge and Lady Augusta Gregory in their various ways worked to combine the older English dramatic tradition of Shakespeare with the new naturalism and vivid colloquial forms of Irish speech.

But already in the 1890s, two Irishmen, Oscar Wilde and George Bernard Shaw, were the most important dramatists of the London theatre. The former worked in the mainstream of European drama, combining popular nineteenth-century dramatic forms with the earlier comedy of wit and manners. Shaw, like Wilde a man of great verbal gifts, was less concerned with the social manners of a particular class than with the overall social structure. Unlike Wilde, he was strongly influenced by Fabian socialism and the middle class, tragi-comic naturalism of Ibsen. From this and from experiments with a variety of dramatic styles he developed a new form of discussion play. His methods and his relation to subsequent political theatre will be considered in a later chapter.

Oscar Wilde (1854–1900) was a European writer. His *Salomé* (1892), a one-act play on a biblical theme, was first written in French and produced in Paris in 1896. It had a phenomenal success with Sarah Bernhardt in the title role but the solemn and timid English establishment banned it for religious reasons. For any director drawn to the more spectacular and musical European tradition, the subject held great appeal. Wilde was no doubt impressed by Maeterlinck, perhaps especially by the Paris production of *Seven Princesses* (1891). The play is still revived and yields to more than one theatrical style – as Steven Berkoff demonstrated in a startling 1989 National Theatre production which made extensive use of mime.

Wilde's other early apprentice work, *Vera* (1882) and *The Duchess of Padua* (1891), unsuccessfully explored the realm of melodrama and verse tragedy, a medium essayed by most of the major Romantic poets, including Keats, Shelley and Byron. His subsequent success lay in parodying these modes in a series of brilliant and witty plays: *Lady Windermere's Fan* (1892), *A Woman of No Importance* (1893), *An Ideal Husband* (1895) and especially the late comedy of manners, *The Importance of Being Earnest* (also 1895).

Wilde's continuing popularity derives from the brilliant plotting and devastatingly witty dialogue of characters who invent new roles for themselves in the elaborate social games they play. Wilde attacks solemnity and the apparent incapacity of a Victorian middle class to respond ironically, and on several levels, to the process of living. His light-hearted advocation of social games-playing may have seemed frivolous to the high-minded Victorians who either did not possess such skills, or realized that they, too, played games. But Wilde was serious and subversive in his frivolity.

His success with audiences largely drawn from the classes he mocked invites the standard charge of irresponsibility and compromise. In *The Importance of Being Earnest* the foundling, John Worthing, in the long tradition of bastards and outsiders who enliven fiction from the Spanish 'rogue novel' to Fielding's *Tom Jones* and beyond, gets the girl and is finally allowed to marry into the social structure. This outsider-become-insider represents, so the argument runs, a contained threat. The happy ending confirms audience prejudice that society is a good thing to marry into, and the discovery that the foundling is not in fact illegitimate confirms the validity of barriers of birth.

Of course there is a degree of compromise here, yet in this ambiguous play subversive elements remain. Defeating the social conventions is the play's main subject, for Wilde creates a spectacle of people seeking control over their lives by creating double identities. The idle aristocrat, Algy, invents a sick invalid,

Bunbury, to avoid unwanted social demands. More pertinently the outsider, John Worthing, pretends to be 'Earnest' in town and Jack in the country. Their future partners, Gwendolen and Cecily play their social games in the search for a mate who is both respectable and not respectable, responsible and irresponsible, inside the social group and yet outside it. The first seeks to acquire a husband with money and no name; the other is attracted to a man who has a name but no money. Behind the lightness of touch, and the dramatic sympathy felt for the successful gamesters, the play hints at personal needs which lie beneath social play and conventions. They also suggest, in the tradition of the comedy of manners, not only how important for the enjoyment of life and the achievement of ends is a mastery of play, but also how impoverished is the community which does not recognize this.

Wilde's concern with the relation between the theatrical and the social process carries his drama beyond a comedy of stereotypes. His people play their roles with a comic gravity and verbal skill that give them an extra dimension. They seem to possess a personal independence which only the great comic characters of English drama enjoy. Though they closely resemble stage stereotypes (Miss Prism, for example is a 'Woman with a Past' and Lane is the perennial stage butler) Wilde parodies the codes they practise by giving them such exaggerated gravity as to belie their utterances. From the imperturbable Lane to the gorgon, Lady Bracknell, the characters have a verbal control, and a desire to control their situations, which enlists our sympathy. Wilde's comedy is warmer than the more savage French tradition. His characters defend their positions in ways which take us by surprise, and their performances engage the audience because only fine actors can perform the games they play so convincingly. We may repudiate Wilde by talking of 'compromise' but something in this apparently frivolous drama goes beyond our moral and rational critiques. The free play at the ambiguous heart of his comedy ensures a continuing appeal.

All the main comic theories apply to Wilde's work. He illustrates Bergson's theory, developed in *Le Rire* (1900), that comedy is health-giving. Humanity so easily encrusts itself with routine behaviour, compulsions, and mechanical thinking that it needs comedy to cure it. Other theories of comedy, such as Freud's, are also applicable to Wilde. Freud argues for the anarchic nature of comedy. Laughter indicates the presence of social subversion. It recognizes our shared awareness of the cloaked existence of sex and desire, providing relief for the feelings not normally directly expressed. Bergsonian 'superiority' laughter and Freud's 'relief' theory mingle in Wilde's play. The laughter he evokes cures by taking stock of the self's denial of freedom. It is a recognition of the dangers of fixation and rigidity.

Of course, laughter which mocks individuals, groups, races, and classes without recognizing the fixity of its own standpoint invites repudiation, but Wilde's standpoint is fluid. Just as his famous aphorism: 'Work is the curse of the drinking classes' could either provoke laughter at the expense of a working class which was supposed not to work, or of a middle class which perpetuated solemn clichés, so his plays work with superiority from above or subversively from below. They also illustrate that collision of logic which Kant, in the third dominant theory of laughter, suggests is the root of comedy.[1] It can be seen as reactionary, progressive or simply anarchic.

Much of the laughter in Wilde's most famous play is similar, for he attacks the concept of seriousness itself, making a fool of those who argue seriously for it. Yet he raises serious questions about the nature of role-play, the relation of language to reality and the dualism of the self. The play mocks a particular class of people, at the end of the nineteenth century, who perhaps deserve some derision. But beyond the mockery is an invitation to recognize the self in the dualisms of these people.

A sombre Marxism, of course, may argue that both mockery and self-recognition are feelings which obstruct the realization of a better society. Bergson's 'superiority laughter' is an expression of class-consciousness. Freud's 'relief' laughter disperses the head of steam necessary for social revolution. The third kind of laughter, arising from a recognition of the disparity between language and the world, anarchically undercuts the solemn words of its political and religious prophets.

But if Wilde's comedy did not work towards revolution, it may have encouraged forms of cultural progress and personal freedom. The Irish and Gallic traditions of wit, anarchic as they were, targetted in the 1890s a characteristic English solemnity, which permeated a whole social class of spectator/readers and the styles of poetry and drama they favoured. Wilde devastatingly punctured this solemnity.

It is worth remembering that a certain satirical tone, sought and found in France, helped the young T. S. Eliot to liberate himself from nineteenth-century forms. With the partial exception of Byron and Browning, English poets and aspiring dramatists were afflicted by high seriousness. The major romantic poets had attempted to compose drama on Shakespearean lines but were unable to equal the success of Schiller and Goethe or de Musset's *Lorenzaccio*. Nor were the later romantics successful. They lacked classical irony, without which both audience sympathy and dramatic suspense were largely absent.

A Wilde and a Shaw were needed to humanize the theatre. However the audience chose to take them, they offered an awareness of human limitation, and re-established a link with the long comic tradition stretching back to the Greeks. Writing for the commercial theatre, Wilde, unlike Shaw, did not try to break through to a new audience. He was no conscious revolutionary inaugurating a new political theatre. But he reinvigorated a comic form which both subverts and consoles. As we look back, his vitality condemns the inflexibility of a society which could accept his art but not his life.

In Ireland the major figure behind the rise of Irish theatre was W. B. Yeats (1865–1939), who tried to retain in his drama what Wilde discarded. The new Irish drama did not develop out of the comedy of manners as with Wilde, or directly out of Ibsen and socialist writing, as was the case with Shaw. It came out of a growing Irish nationalism and it sought to work, like romanticism, in a tradition which was lyrical and poetic. Fortunately it also sought to establish itself in a specifically Irish popular tradition, and it formed an alliance with the new naturalism.

The famous Abbey Theatre began with a manifesto in 1897 proposing to build an Irish school of dramatic literature with a 'freedom to experiment which is not found in theatres in England'. It rebelled against the presentation of the stage Irishman: 'We will show Ireland is not the home of buffoonery and easy sentiment' (even if later plays by Synge and O'Casey depicted ways in which the Irish imagination ran to such sentiment and buffoonery). At first the insistence was on the importance of the spoken word. In 1904, when it first acquired its theatre, the principles of the new school were literary. The plays had to be 'literature'. The drama had to be one 'of energy, of phantasy, of musical and noble speech'. With this emphasis it could not be comic, nor, in its search for 'a new kind of scenic art', was it naturalistic.

This programme, however, was not fully achieved. According to the later, disappointed Yeats, it achieved a theatre 'all objective, with the objectivity of the office and the workshop, of the newspaper and the street, of mechanism and of politics . . .'. He adds: 'We did not set out to create this kind of theatre and its success has been to me a discouragement and a defeat.' They had set out 'not understanding the clock' . . . 'to bring again the theatre of Shakespeare, or rather perhaps of Sophocles.' The Irish school looked towards 'the imagination and speech of the country, all that poetic tradition descended from the Middle Ages'.[2] In so far as it was an Irish national drama and thus imbued with a desire to be free of English rule, Yeats looked to traditional Irish mythology rather than the contemporary social scene. But what the Abbey achieved, in the work of Synge and Sean O'Casey, was, like Ibsen's, a drama of conflict between dreamer and reality. *The Playboy of the Western World* (1907), *Juno and the Paycock* (1924) and *The Plough and the Stars* (1926) mingled lyricism with social concern and a naturalist tradition, retaining a powerful comic tone.

Yeats contributed immensely to the Abbey's achievement, however much it later departed from his personal vision, and his influence was widely felt. He encouraged Eliot, Auden and Fry to combat the dominant naturalism and bring back an older tradition of poetic language, while he himself went on to experiment with oriental theatre, ancient myth and poetic forms of staging, as he moved well away from his earlier, more popular drama and looked back on his early phase with considerable misgiving. In the poem 'The Man and the Echo', written in July and revised up to October 1933, three months before his death, Yeats wrote:

> All that I have said and done
> Now that I am old and ill
> Turns into a question till
> I lie awake night after night
> And never get the questions right
> Did that play of mine send out
> Certain men the English shot?

The poet in old age is haunted by what Eliot in 'Little Gidding' called the 'rending pain of reenactment/ Of all that you have done and been.' His early use of theatre as an instrument of freedom brought with it the pain of responsibility, which then flowered as poetry.

Despite Yeats's misgivings, his early drama is a considerable achievement. In it, the naturalist style is more strongly present than his observations would have us believe. The play Yeats refers to in his poem is *Cathleen ni Houlihan*, performed in Dublin in 1902 with Maud Gonne in the leading role. In 1899, Maud Gonne had played the title role of an earlier apprentice play *The Countess Cathleen*, which Yeats wrote specially for her. Eight years before, Yeats had proposed to her for the first time (the last was in 1917): she always refused. ('The world will thank me Willy Yeats'.) She had fallen ill with overwork during a threatened famine in Donegal and Yeats told her she had enabled him to understand an Irish tale about a woman who bartered her soul for bread to feed the peasantry. Her nationalism, her effect on Yeats and her work as an actress make her an important figure in the story.

Cathleen ni Houlihan was Yeats's third play and very success-ful. In it, Yeats married naturalism to Irish mythology; Maud and Ireland appear in a new guise. But the immediate stimulus, as is often the case with Yeats, was a dream, 'almost as distinct as a vision . . . of a cottage where people were talking in the firelight. . . . Into the midst of that cottage came an old woman in a long cloak. She was Ireland herself . . .'[3]

When the play begins there are three people in a cottage, a woman, her husband, Peter, and one of his sons, Patrick, sitting on either side of a burning fire. The play uses the fourth-wall convention, with no asides or soliloquys. The people appear to speak the language, wear the clothes and sit amid the props and furniture of one place and time. It is a historical reconstruction of a moment when at Killala in 1798, a French force landed under General Humbert. People do ordinary things. One opens a parcel, another the window. But as Ibsen and Chekhov had shown, the naturalist concern with surface accuracy, in costume, props and set, led beyond the pictured room to a concern with the unseen spaces: the house, garden, forest, town, fjord, steppe or railway which lay outside. Naturalism forces the actors to create space and in *Cathleen ni Houlihan* the outer world enters through sounds the actors hear down in the town. The audience hears of strangers walking the road, pausing by places where unseen people work. The unseen, left unexplained, leaves a sense of unease, as the characters shift back into their on-stage activities. One opens a door, the others examine wedding clothes. The play expands in time rather than space as the characters recall past weddings and anticipate the immediate future.

The man who enters, Michael, Peter's other son, brings with him a bag of money from the bride's father, which Peter handles with satisfaction. They talk of the immediate use of this dowry and of the girl Delia who brought it. Then they hear cheering in the town and Patrick goes out to discover the cause. Father and mother talk on, concerned with their rising social status which is a matter of indifference to the young around them.

Michael goes to the window. An old woman is coming up the path. Michael hides the money. The woman passes the window slowly before entering. She is welcomed and sits by the fire, warming herself and creating a sense of the difference between this warm interior and the cold wind outside.

The woman is unknown, unnamed. She is a traveller who has lost her land which consists of four beautiful green fields. Too many strangers in the house caused her to leave. At this point, the play moves from naturalism into allegory. The unnamed woman is Ireland; the strangers in the house are the English; the four fields are Ulster, Munster, Leinster and Connaught. The unknown noise, too, also takes on the power of the past: 'It is the noise I used to hear when my friends came to visit me. The sound of gaiety and hospitality before the English took over.' The woman begins to sing. Music, allegory and natural setting make a combined appeal, which to an audience rebelling against English rule was very powerful:

O we'd have pulled down the gallows
Had it happened at Enniscrone

The old woman then names people who have died for love of her, all figures mythologized as national martyrs: Red O'Donell (d. 1602) Donal O'Sullivan Beare (d. ca. 1618) and Brian Boru (d. 1014). Maud Gonne brought a very strong stage presence to her characterization and 'stirred the audience as I have never seen another audience stirred' (Stephen Gwynne, *Irish Drama*, 1936). Maud's great height made her seem, Yeats thought, 'a divine being fallen into our mortal infirmity'. She played Cathleen 'centuries old' but with a magnetism which draws away the young bridegroom, Michael, to die in his turn for Ireland. With his death the material hopes of his mother and father collapse.

The play is about a choice between personal or family commitments and the whole community. When Cathleen sings another song and the French arrive in the Bay of Killala the cheering draws Michael away. What is local has become strange. The young man has chosen Ireland. The old woman is now, says Patrick, a young girl 'and she had the walk of a queen'.

The play therefore links naturalism with folk legend and makes a passionate appeal for national freedom: therein lay its energy. Yeats called it the first play of the Irish school of folk drama. It was performed by William Fay's Irish National Dramatic Society, with Fay himself playing the father Peter Gillan. This company had evolved from the Irish Literary Theatre and played its first season in 1899. William's brother Frank, in articles in *The United Irishman*, insisted that a troupe of Irish actors was required to perform the new Irish drama: 'Antoine did it in Paris and trained himself as well,' so the Fays sought a permanent home for the Irish Literary Theatre where 'they will get the support of the immense and delightful audiences who are supporting the movement that is reviving our music'. Both Fays, especially the older Frank, had studied European drama and knew the work of Ole Bull at the Norwegian National Theatre and of Antoine's naturalist *théâtre libre*. Yeats entered into correspondence with them, then saw the company perform a historical play: 'I came away with my head on fire. I wanted to hear my own unfinished *On Baile's Strand*, to hear Greek tragedy spoken with a Dublin accent.' The Irish Literary Theatre offered Yeats the company he needed. It was amateur, like Antoine's original company, but therefore flexible. It brought with it the new naturalist methods and it was above all Irish.

Yeats offered them *Cathleen ni Houlihan*: 'The first play where dialect was not used with an exclusively comic intention' and it was presented at St Teresa's Hall in Clarendon Street, Dublin on 2 April 1902 as a curtain-raiser for his longer play *Deirdre*. According to Joseph Holloway, the tension between 'the matter-of-fact ways of the household and the weird uncanny conduct of the strange visitor made a very agreeable concoction' . . . 'the tall and willowy Maud Gonne chanted her lines with rare musical effect, and crooned fascinatingly if somewhat indistinctly, some lyrics . . . The audience applauded each patriotic sentiment right heartily, and enthusiastically called for the author at the end and had their wish gratified.'

If Yeats later had misgivings about the play's patriotic appeal and moved steadily towards a less popular theatre, it is arguable that much of Yeats's early strength lay in powerful and recognizable characterization in a natural setting. He then introduced a strangeness among the familiar objects, disturbing the spectator's sense of control. Out of a collision of genres and acting styles Yeats offers the spectator an uneasy freedom, the need to resolve a mystery. And, as Eliot said in *The Cocktail Party* (a play which also uses strangeness as a springboard into another form): 'No one likes to be left with a mystery'.

The production of *Cathleen ni Houlihan* established a company, a style and a theatre from which John Millington Synge (1871–1909) and Sean O'Casey (1880–1964) were to emerge. Yeats defined the style as 'That way of quiet movement and careful speech . . . arising partly out of deliberate opinion and partly out of the ignorance of the players, and asked the question, 'does one owe most to ignorance or knowledge?' The players acted naturally, imitating, for example, the physical movements of the peasantry, 'the awkwardness and stillness of bodies that have followed the plough', without convention or caricature'.[4]

The Fay Brothers' Irish National Dramatic Society was a naturalistic mimetic theatre and this underpinned Yeats's main concern which was to create a feeling of strangeness, of the supernatural and heroic. Lady Gregory helped Yeats to acquire the peasant dialogue that gave his play a solid basis: 'I could not get away, no matter how closely I watched the country life, from images and dreams that had all too royal blood' . . . 'I wished to make that high life mix into some rough contemporary life'. It was Lady Gregory's knowledge of country life that brought Yeats's aristocratic dream the earthiness it needed.

Mingling dialogue with songs derived from native airs, Yeats sought to fuse the traditions of 'high' and folk culture. He took as models Shakespeare, Cervantes and Pushkin, who generate an intense dynamism from the combination of cultural extremes, one literary, the other oral and colloquial. The play's music was there to strengthen the language, not take what Yeats called 'the keenness and the salt' out of the words: 'No word of mine must ever change into a mere musical note, no singer of my words must ever cease to be a man and become an instrument.' Behind the theory lay the example of Shakespeare who established the same tension between rhythmical pattern and colloquial flow at which Yeats (and later Eliot) aimed.

Yeats was to declare in the 1902 issue of the organ of the national theatre movement *Samhain*: 'Our movement is a return to the people. The play should either tell them of their own life, or of that life of poetry where every man can see his own image, because there alone does human nature escape from arbitrary conditions.'

Yeats's experience with the Fay brothers was followed by a growing friendship with Edward Gordon Craig. Out of this came Yeats's lecture 'The Reform of the Theatre', published in *Samhain* in 1903, in which he argues that the theatre is a place 'where the mind goes to be liberated, as it was liberated by the theatres of Greece, England and France at certain great moments of their history, and as it is liberated in Scandinavia today.'

By liberation he meant a freeing from both convention and ideology. His watchwords, Beauty and Truth were justified in themselves and offered 'a greater service to our country than writing that compromises either in the seeming service of a cause'. It is not surprising he had late misgivings about the political effect of *Cathleen ni Houlihan*, though he denied that the play was that kind of compromise.

Yeats placed great emphasis on form, and particularly on forms of words. Words were sovereign; cadence must be varied. Unnecessary movement, indeed anything which distracts from the speaking voice, was to be eliminated. Gesture must be simplified; scenery such as trees should be treated decoratively. Greek acting, he argued, was great because it did everything with the voice and modern acting may be great when it does everything with voice and movement. But an art which smothers these things with bad painting, with innumerable garish colours, with continual restless mimicries of the surface of life, is an art of fading humanity, a decaying art.

It is as well Yeats's aestheticism at this stage was reined in by Lady Gregory and others who had a greater respect for the surfaces, and a less platonic view of existence. His drama needed the surface. Without it, Yeats's own drama, as well as the simple naturalism he deplored, was arguably in decay. Drama thrives on recognition of what exists, more than on visions of the essence of things. Yeats's impatience with the imperfections of humanity lay in the way of his ambitions for the Irish Theatre, whose achievements now seem to lie more with the greater naturalism of O'Casey and Synge. The ultimate effect of Yeats's dreams was an isolation from the Irish community to the detriment of a public drama.

Yeats and Eliot

Poetic drama, freedom and transcendence

If it has been argued that poetic drama acquires dramatic conviction from a ballast of prosaic normality it can equally be argued
that prose naturalism requires to be lifted from its pedestrian level
by an infusion of poetry. Prose drama, of course, works by many
means besides prose dialogue, some of them poetic. Yet a number
of major twentieth-century poets have still sought to recreate a
drama of poetic speech which communicates states of feeling the
prose drama is thought incapable of conveying.

Claudel (1868–1955) in France, Lorca (1898–1936) in Spain
and a number of major poets in England chose to work in poetic
forms. In England the example of Yeats (1865–1939) lay behind
the poetic experiments of T. S. Eliot (1888–1965) and the
'Thirties poets', W. H. Auden (1907–72) and Louis MacNeice
(1907–63). The latter, along with Dylan Thomas (1914–53),
experimented with verse forms in the new medium of radio
drama. Although arguably, much of this work is eclectic and the
writers are poets first and men of the theatre second, their work
throws considerable light on the nature of dramatic form.

This is especially true of Yeats and Eliot who commented
on and experimented with various forms of theatre: Greek,
mediaeval, Elizabethan, oriental, comic and prose naturalist. For
Eliot later, and Yeats throughout his life, the theatre was a major
concern. Each attempted to work in the long tradition of poetic
drama which goes back through the earlier works of Ibsen to
Schiller and Goethe, and then to Shakespeare, to the mediaeval
theatre and the Greeks. Eliot argued that prose drama is a minor

current. Poetic drama is the mainstream of dramatic tradition and verse its natural form.

During the twentieth century (and in the comic tradition leading into it) prose dialogue has been dominant. Yet poetry has been present in various forms. Dramatic tensions have, from Shakespeare's time, been identified as conflicts between the colloquial and the rhetorical, the popular and aristocratic, the comic and the passionate; between speech and music, the individual and the group, actor and chorus, sub-plot and main plot, the present and the past, the near and the far. Such tensions often express themselves formally as an opposition between prose and poetry. Poetic drama needs to be anchored to the earth, just as naturalistic drama benefits from a powerful poetic undercurrent. Drama thrives on contrast and opposition, as it embodies the social and human contradictions of its time.

In Elizabethan drama, Eliot reminds us, the verse medium was flexible enough to allow actor and audience to pass convincingly from the poetic and passionate to the prosaic and functional. One thinks of the political 'business sections' and the tragic lyricism of different scenes in *Antony and Cleopatra*. In the twentieth century, Eliot tried to recreate just such a flexible instrument.

Yeats's example is also instructive. His concern with poetic verse was an intrinsic part of his concern with raising the cultural level of audiences at the Abbey. As we have seen, this did not mean abandoning vigorous prose drama, though Yeats steadfastly refused to give the audience the prose plays which were most popular and easy. He wished in the first place to make an appeal to a high quality both of feeling and intelligence and when Synge's *Playboy of the Western World* detonated the famous riots on 26 January 1907, he deplored the absence in his audience of civilized qualities. Yeats was interviewed for the *Freeman's Journal* and stated:

'Instead of a Parnell or a Stevens, or a Butt, we must obey the demands of commonplace or ignorant people, who try to take on an appearance of strength by imposing some crude shibboleth on their own and others' necks. They do not persuade, for that is difficult; they do not expound, for that needs knowledge . . . There are some exceptions . . . but the mass only understand conversion by terror, threats and abuse.'

Yeats respected civilized prose and hated false poetry with a nationalist appeal. The poetry he respected was one of understanding and intelligence. When an article in *Sinn Fein* charged Yeats with approving: 'the staging of squalor and the one-sided view of that which plays in the human economy the part that sewers may be held to play in the economy of the town . . .' it accused him in the terms which had greeted Ibsen's *Ghosts*. Yeats was too earthy. *Sinn Fein* obviously preferred high national rhetoric but Yeats's conception of language in the service of community was other. Dramatic language in prose or verse needed to tell the truth: 'A writer must be free to ripen weed or flower as the fancy takes him . . . the moment a writer is forbidden to show the weed without the flower, his art loses energy and abundance'. Yeats is arguing for good prose as well as for poetry; for the acceptance of a prose play which looked with some irony on an Irish propensity to dream in bad poetry.

This said, Yeats ultimately wanted a theatre and an audience capable of rising to those moments of intensity for which poetry was the natural expression. Freedom and realism led towards poetry. He sought a cultural aristocracy and was contemptuous of the *Playboy* riots which were a manifestation of 'the old Puritanism, the old bourgeois dislike of power and reality'. This was defined in his essay 'Poetry and Tradition' (written in 1907 after the death of John O'Leary) as the sentiments of a class 'which had begun to rise into power under the shadow of Parnell'. It would change the nature of the Irish movement. It was a class dedicated to its own security which, 'needing no longer great sacrifices, nor bringing any risk to individuals, could do without exceptional men and those activities of the mind that are founded on the exceptional moment'. It was a loss of a sense of the importance of 'those moments out of which poetry comes, and of a sense of tragedy as life grew safe'. The language of poetry was a necessary guarantee of a liberation of the spirit and this audience was not mentally free. In this way realism and poetry were connected, as Zola had argued in the previous generation.[1] The purveying of facile comedy, 'the social bond in time of peace' had, Yeats thought, taken over. 'Ireland's great moment had passed.' Thus came his disillusionment with the public theatre.

Yeats's temperament and experience inclined him to dwell on these 'moments out of which poetry comes' and he sought to convey a quality of tragic feeling which by his own account was unlikely to be popular. When he turned towards verse writing he was turning away from the general public. One remembers the heartfelt words of Henry James after his painful post-Ibsen foray into the West End to receive the catcalls of the gallery.[2] God knows he was made for drama but not for the theatre. Yeats was altogether tougher, possessing a public and combative personality which kept him involved in practical theatre concerns. He was made for the theatre, but his drama dwindled in popular appeal as he loaded it with symbolic writing which had more in common with magic and mysticism than the contemporary scene. The kind of reality he sought to convey was caught up in myth, in the drama of the past and in the supernatural. It was not a vision his audiences could readily comprehend.

At first he managed to reconcile his audiences with his aims. Of *Deirdre* (1907) he says: '(It) is my best play and the last half of it holds an audience in as strong a grip as does *Cathleen ni Houlihan* which is prose and therefore a far easier thing to write'. His fundamental intentions are revealed in 'An Introduction for My Plays', later published in *Essays and Introductions* (1961). For him the London stage was full of 'irrelevant movement' and words that had no vividness 'except what they borrowed from the situation'. Something other than the situation was paramount for Yeats, which could be communicated only by the music of poetry and musical speech. It was a quality the great poetic drama of the past had known. Racine and Shakespeare, he believed, wrote and were declaimed musically. The speaking was crucial and the effect more than prose drama could achieve.

Yeats aimed at a spare clarity of production, staging, and speech. He turned away from the naturalist stage towards other forms of drama, in particular the Japanese Noh Theatre. He wrote a sequence of 'Plays for Dancers', putting them on in drawing rooms for a select few, renouncing popular appeal for 'an unpopular theatre and an audience like a secret society'.[3] He was drawn to the austerity of Gordon Craig and sought to achieve a symbolic concentration which communicated a state almost of trance. Character was presented at the point where individualization merges with type. Acting was stylized and the performers were apt to remain still for long moments of great muscular tension. In these conditions, the words could work to greater effect. For such a theatre, however, there was no large public audience.

In his essay, 'The Cutting of an Agate',[4] he describes the effect at which he aimed. 'The arts which interest me enable us to pass for a few moments into a deep of the mind that had hitherto been too subtle for our habitation'. This it does while 'seeming to separate from the world and us a group of figures, images, symbols . . .'. His theory is highly suggestive of the work of Jung. He seeks to express the archetypal images which reside in some 'collective unconscious' lying beyond the individual mind. Naturalism cannot reach such platonic realities. Familiar surfaces and accurate historical representation of scene and costume were distracting. Even the actors' faces could distract. Hence facial expressions were covered by still masks. One could only gain by substituting 'the fine invention of a sculptor' for 'the face of some commonplace player'. The whole body expressed feeling, while the face, like Buddha's, remained immobile.

So, in *At the Hawk's Well, The Only Jealousy of Emer* (1916), *The Dreaming of the Bones* (1917) and *Calvary* (1920) Yeats moved away from the Abbey Theatre, which was passing its peak as Irish Home Rule passed into law. The incandescent nationalism faded, together with the brilliant team of actors who sustained the theatre and the group of talented aristocrats (amateurs in Tyrone Guthrie's view)[5] who had controlled it. Power moved back into the hands of business and despite the achievements of O'Casey the theatre waned artistically.

Yeats continued to write to the end. *Purgatory* (1938), was a one-act allegorical dream play about Ireland and the relations between a father and a son, representing the older generation and its betrayal by the new. In the play a house window lights up and within the frame the living characters see past events unfurl before their eyes. In *Ghost Sonata* Strindberg had done something similar. It is a haunting stage image of the way the dead exist in the minds of the living. More than that, at times Yeats speaks as though the dead had an existence outside memory: . . . 'I think the dead suffer remorse. There are mediaeval Japanese plays about it . . .'. 'In my play a spirit suffers because of its share when alive in the destruction of an honoured house; that destruction is taking place all over Ireland today'.[6] For Yeats the supernatural was more than a psychological phenomenon.

In his late drama, Yeats aimed to induce in the spectator a state of heightened consciousness or trance. Nietzsche had argued in *The Birth of Tragedy* (1871) that such was the effect of the chorus in the ancient Greek theatre. Choral speech and movement, he said, operates musically to break down individual barriers, achieving the central tragic effect by absorbing the ordinary mind 'like lamplight into daylight' (he quotes Wagner). In *The Trembling of the Veil* Yeats argued that the sub-plot acts similarly, like an echo chamber, extending the effect of the main drama by a species of reverberation in the audience which he called 'emotion of multitude'. To a similar end Yeats used the Japanese Noh drama, which represents the supernatural in the form of apparitions which haunt the places where they have formerly lived. Yeats speaks of these apparitions as both outside and inside the mind. They are 'spirits who suffer remorse' yet at the same time they inhabit our unconsciousness; they are (Yeats quotes Swedenborg) the 'Dramatis Personae of our dreams'. To convey his vision, Yeats employed not only poetic speech but such resources of the theatre as chorus, music, dance, stage effects, sub-plot, myth, legend and supernatural story. Event and character demanded appropriate language, further reinforced by dramatic structure. Yeats drew on traditional means and his example is fascinating. Whether his later plays attempted to convey a state of mind which, as Dr Johnson once suggested, is beyond the range of language, is a question for the individual spectator.

Certainly poetic drama endeavours to convey states beyond the reach of prose naturalism. The danger lies in its losing contact with the reality which the naturalists, reacting against the failures of romantic drama, sought to regain – a sense of present social conditions and of suppressed psychological needs behind the idealization of woman or country or ideology. At times Yeats loses this sense and the drama fails, as he seems to recognize in a famous, bitter poem which scrutinizes the mental processes behind his early drama. In 'The Circus Animals' Desertion' (1938), he discusses the growth of ideal images and pins them down to their human origins:

> Those masterful images because complete
> Grew in pure mind, but out of what began?
> A mount of refuse or the sweepings of a street . . .
> . . . Now that my ladder's gone,
> I must lie down where all the ladders start,
> In the foul rag and bone shop of the heart.

When Yeats seems, not only in early but in later plays like *The Herne's Egg* (1938), to disappear into a complex web of mysticism, these lines are worth remembering. Yeats comes down to earth with this devastating analysis of the sources of his work.

T. S. Eliot acknowledged and built on Yeats's contribution to modern poetic drama. His ear for dialogue was already evident in the early poetry. Full of varying registers and discordant voices, his fragmented structures also suggest his growing need to examine dramatic form and language, whether it was Greek, mediaeval, Elizabethan or modern. For this reason his recorded experimentation, his body of dramatic criticism, and his work in the theatre are equally illuminating. His contradictory impulses towards the comic and colloquial on the one hand, and the choral and liturgical on the other, point towards tensions and contradictions he found within himself. They find expression in his embracing of opposite styles and mixing of dramatic traditions.

Eliot had always been interested in drama. His early poems are narratives, interweaving dialogue with thought and setting. 'The Love Song of J. Alfred Prufrock' (1915) is a dramatic monologue addressed to the reader which also takes the form of a narrator having a dialogue with himself. The timid Prufrock wonders whether he can change his life, imagines the consequences: 'Would it have been worth it after all?' Then he decides it is too late to live and wakes up to a future created not by his desires but his fears.

The next poem, 'Portrait of a Lady' (1917) is a step closer to drama. It moves from monologue to dialogue and is written in 'scenes' set in differing places and at different seasons. It has two characters, a young man and an older woman. The young man tells his thoughts to the listener. The lady's thoughts we do not hear, only her spoken words. The man, like a Shakespearean fool or villain, has the dramatic advantage. He stands down-stage and has the ear of the audience. The poem resembles a radio play for voices and again reveals a highly sensitive ear for dialogue, as do such later poems as 'Gerontion' (1920) and 'The Waste Land' (1921–2).

Eliot's first play, *Sweeney Agonistes* (1932), which Eliot calls 'Fragments of an Aristophanic Melodrama', is vivid and anarchic. It is very much a musical and spoken piece, as a subsequent musical and vocal setting by Johnny Dankworth and Cleo Laine entertainingly demonstrates.[7] It also possesses the grotesque and caricatural quality found in Eliot's poetry before his conversion to Christianity in 1925. Later, the humour, questions, pain, silences, broken images and rhythms fall away as the poetry moves towards liturgy.

At first, this is also the case with his drama, as it develops from *Sweeney* to the pageant play with choruses, *The Rock* (1934) followed by his festival play on Thomas à Becket, *Murder in the Cathedral* in 1935. Eliot's conversion prompts him to desecularize his drama. Working against the current of history, he chooses a mediaeval subject and sets it in a church. Eliot was not interested in the kind of secular humour which caused the mediaeval drama to move from church to market place. He sought, like Yeats, to recover what drama began to lose in moving out of the church – a sense of the supernatural.

In the early, incomplete and experimental *Sweeney Agonistes* Eliot had not written a full drama. It was a dramatic poem which could be spoken standing still, as if for the microphone. He only began to confront the problems of live performance with the early religious dramas: *The Rock* was written for a pageant and *Murder in the Cathedral* for performance in Canterbury Cathedral. Their emphasis was liturgical but they demonstrate a growing interest in the way mediaeval pageant plays and the Greek chorus use theatrical space.

In the later plays the use of Greek elements was extended. Eliot continues to experiment with the choral form but also employs Greek myths to parallel the surface plot. It is reminiscent of the way James Joyce had used the Ulysses story to parallel the various episodes of 'Bloomsday' but does not achieve the same effect. Joyce's method unifies his comic epic, enriching the everyday surface of his story as well as conveying a depth behind surface appearance. Eliot's handles the comic disparity between surface and myth with much less confidence; rich surface detail interests him less than a sense of spiritual depth.

The events and characters of Aeschylus's *The Oresteia*, lie beneath events and characters in *The Family Reunion* (1938). Clytemnestra finds an equivalent in Amy the dominant mother, and Harry parallels Orestes, the returning son responsible for his mother's death. In a similar and more disguised way Euripides's *Alcestis* was the preliminary basis for *The Cocktail Party* (1949).

forced the French patriot either to ignore or deny the facts, or else to free himself of bias and recognize in Frantz, the German torturer, a fellow (fallible) human being. *Altona* demanded a recognition of national guilt, not a violent response against an invader, as in the earlier play. *Altona* made, perhaps, the more painful demand. Sartre was saying to a bourgeoisie that insisted that Algeria *was* French, that, like Frantz, French colonial rule had no future. This sombre play asserted that just as the Gestapo's methods in France constituted a rear-guard action against the movement of history, so did the extreme methods adopted by the French army to win an unwinnable war.

Altona examines the condition of those who attempt to rule. (In this it is arguably braver and less sentimental than political plays which dwell only on the problems of the victim.) *The Flies* examines the problem of the revenger faced with the usurper and in it the murder of tyrants is embraced as a necessary courageous act. Orestes makes his choice, which, like Frantz, he acknowledges as his own and not the gods' – for we invent gods only in order to justify our own desires. The gods lift the burden of choice from our shoulders. In *The Flies* the citizens of Argos, resembling those of Paris Sartre implies, are trapped into believing they have no choice. Fearing to admit their responsibility, they embrace an ideology which relieves them of the charge of cowardice. Political action, not blindness or suicide is the valid response. The early play asks the audience to embrace an evil means to a good end. The latter asks them to admit to evil means used in its name to an evil end.

Over the 17 years between the two plays Sartre came to embrace a darker view of the possibility of free action. He had declared Orestes was free. 'Can I ever have believed that?'[5] he later asks. Human action, he began to argue, was socially determined. Thus the priest, Heinrich in *Lucifer and the Lord* (1951), refuses to countenance an act of betrayal, then betrays the people from whom he originates in the interests of the church which has formed him. The element of freedom remains only in Heinrich's anguished consciousness of his choice.

As Sartre sought to reconcile his existentialism with his Marxism, his optimistic sense of individual freedom decreased. *Altona* is still a play about choices and about a change of consciousness, for the torturer, Frantz, recognizes his deed. The moment of his freedom to act, however, has passed. Frantz acknowledges his helplessness and the play ends with his calmly deliberated suicide. It is the only way he can take control of his life, for he has no future. In a final powerful scene, Frantz's tape-recorded voice speaks from an empty stage.

Frantz's suicide signals the approaching end of Sartre's dramatic work. In 1960 Sartre reached a point where consciousness, and even the consciousness we take of our own consciousness, is entirely determined by our upbringing. 'Childhood decides everything' he declares in *Les Mots*. If a dramatist needs to believe in some kind of individual freedom of action or consciousness even whilst recognizing the forces that restrict it, Sartre's abandonment of the medium of drama is not surprising. One of the polarities of conflict had disappeared and a single viewpoint had taken over.

In *The Flies*, Sartre was far from embracing that combination of Marxism and psychoanalysis which ultimately led him in 1968 to act as a 'megaphone' for the will of the 'masses'. The early play has an individualist ethic. When Orestes kills his mother and the tyrant Aegisthus he comes to consciousness of himself (albeit, I shall argue, too suddenly for dramatic conviction) and chooses to be an unthanked saviour.

Electra, the sister and helper, also represents an active consciousness at first. She is the Resistance Movement. Later she repudiates her rebellion and the necessary guilt it implies. She comes to signify the section of the French people who deny free consciousness and are appalled by the means employed to achieve a necessary end. They are the people of 'bad faith', the section (especially of the bourgeoisie) which refused to employ means which would expose as hypocrisy its desire to pretend to itself that it was innocent. The crime was one of evasion, of lying to the self by inventing a self-justifying ideology and leaving events in God's hands. In *The Flies* Sartre and Orestes argue that men and women are tied because they prefer to be tied. They fear to admit they are free. Electra, however, the unfree character, is psychologically more convincing than Orestes, the embodiment of Sartre's views. The play's dramatic weakness works against the general statement.

The tension between freedom and constraint is more convincingly presented in the other, less wordy, more intense and highly organized play he wrote during the war years: *In Camera* (*Huis Clos*) (1944). The three characters in this play are in Hell. For them there is no active future. They sit in a windowless room with no mirrors. The only diversion comes when the living who remember them speak of them back on earth, but they are soon forgotten and left to defend their illusions by lying to themselves and one another.

In Camera dramatizes the bad faith of those who wish to make life easy. The characters flee the judgements of other people; they sleep or take refuge in conventions; they set up a system of mutual flattery, telling lies to one another in order to be lied to. But the presence of a third person exposes the practice of reciprocal lying and the result is a Hell where people torture one another by telling them they see them for what they are. Thus in the play Estelle has killed her child, Garcin has failed to die a hero's death, and Inez has been responsible for the death of others. In this triangle Garcin attempts to convince Inez he is courageous, only to receive the answer: 'You are a coward because I will it'. Garcin wants Inez's approbation because he respects her judgement. Estelle seeks Garcin out of physical desire and because he is a man. Inez seeks Estelle out of desire and because she is beautiful. Each is tortured by the others in a facsimile of the triangular situations they have met in their previous lives. There is, it seems, no escape. In Hell all is over. The people are fixed for ever. They are what other people choose to make of them. After death no one can alter the image others have of them. That, too, is in the hands of others: *L'enfer c'est les autres*.

The play would therefore seem to take a tragic, even 'bourgeois'[6] view of an unchangeable human condition, yet there remains a ray of light. The characters may be dead, but they also allegorize states of mind of living people who may be capable of change. In fact, the characters are allowed a chance of escape: at one point the door opens. (One of the English titles, *No Exit*, is therefore not fully appropriate.) The characters, however, are afraid of freedom and refuse to go through into the unknown. They prefer talk to action. Even Inez, the most 'authentic' character, the one who does not lie or accept other people's lies, refuses to be pushed out of the door. Is it that she cannot, or will not? Has the spectator the right to condemn her fear? The play, if it is an allegory, represents a particular imprisoning psychology which threatens our freedom. It afflicts even the courageous and must be fought. In eternity all is over. But do we sometimes choose eternity? Sartre later argued that this is what he meant.

The play can be seen both as tragic and universal or as allegorical and particular. It is closed or open depending on the angle chosen. A director who chooses a stylized half-speed delivery which prolongs the play by 40 minutes (as in Claude Berri's 1990 Comédie Française production) seems to have opted for a closed interpretation. Setting the three characters in front of two huge doors which open and thud shut reinforced this effect. However, in retrospect, the two doors, when open, did let fall the other possibility.

Later, in *Lucifer and the Lord* (1951) Sartre built a play upon a series of offered choices, each of which had to be made without certainty of the outcome and in the service of a belief which proves delusory. Only when the central character Goetz achieves a state of mind in which people become real to him, more real than the images in his head, more real than the illustrations in the *Grand Larousse*, more real than words, is there a chance of success. Liberty has become dependent on the achievement of a capacity to acknowledge the existence of the other. Only then, as Sartre said in 1946, should he 'play his cards and take his risks at whatever the cost'.

Sartre's play becomes a drama of means and ends, where good means can issue badly and bad means may issue well. It is a drama about decisions and modes of action, about value systems, about the constraints which imprison the self, about how one may confront a situation which threatens liberty. His drama confronts tragedy and seeks an escape, just as the tragic hero seeks freedom within a situation which ultimately destroys him. The emphasis, however, shifts to the importance of solidarity. Sartre finds his ethic ultimately in a form of love. The individual can only act well when he recognizes his isolation yet cares for others.

Sartre's ideas carry conviction in those of his plays which exhibit great dramatic power, and perhaps most convincingly where they are more implicit, as in the economical dialogue of *Huis Clos* rather than the long speeches of *The Flies*. His intellectualism is sometimes at odds with his formidable powers of dramatic construction, but he has the important gift of creating living characters who possess both dynamism and a mocking self-awareness. In the self-awareness lies a potential liberty, which is arguably why the voices which speak from his pages are convincingly alive. Sartre had a gift few possess and without it his plays and fiction would mean little.

His characters seem to derive their reality from a central experience – that of emerging from what Sartre called 'aesthetic contemplation . . . an induced dream' from which 'passing into the real is an actual waking-up'.[7] This aesthetic form of awareness, whose limitations Sartre discovered when confronted with the realities of power, is found again and again within, and in contrasts between his characters. It is this experience which lies behind his early pre-war studies *Imagination* and *Psychology of the Imagination*. There he asserts that 'the real is never beautiful', and it is this tension between actuality and images of the ideal which underlies his celebrated work *Being and Nothingness* (1943). He returns to it in different ways, whether it is in Frantz in *Altona* (1959) emerging into the realities of the post-war world from the room in which he has shut himself up with his dreams and his guilt, or in the comparison in *Les Mains Sales* (1948) between the little bourgeois Hugo and the activist Hoederer, the first of whom loves an image of men as they ought to be, whereas the second loves them for what they are.

Maturity and a greater freedom come when we rid ourselves of images and dreams – or such seemed to be Sartre's experience. It is an opposition found in the light-hearted play *Kean* (1953) when the famous actor has problems in separating the fictive from the real, and it is obviously there in the way characters in *Huis Clos* play games to keep reality at bay.

Sartre created autonomous characters with individual voices and separate selves. Only in *The Flies* does Sartre try to show a character escaping from the self (and there he is unconvincing). In the later plays, characters like Frantz and Goetz change, yet remain convincingly themselves. Sartre may in early days have claimed that there is no such thing as human nature and that characters can recreate themselves by a free decision, but even the chameleonic Kean and the bastard Goetz seem to have a centre. Sartre fails to convince where he tried to enact a sudden and permanent character change. In *The Flies*, Orestes repudiates the Gods and changes personality. The character acts in the service of an idea of freedom, but the idea does not serve the character. The dialogue is forced and solemn and when Orestes effects his change from itinerant lecturer to avenger it requires a consummate and deceptive piece of acting to convince the spectator. Changing the self is not so simple – as Sartre later acknowledged: 'How could I ever have believed that!'.[8] Character-changes at a drop of a hat are the stuff of comedy, not tragedy. In tragedy the fragmentation of personality into madness, whether of Ophelia or King Lear, or in Hamlet's rapid changes of self, is deeply disturbing because we sense a potential integrality of identity. But Orestes simply throws the self unconvincingly aside. No 'free' consciousness is made real.

The conventions Sartre employs are predominantly realist and such sudden shifts as Orestes is supposed to effect are especially unconvincing in a realist mode. Only when the comic convention that audience, author and character are playing an elaborate game, or when in realist genre the characters are shown as play-acting a role, are such violent changes of behaviour acceptable. An audience needs to recognize the difference between self and persona, as it does between role and role. A drama in the Pirandellian tradition in which character is 'one thing, nothing and a hundred thousand things' may be acceptable within the conventions which the absurdist theatre was soon to establish. But the forms of classical naturalism which *The Flies* embraces (despite the introduction of a comic and supernatural Zeus) work against acceptance of Orestes's character change. Freedom we must assume, but not such freedom as that.

Sartre's work acknowledges the difference between the world of the imagination and the world of fact. The recognition is itself a kind of freedom. Liberty, he was to say in *A Theatre of Situations* (1947), is the principal spring, the *'ressort principal'* of ancient theatre. Fate is only the reverse side of the coin. We feel the existence of material constraints when they are set against our need for freedom. We feel the need for freedom when oppressed by material constraint. Characters (and authors) are more convincing when they consciously react against the way societies and ideologies, parentage and childhood have shaped them, than when they obey without question their inner material determinants. Drama emerges from the attempt, successful, part-successful or unsuccessful, to throw off these determinants. Both tragedy and comedy arise out of this collision between automatism and freedom, or as Bergson said, between the mechanical and the living: *du mécanique plaqué sur du vivant.*

Sartre, despite an early half-failure with Orestes, succeeds in creating ironic, witty, convincing characters who take consciousness of themselves in the act of choice. In classical manner he places them in extreme situations. Their decisions recall the choice of Galileo to capitulate to the Inquisition; the choice of Joan of Arc not to do so; the choice of a Macbeth or Hamlet before the act of killing; the choice of characters in Brecht's *Lehrstücke* to place the group before the individual self; the choice of Kattrin to sacrifice wagon and self in an attempt to raise the sleeping town in *Mother Courage*, the failure of other characters to choose in these same extreme situations. Sartre relates to theatres both contemporary and past. Sartre, like Brecht, is following the example of the ancients, perhaps the supreme example of Sophocles's *Antigone*, in the presentation of the conflict between might and right, between the requirements of order and individual need.

A final observation on the relationship between Brecht and Sartre may be made. If Sartre's intellectual distinction equals and probably exceeds any other dramatic theorist of the twentieth century, it is surprising that his impact has been far less than that of Stanislavski, Brecht, Artaud and others. This is probably due to the comparative and surprising conservatism of his dramatic theory. He was making a claim for a traditional form of theatre which shows the world as process, not as fixity, a theatre which raises questions of rights and examines the contradictions within man, retaining the complexities which caricatural or stereotypical representation denies. Like Brecht, he was concerned with a dialectical drama which looked forward to a reconciliation of contradictions, but he generally and courageously presented it through an examination of the struggles for freedom and rights (whence 'passion' arises). In the tradition of Ibsen's *An Enemy of the People*, he explores the situations and responses of people who rebel against, struggle for or wish to retain political, commercial or even aesthetic power (Goetz in *Lucifer and the Lord*; the Father in *Altona*; Kean in the play of that name). As with Brecht, an immediate ancestor is Hegel; another less often acknowledged is Henri Bergson. But Sartre's is a 'dramatic'[9] rather than an 'epic' theatre. His characters speak with sufficient fullness to support his point that Brecht's formulation of epic theatre had 'a clear insufficiency . . . Brecht never realized the problem of subjectivity and objectivity . . . never created the subjective as it should be'.[10]

Sartre, however, did not repudiate epic theatre. Indeed, as he says in the essay quoted previously (written in 1960), 'there is no real opposition between the two forms'. He sought neither extreme identification with character – which seems at times the aim of Stanislavski (though not of Chekhov), nor the extreme epic theatre 'which tries to present man and society as object'. This is doomed to failure because no man is completely object, and no individual is fully defined by class or gender, as Brecht declares in *The Messingkauf Dialogues*.

Sartre gave less of his life to the theatre than Brecht and the forms he chose were more traditional. Brecht, the director, worked intensively with actors and was able to combine a theory of dramatic structure with a political philosophy and a practical theory of performance. Sartre's dramatic theory was less central to his political philosophy but his plays and writings provide evidence of great intellectual and imaginative gifts and should be studied alongside the dominant dramatic theories and practices of the last 50 years.

Absurdism in France

Anouilh, Sartre, Beckett and Ionesco

Mention was made in the previous chapter of the use of ancient myth in Jean Anouilh's play *Antigone* (1944) which ran for 500 performances during the war years, playing right through the Normandy landings and the liberation of Paris. Audiences saw Antigone as a symbol of resistance to tyranny and the play propelled Anouilh to international fame. But Anouilh does not seem to have been writing political allegory and he was far less concerned with social and political action than Sartre. Sartre's view of him as an 'anarchic pessimist', in the tradition running from Pirandello to Genet, Beckett and Ionesco, now seems more accurate than the popular view taken of him during the war. His principal themes, handled always with wit and a Gallic shrug of the shoulders, are Play, Time, Isolation, and Death.

A collection of quotes suggests the characteristic tone:

'God turns away from men over forty' (*Ornifle*).
'Everywhere we hear conversations between deaf people' (*Ne Réveillez pas Madame*).
'We are in the same train compartment and there is someone who exits at each station. So let's share our last sandwiches and talk about the scenery in order to forget the terminus' (*Cher Antoine*).

The distanced, sceptical, jesting note is frequent among his characters. It is not a note he shares with Sartre. It is hard to imagine Sartre, or even one of his characters, saying with the same joking detachment: 'During the occupation one half of the French people denounced the other half. After the liberation the other half denounced the first half. Some reliable historians wonder if it was not the first half that denounced in both instances.' (*Les Poissons Rouges*.) Sartre's wit had a greater sense of human commitment; he did not admire defensive irony. If man's situation in the world was absurd, if God was deaf, or was a mere 'hole in the sky', if no absolute criteria of value existed, Saₜtre's writing is yet full of urgency and a need for solidarity. Though he could write a light-hearted play such as *Kean*, life for him was not a jest. Although he shared a sense of the absurdity of things with Anouilh, he felt it with nausea and anguish. He did not say with the Anouilh character: 'If this is life they should have told me in advance. I would not have bothered to come.' (*Le Boulanger, la Boulangère et le petit Mitron.*) If life outside the theatre did not make sense that was no reason for sitting indoors with an audience, but for venturing outside to make sense of it. For Sartre, to choose the theatre as an alternative to living was to refuse an obligation.

Anouilh, on the other hand, finds freedom in withdrawal to the realm of play. Here he exercised his gift to the full and it is within this realm that his character Antigone, who never grows up, wishes to remain. The power of *Antigone* resides in the conflict between a character who wishes to play a heroine and a character who plays the necessary game of a political realist. If the first French audiences embraced Antigone, her antagonist Creon now emerges with more sympathy. The writer, one suspects, regarded their conflict with wry detachment and did not attribute to life the value Sartre insisted upon.

An early fifteen-minute burlesque called *Humulus le Muet* (pub. 1958) exhibits Anouilh's gift and his relation to the absurdist school of writers. Humulus is a character who can speak but one word a day. By remaining silent for a day he can speak two. Once a year he stays silent for three days in order to utter the family motto: 'Honour above all!' on his grandmother's birthday. One year, however, he falls in love and retreats into total silence for 30 days so as to declare his passion. Unfortunately the girl he loves is deaf and after he has used up his 30 words she asks him to repeat himself. He must now wait another month to make his declaration – with no guarantee even then of being understood.

The crazy logic of this failure of communication is familiar to those acquainted with the absurdist theatre in which characters seek explanation of a world which denies them – the gods are absent, deaf or sadistic. The grotesque situation is treated by the characters with great seriousness whilst the author and audience are aware that the situation is grotesque. When author and audience take the situation seriously the mode becomes tragicomic or even tragic. It recalls the way Shakespeare's protagonists take stock of the apparent futility of things. For Gloucester in *King Lear*: 'As flies to wanton boys are we to the gods/ They kill us for their sport' (Act IV i 37–8). For Macbeth the gods are not sadistic but absent. Life is 'a tale told by an idiot/ Full of sound and fury, signifying nothing.' (Act V iv 26–8). In both cases there is a vision of absurdity. But the audience cannot, if the acting does justice to the play, maintain a comic detachment. The character's suffering implicates the audience and keeps the play within the tragic mode. A distant god's eye view, on the other hand, moves the play nearer to farce. We laugh when people look small. When they loom large the Aristotelian elements of pity and fear are strongly present.

If absurdist theatre lies in a region midway between tragedy and farce, Sartre is closer to naturalism and classical tragedy whilst Anouilh is closer to farce. In *Antigone* he managed, with brilliant theatrical use of a classical Chorus, to effect a distancing which is not jesting but compassionate. But the general effect of Anouilh's work is to remind us how close tragedy is to farce. When the pity it evokes is close to compassion tragedy is near; when it is close to contempt, farce approaches. The plays shift between the 'pathetic' and 'pitiful' in both the positive and negative senses of the words.

Theatre of the Absurd may be closely related to tragedy but its more recent ancestors are Jarry's *Ubu Roi* (1888), surrealism and the plays of Pirandello. Sartre's novel *La Nausée* (1938) and Camus's *L'Etranger* (1942) focus on states of mind arising from a sense of the world's absurdity but they do so within recognizably human situations and avoid grotesque allegory. Sartre is concerned with a painful form of linguistic and personal breakdown. Camus's Meursault may have been called an absurdist hero but the situation is too painful, too naturalistic in its treatment to provoke laughter. The grotesque element is missing. This is also true of the drama – Camus's treatment of the grotesque *Caligula* (1945), for example, is still too traditional to be called absurdist.

Camus and the early Sartre are philosophers of the absurd, rather than absurdist playwrights.

The term 'absurd' was defined by Camus in his book *The Myth of Sisyphus* (1942) which derives in the main from a study of Dostoievski and Kafka. It implied atheism, the absence of valid moral categories, the insufficiency of reason and the need to create one's own standards. It gave priority to 'existence' over essence. Man created God; the world came before the Word.

Theatre of the Absurd embodies these feelings and ideas. The term was popularized in England by Martin Esslin in his standard critical book of that name. Dramatists including Sartre deride it: 'The title is itself absurd since none of the writers believe the world or human life to be an absurdity, not Genet, who considers the relations between reality and fantasy – nor Adamov who is a Marxist, and has written "No theatre without IDEOLOGY" nor even Beckett.'[1] The phrase, however, remains useful if it is taken to mean the non-realist theatre that was launched by the success in Paris in 1953, and in England two years later, of Beckett's *Waiting for Godot*.

This play embodied many of the feelings Camus and Sartre described and made as sombre a statement as had any writer since Kafka. The anguish of seeking for meaning, in a world which denied it, was distanced by comedy. At the same time the play alerted the audience to what it was doing, causing it to take stock of the defensive function of comic distancing. A play was a 'passtime' and presented characters who, like actors and audience, were engaged in protecting themselves against the pain of exposure to the processes of time. Defence lies in joking, in playing games. 'How time passes when one has fun!' It is a defence that is not ultimately successful.

This sombre vision, far from depressing its audiences, had two active effects: it sent irritated spectators away in droves and it stimulated immense creativity. If plays are to be judged on the impact they have on others, then *Godot* was a very positive play. If nature hates a vacuum, Beckett's play about time and nothingness, and his subsequent refusals to give any explanatory comment, provoked critics to fill the void with speculation. This served as good publicity, but more importantly Beckett broke out of the still dominant naturalist mode, returning to forms of recognizably expressionist theatre. His twisted stagy tree in *Godot* and the circular room with two windows on the world in

Endgame (1956), are intriguingly close to the symbolic sets of Reigbert and Sievert in the expressionist Weimar theatre. The success of Beckett's 'anti-theatre', also very importantly, encouraged theatre management to believe new forms of plays were commercially viable and offered dramatic forms which released the talents of many new writers.

'We're not tied?' Gogo asks Didi. Among the vivid memories left by Beckett's extraordinary play is the theatrical image of two beings, the grotesque Pozzo and the aged and frail Lucky, tied to one another, in the first act by a long rope, in the second act by a short one. In the first act Pozzo is in control and whips Lucky like an old nag. In the second act it is Lucky who pulls along a Pozzo who has gone blind. What is presented are images of imprisonment and these reflect the conditions both of spectators in the auditorium and of the characters who watch on stage. The audience is tied to the performance (those at least who do not walk out); the actors are tied to the characters they play; Gogo and Didi are tied to their spectacle (Pozzo and Lucky) and also to each other. Gogo is tied to Didi, Didi to Gogo, and they are both tied to Godot, since they wait every evening for him to appear. They all wish, yet fear, to be free of these ties. Thus the visual symbol of Lucky physically tied to Pozzo, yet not wanting to leave, reflects not only the relations between human beings but also the relations between humanity and whatever you take Godot to represent. The play is, among other things, about habit and mental and emotional dependence.

The play is also about time. Men and women may depend on each other because they are subject to time. The play constantly reminds us of how they experience its processes in the decline of their own bodies. The autocratic Pozzo, who has believed in Act I he was young, is pulled along in Act II by his vassal, Lucky. The pair here symbolize the relation between Man and Time.

To combat time, Gogo and Didi hope for rescue in the shape of Godot – and Godot can come in many shapes, one of which is Pozzo. 'Are you Godot?' they ask. Evidently if Godot came, even if Godot were God, they would not recognize him. Pozzo, in his apparent omnipotence in Act I, may be a parody of God, in control of man on his first appearance, then under his control later. 'God makes man' has given way to 'Man invents God'. An essentialist view of God: 'In the beginning was the Word' has given way to an existential view: 'In the beginning is the world'.

129

If Pozzo is God, He behaves abominably, is cruel to his slaves, and affords Gogo and Didi negligible relief. If Pozzo is not God then whatever replaces him does not appear.

He does, however, send a representative in the person of a Boy. On two occasions the stage sun goes down, the stage moon rises and a boy messenger announces that Godot is not coming. Interestingly, the Boy stands in relation to his master as does Lucky to Pozzo. He cringes (at least in Peter Hall's production of 1955), dithering with his hands held out before him like a begging dog. Despite the message, the two tramps remain, tying themselves to the hope they will be rescued. They are tied to time, to God perhaps, to the idea of some absolute, some Meaning. They remind one of similar dependencies: man and woman; wife and husband; father and son; mother and child; King and Fool, master and servant; factory owner and worker; landowner and peasant; society and artist; man and man. The characters are vivid human presences. They also represent a multiplicity of possibilities which lie within and outside the audience's heads. They are vigorous and alive but they are also incomprehensible and stand as invitations to the spectator to find an explanation of their mystery. What do they represent? The spectator invests a meaning, fastens on perhaps one of the many suggested. Gogo is Oedipus, because his foot is 'swelling visibly' or he is Adam. Pozzo is a ringmaster because he 'took a knouk' (clown). But the spectator who fastens on only one meaning suffers bewilderment and irritation because many interpretations are possible. The play mocks the audience's needs. It is a deliberately open framework, an invitation to reconstruct. Were a single explanation possible the play would cease to work, yet it sympathizes with the obsessive need to find explanations, for the character Didi wants to be sure of things. It also sympathizes with Gogo who does *not* want to be tormented by such things. It is aware of the need for 'truth' yet it mocks dogmatism and the single intellectual theory. It celebrates the multiplicity of art and the conflicts between possibilities on which drama depends. This is one explanation of its fertile impact.

Beckett also operates by repetition of an image. Figures enter a pool of light, exit, re-enter, re-exit. Their postures, sudden, grotesque, and yet amazingly human, cut deep into memory. They inherit the patterns of Everyman confronted by death: the King talking to his Fool; the Fool conversing with his bauble; the ventriloquist talking to his dummy or the straight man attempting to cope with the funny man. Morecombe and Wise, the Fool and Wise Man, Fool and Madman, are patterns not far distant.

The play's language must also be mentioned. It is musically orchestrated, leaving silences, precisely calculated, which fill with the play's multiple suggestions.

'The sun will set, the moon will rise and . . . who said that?' The answer is Marlowe's Faustus said it, and the image of Faustus near to damnation (another subject toyed with in the play) rises with the words, together with associations which vary with each playgoer: Helen of Troy, Marlowe and Ingram Frazer[2], great reckonings in little rooms, devils on trapezes, Everyman I will go with thee, the end-pages of Dent's popular series . . . the mind goes off at tangents, but the play reasserts its circles, filling the air with further echoes: personal, idiosyncratic, general and shared. That this is deliberate is hard to doubt. The names themselves of Beckett's characters both invite and mock allegory. Hamm in *Endgame* may remind us of Hamlet, ham actors, Ham the son of Noah, a hammer (in the way he treats Nagg and Nell, whose names together suggest *Nagel*, German for nail), even ham and cloves, since the son is called Clov. At this point the allegorizer may start to feel his leg is being pulled.

Beckett liberates the mind. He also ties it to a rhythmical form. When the timing is precise, the form holds the multiple voices and personal reminiscence and the transaction between actors and spectator is maintained. We are confronted with what we prefer not to be confronted with – our own desire not to watch, not to listen to painful and obvious truths. At the same time a spectacle of heroism is presented. When the characters together suppress Lucky's long monologue by taking off his thinking cap we watch the cowardice and heroism of our struggle not to know.

It is sometimes said a Beckett play leaves one where one was at the beginning, but this need not be true. Beckett may attack Aristotelian assumptions that a play like other forms of life, animal, vegetable and human, has a beginning, middle and end. Beckett's plays (like Shakespeare's *Troilus and Cressida*, for reasons not dissimilar) begin and end in the middle. But Beckett's characters move slowly on – if only towards immobility and the loss of mental and physical power. The audience has also moved on, both in time and possibly in awareness. The minds of those who register, even against their will, the nature of what Beckett says, must change. A form of expansion, of liberation, can arise out of the very recognition of limitation. In this, and no doubt other ways, *Waiting for Godot* in the mid-1950s, superannuated older forms of writing and fertilized the minds of a generation. To the many anecdotes about Beckett I can add the following. Imagine two people, married, very different from one another: the man reflective, sensitive, unassuming, the woman odd, lively, obsessive. The woman's brother, a demolition worker, is electrocuted whilst knocking down a house, because someone has forgotten to switch off the mains. The woman identifies her brother's body and writes to Beckett that her obsession with his work gave her the strength to go through with it. Beckett replies courteously, says that if ever they go to Paris they should let him know. Some time later they go to Paris and write to say so. Nothing is lost by writing. Something might be lost by not writing. Beckett comes to their hotel. The husband introduces himself saying 'I'm nobody'. Beckett talks for an hour . . . says he has done nothing. 'The Greeks have said it all.' When they shake hands at parting he says he is happy to have met Nobody.

This true story is hard to square with rumours of the death of the Author. Creative transactions between writer and reader, author and spectator are fortunately possible. If, as has been said, nothing is more real than nothing, then Nobody is very real. The admission that one is nobody or has done nothing, may warm the heart in recognition or denial. A form of freedom exists in the recognition of a transaction between people, made possible by an art as apparently bleak as Beckett's. The wife has now become a Nobody and so has Beckett. But the voices of the dead speak on like leaves. 'Like ashes,' replies Didi. 'Like leaves,' insists Estragon. 'To have lived is not enough for them', says Vladimir. 'They have to talk about it', says Gogo. It is as well they do. A certain value may reside in our freedom to listen in.

Beckett is often linked with Ionesco as a dramatist of the absurd. Their plays were performed at almost the same time in France, although Ionesco began earlier. His *The Bald Primadonna* began a record run at the tiny Théâtre de la Huchette in the Paris Latin Quarter in 1950 and this first play, together with the short plays *The Lesson* (1951) and *The Chairs* (1952) illustrate the parodic nature of Ionesco's work. In the latter an old couple, living in isolation, people the stage with chairs for guests who exist in their imagination. There is a knock at the door. No one enters and the old couple conduct this empty presence to a seat. They move about, bringing in chairs from the 14 doors which open onto the stage, talking excitedly to the swarm of invisible guests and creating the sense that a great event is about to take place. A Message is to be delivered as a climax to the evening. Amazingly, after so many nobodies, a 'real' guest finally arrives. An Orator, looking very theatrical in evening dress, strides in, makes a series of choking noises, then delivers an incomprehensible message, ANGELBREAD, by spelling it on a blackboard. *The Chairs*, like *Waiting for Godot*, frustrates our need for confirmation and security. Ionesco might well say that the performance he preferred was when there were only two people in the audience. Empty chairs on stage, empty chairs in the audience, and two couples reflecting one another.[3]

The play is a fine vehicle for two actors. The double bill at the Royal Court which established Ionesco's name in England also established Joan Plowright as a leading actress, since she played the young girl who is assaulted by a mad professor of linguistics in *The Lesson* and the old old lady in *The Chairs*.

These early plays are short and allegorical. Of single rather than multiple meaning, they dwell on themes such as the nature of language, or power relations. Like most absurdist plays they lack the consistency of plot and characterization which informs a longer drama. Occasionally Ionesco was more ambitious. *Rhinocéros* (1960), produced by Jean-Louis Barrault at the Odéon, Théâtre de France, at the time of the Algerian war, has three acts. It is a political allegory in an almost Swiftian or Orwellian mode, though it hints, too, at the animal fables of La Fontaine and those of central Europe.

In 1960, De Gaulle had sacrificed his nationalism to his good political sense and outmanoeuvred his own right wing. Shouts of '*Algérie Française*' were echoing up and down the Champs Elysées. Helmeted baton-wielding RSF police were barging cinema queues to reach the demonstrators. Senators were arguing that Algeria was part of France. The rhinoceros herds seemed to be growing in strength and students set watch on the police to see which way they would jump if Salan and his paratroopers descended on the capital. Fortunately there was no civil war but the threatening danger made manifest the purport of a play whose characters turned one by one into rampaging rhinoceroses.

It is true the play was about Ionesco's youth in the 1930s in

Roumania, when the fascist greenshirts began to proliferate. But like Sartre's *Altona* in the same year, it seemed strangely apposite. The play was not naturalistic and traditional in form, as was Sartre's nor was it haunting and multiple in meaning, like Beckett's *Endgame* (1956). *Rhinocéros* is a brilliantly theatrical, if overstretched allegory about the various reasons why people lose their identity and mental independence.

The play begins with a contrast between the bourgeois Jean, always immaculate, accepting the routines of his working life as a social duty, priding himself on his will-power, and freely criticizing any departures from the norm – such as his friend Bérenger's hangover, his not wearing a tie and his lack of punctuality. Jean is at home in the world, Bérenger is not. His existence fills him with an anguish which he drowns in drink. Soon a rhinoceros gallops past, then another. It appears all the townspeople are turning into rhinos – all except the man who does not fit – Bérenger. Rhinos have thick skins and uncertain tempers, they charge and they proliferate as did the Roumanian greenshirts. The transformation is an allegory of the herd instinct which made fascists of those who lacked independent judgement and human concern.

Ionesco defines the various ways in which human beings lose their humanity. There is the horny-handed old boss, Papillon, who handles Daisy in a pachydermatous way. There is Mrs Boeuf, who loves a man/rhino and becomes one by attraction. There is Jean, who lives by tags and has no independence of spirit. He has one aim in life, he says 'And I'm aiming straight for it'. He bellows and trumpets and scratches himself into the semblance of a beast.

Rhinocéros is about transformation. For varying reasons different people become very similar; the more they are in number the more acceptable it becomes to join them. Characters begin to feel it is normal to have a thick skin and use linguistic tags to seal out unease. 'Don't worry. You've got to go on living' is the motto of Dudard. Fatalism and indifference become 'common sense'. When the sympathetic Bérenger declares 'They should all be rounded up and placed in one enclosure' one begins to assent.

It is true that Bérenger at this point approaches the mentality he stands against. If the Nazi rhino mentality was herd-like it also exhibited a strong desire to herd others into enclosures – in particular the social group it was convenient to blame for economic ills. One wonders for a moment whether Bérenger will go the way of the rest, although in this instance he is right to assert his difference.

What is so compelling and convincing about Ionesco's presentation of the rhino mentality is not so much that it thrives on the condemnation of others, but that it is reinforced by kinship patterns. 'Everyone has a relative or close friend among them', says Daisy. Family feelings override what should have overridden family feeling. The herd refuses recognition of the essential difference between us which makes us free.

It even does this by making the doctrine of freedom an excuse for joining the herd: 'People are free to do as they like.' A chained mentality is claimed as freedom by a logic used in the service of the herd instinct. A relativistic morality, which says that evil is only the material product of a particular culture, is, for Ionesco, a dangerous misuse of intelligence. For him, the anguish of an Antigone, a Hamlet, a Lear, a Dimitri Karamazov, testifies to the unprovable existence of an ethic which goes beyond relativistic goodness and badness. There is a point at which tolerance must stop. The tolerant are assimilated. Ionesco had lived through that, yet it was still true in 1960 when the RSF baton-charged the rhino herds of right-wing protestors the boulevards.

The Theatre of the Absurd is not a single genre and its apparent anarchy conceals serious concerns. If at times the crazy vehicle takes over from the tenor, the form from the content; if the imagination that went into creating a fable becomes more important to writer or spectator than the original impulse behind the writing of the piece, then the absurdists can claim kinship with other allegorists – with Yeats who had proclaimed that his 'circus animals' took all his love 'And not those things that they were emblems of'.[4] There is also the example of Swift himself. It is in the nature of satire to become at times absorbed in its own inventions to the detriment of the message. And, of course, the absurdists, although like Ionesco they might have a 'message' of an important kind, were very uneasy about the didactic role of drama.

Sartre and Camus were not so uneasy, and were more allied to each other than to Beckett, who remains more open than any. The absurdists are very different writers. Genet, Adamov and Pinter are distinct from the other absurdists, and from one another, but the umbrella title still usefully relates to all of them and helps define aspects of writers, such as Stoppard (who were to make their impact in the 1960s). Before discussing that, something must be said about American and British naturalism in the 1950s, as well as about the impact of Brecht on British drama and the visit to London of the Berliner Ensemble in 1956.

American Naturalism

Miller and Tennessee Williams

The Theatre of the Absurd was a composite genre which began powerfully to affect the English scene in the mid-1950s. Other dramatic styles also made their impact, including 'kitchen sink' naturalism, ushered in by John Osborne's *Look Back in Anger* in 1956 and epic drama, resurrected by Brecht in post-war East Berlin and brought across to England by his company just after his death. Absurdism probably made the strongest immediate impact but Brecht's influence has strengthened with time. Osborne, for his part, extended the acceptable range of character and setting. His commercial success also enabled the Royal Court Theatre to subsidize plays of a more original dramatic form, such as those of John Arden, which made a consistent loss.[1]

It has become customary to date the resurgence of theatre in England to the years 1955–6, though as usual with such watersheds some qualification is necessary. It is true that in the years after World War II much of the vitality of a highly gifted generation of actors was channelled into revivals and well-crafted, but relatively conventional plays such as those of Terence Rattigan (1911–77). Verse drama, too, was successful, attracting major actors, and filling theatres. Besides Eliot's *The Cocktail Party* (1949), Christopher Fry enjoyed his most productive years with *A Phoenix too Frequent* (1946), *The Lady's not for Burning* (1948), *Venus Observed* (1950) and *The Light is Dark Enough* (1954). John Gielgud, Alec Clunes, Laurence Olivier and Edith Evans performed in plays which seem now to have been superannuated by the 'mid-fifties revolution'.

There was, however, another source of vitality on the London scene before the mid-1950s. This was American naturalism, represented by the plays of Arthur Miller (1915–) and Tennessee Williams (1914–83), and the films of Elia Kazan (1909–85). Miller's *All My Sons* and *Death of a Salesman* came to London well before the arrival of Beckett and Osborne, although productions of *The Crucible* and *View from the Bridge* (both 1956) were caught up in 'the new wave'. Williams's productions, too, had an earlier impact. *A Streetcar Named Desire* was seen in 1949 and *Summer and Smoke* in 1951. Through these plays and Kazan's films the Stanislavski-inspired 'method' school of acting, of which Marlon Brando and Paul Newman are well-known products, was already dealing seriously with working class experience. Before we can discuss the resurgence of English naturalism some description of earlier, and major, American theatre is required.

The 'method' developed out of Stanislavski's published writings and his work in the theatre. *An Actor Prepares* was published in English in 1936. It had a strong effect on the pre-war American Group Theatre which had produced in the 1930s the work of Maxwell Anderson (1888–1959), William Saroyan (1908–81) and the social plays of Clifford Odets (1906–63). Elia Kazan, who had been closely involved with the Group Theatre, founded the New York Actors' Studio in 1947. Here Kazan and fellow directors Lee Strasberg, Harold Clurman and Cheryl Crawford brought method acting both fame and notoriety.

English actors tended to reject the style. Some felt it emphasized individual performance at the expense of ensemble acting and character relationships; others felt it was relevant only to psychological naturalism and not to other styles of theatre. Yet the Stanislavski basis of method acting already formed an important element of most English actors' training and there is no doubt that it brought to screen acting, with its emphasis on facial expression in close-up, a deeper realism.

Antecedents of this post-war American naturalism included Thornton Wilder (1897–1975), whose dramatic aims were more classical than naturalist. His most famous play, *Our Town* (1938), first seen in London in 1946, was an attempt, said its author, 'to find a value above all price for the smallest events of our daily life'. The dialogue and costuming are naturalist and the atmosphere of village life is powerfully created. However, the situation is generalized in the manner of classical tragedy. The direct choral commentary of the Stage Manager sets the characters and the fugitive nature of their everyday small-town talk against a broad backdrop of time and space. The absence of scenery reinforces the impression of individuals caught in time who become aware of the necessary transience both of themselves and of the props they accumulate around them. The scene in which the dead Emily revisits Grover's Corners, takes the play out of natural time, presenting a situation of deep poignancy:

'Here the method of staging finds its justification – in the first two acts there are at least a few chairs and tables; but when she revisits the earth and the kitchen to which she has descended on her twelfth birthday, the very chairs and tables are gone . . . The climax of this play needs only five square feet of boarding and the passion to know what life means to us.'

Like many major writers, Wilder mixes genres; he invokes names such as Shakespeare, Dante, Molière and Joyce. His naturalism supplies an apparently solid human basis for the play. The solidity then poignantly gives way to a more generalized tragedy. 'I am not an innovator', said Wilder with humility in his Preface, 'but a rediscoverer of forgotten goods'.

J. B. Priestley, who deserves more than a brief mention for his work in the naturalist mode, achieves similar, poignant distancing effects in his 'time plays', *Time and The Conways* and *I Have Been Here Before* (both 1937–8), by rehandling the chronology of his scenes.

Another antecedent, and the dominant figure in pre-war American drama, is, of course, Eugene O'Neill (1888–1953). O'Neill, like Wilder, uses naturalist theatre techniques, yet his methods also invoke the big writers, and big intentions are written all over his work. He calls on Sophocles and classical myth in *Mourning Becomes Electra* (1931), and a moving tribute to his (and his father's) literary masters may be found in the stage directions of the autobiographical play *Long Day's Journey into Night* (1941). There, in the detailed description of the set, he spells out the titles of the books on the shelves. No audience would have been close enough to read them, and even the front stalls might not notice that the books 'astonishingly . . . have the look of having being read and re-read'. But O'Neill wrote these directions for his interpreters since he wished to point out important literary influences on the family he portrays – his own. Under a picture of Shakespeare, the family bookcase is loaded with volumes of Shakespeare's plays, the works of Victor Hugo, Dumas, Nietzsche, Marx, Ibsen, Shaw and Strindberg and famous histories by Hume, Smollett and Gibbon.

O'Neill was recreating the family atmosphere of the summer of 1912, when he was 24, a drop-out from Princeton, a guilty, lapsed catholic, a 'Broadway wise-guy' with a famous actor father still playing the 6000 performance run of *The Count of Monte Cristo.* His mother was addicted to morphine as a result of the father's penny-pinching use of a quack doctor and Eugene was in the habit of embarking on heavy drinking bouts with a jealous elder brother. One should add that he was Irish: 'One thing that explains more than anything else about me'. All the gods of the unsavoury Freudian Olympus seemed to hover over him.[2]

Long Day's Journey was a play written to free the writer of a past which obsessed him. In a diary entry his wife notes; 'June 21st 1939, a hot sleepless night. Gene talks to me for hours about a play (in his mind) of his mother, father, his brother and himself . . .'. Later she said: 'He had to get it out of his system. He had to forgive whatever it was caused this tragedy between himself and his mother and father . . . He would come out of his study at the end of a day gaunt and almost weeping . . . It was his way of making peace with his family and himself'.

Long Day's Journey is one of an incompleted nine-play cycle of American life from 1775 to 1932 and is sub-titled: 'A Tale of Possessors Self-Dispossessed'. It is an appropriate play to mention as prologue to the 1950s since it was published in 1956, three years after O'Neill's death. A series of productions in Milan, Stockholm, Berlin, New York, Paris (1957) and finally London (1958) made it part of the 1950s scene. In this decade, however, the expressionistic and melodramatic tone, the heroic energy and tragic intensity of O'Neill's work seemed to speak from an earlier time. Strong emotions, unregulated by irony or reason, tend towards melodrama, the form against which the naturalist movement rebelled. In O'Neill's plays this melodrama operates within a naturalist frame. O'Neill, like the father he depicts in his autobiographical play, was simple and direct. He was also an actor. The staginess of the play and of its characters, the secrets and revelations, the declamation and strong entrances, are naturalized and made acceptable by the way characters oscillate between pretence and sincerity. The audience sees that, for these characters, occasional melodrama was natural.

It is true, however, that O'Neill had a taste for highly theatrical staging. Among interpreters who disliked this aspect of the writer was American academic and man of the theatre Eric Bentley. Of *The Iceman Cometh* (1938), produced in London in 1958, the same year as *Long Day's Journey*, he declared: 'In order to find the essential, or at least better O'Neill, we agreed to forego much 'O'Neillism'.[3] The writer, he admits, has a genuine realist talent and an element 'which we took as an incidental excrescence, being expressionistic'. The Bentley production eliminated 'Rembrantesque lighting', the slanting Caligari corridors, and elements of Strindberg's phantasmagoric *Dream Play*.

Bentley had worked closely with Brecht, whose epic theatre had developed away from early 1920s expressionism. He identifies the expressionist/naturalist duality of O'Neill and, not surprisingly but perhaps unwisely, strives to eliminate the expressionist polarity which he identifies as a weakness. In performance, this very split in styles of producton and character behaviour can generate immense power. Alternations of mood between rage and apology give each character two voices, one civilized and the other violent and uncontrolled. The duality gives O'Neill's plays that variety of level found in the great writers who transcend the limits of genre.

Before *Long Day's Journey* came upon the London scene, but long after O'Neill had made his first impact, the plays of Arthur Miller and Tennessee Williams had made their mark in New York. When they transferred to London theatres they were lauded by Ken Tynan, the influential *Observer* drama critic. It was a judgement he held to. 'America in 1951,' he proclaimed, 'had the best young actors and actresses, the most exciting directors . . . unquestionably the finest playwrights. America alone had built upon the foundations of realism laid down by Stanislavski and Chekhov.'[4] The situation was to change and Tynan came to consider Broadway a 'Death Valley' of theatre where commercial values had entirely taken control. But in 1951 it was for him a 'fertile orchard' where *Death of a Salesman* (1949) and *A Streetcar Named Desire* (1947) were continuing a vital dramatic tradition. They are still key plays in a discussion of the modern evolution of drama and frequent revivals ensure their continuance and testify to their power.

The plays build on a realist or naturalist tradition. But this tradition carries within it an awareness of its own limitations and seeks ways of transcending surface realism. Like O'Neill and Wilder (and before them Ibsen and Chekhov) Miller and Williams were concerned with the familiar collision between private dream and public pressures, between an overriding fate and the individual struggle for freedom and control of the future. The sense of doom, a feeling that most human projects end badly, vies with an American respect for liberty. Miller in a television interview in 1986 admitted as much. He marries lived experience to a classical tradition. His American naturalism, with its close resemblance in structure to Ibsen – 'the birds, one by one, come to settle upon the branch' – found its truth in a lived awareness of human tragedy. Private guilt, created out of a competition between family relations and social responsibility, and fought against, is finally appeased when the self turns against the self. Such is the pattern of *All My Sons* (1947). In similar terms he describes the struggle of his one-time wife, Marilyn Monroe: a condemnation by her mother, and the remnants of a childhood fundamentalism, made her feel guilty in the practice of a profession she chose in rebellion against them. This inheritance led, said Miller, to her tragedy. The terms within which he sees such a struggle owe much to O'Neill, Ibsen and Sophocles. His plays seem consequently to demand more imaginative forms of staging than the limited box-set.

Death of a Salesman stunned the audience into silence on its first performance in Philadelphia. People stood up, put on coats, sat down again. 'Then someone clapped and the house came down.' The audience stayed for hours, hours, Miller insisted, telling each other about their lives. No one wanted to go. It was one of those very rare occasions, resembling the Moscow reception of *The Seagull* when the play breaks through a barrier. Miller was suddenly, after some 15 years of writing, famous.

The play went to New York where it was ecstatically received, before coming to London's Phoenix Theatre on 28 July 1949, with Paul Muni taking over from Lee Cobb as Willy Loman and Elia Kazan directing. For this production, Joe Mielziner designed a multi-levelled, skeletal setting which served, with lighting changes, as the Loman home, suburban backyard, restaurant, hotel room and graveyard.

The multiple set had three rooms and a staircase, with shapes of the threatening city above and around, bathed in an angry orange light. Weimar expressionism is not far away. 'An air of dreams clings to the place' says Miller, and indeed the actors could step through imaginary walls to a forestage when the action shifted from the present to recollection of the past. With this half-realistic, semi-transparent set Miller attempted to resolve the old problems of presenting the thoughts of characters who live within a real situation. By stepping over a wall they seem to escape from a confining situation into a 'freer' world of imagination.

In both public and private worlds, however, the characters are trapped. Dreams of freedom paradoxically tie them down. Willy Loman dreams the American dream and instils it in his sons. They dream of 'coming good', their utopia is just around the corner. Obstacles to its achievement are either ignored or transformed, for the dreams release an imaginative rather than practical energy. Without the projects these characters imagine, life would be impossible to tolerate. When human voices wake us the little men drown,[5] so they prefer to remain trapped in the dream of being or doing something special: to emerge is to commit emotional suicide. Indeed when the truth is told, and Biff can no longer be the accomplice to his father's dreams, suicide is the solution. Willy Loman dreams to justify his labour. Passed on to his sons, his vision undermines their capacity to act or meet responsibilities. Willy's dream helps him to work and support his family, but industry is not for Happy or Biff. They are contaminated by their father's fantasy.

The play was seen in two ways. The political left saw Miller as too soft on the system within which Willy Loman is working, a cruel world in which profit margins are more important than individuals. For them Miller did not adequately attack the capital-ist world of market forces. The right saw Miller as blaming the system when he should blame the individual. For them Willy Loman is responsible for his situation and deserves his fate.

That the play encourages these opposite responses is a form of tribute. A play which argued either the materialist or the individualist (liberal humanist) case would have lost dramatic force. The replacement of conflict by dogma diminishes dramatic possibilities and limits audience response. Both the private and the public worlds, and the conflict between them, need to be rendered. Even Engels supports such a view. It is 'not the case that the economic situation is the sole active cause, and everything else only a passive effect'. Economic base and cultural superstructure are not linked in a simple relation of cause and effect. If this model was encouraged it was because, in Engels's words: 'There wasn't

143

always time, place and occasion to do justice to the other factors in the reciprocal interactions of the historical process'.[6]

Engels still tried to argue for the ultimate dependence of the individual on economic forces. Miller represents a reciprocal interaction and implies a double responsibility. The pain of the tragedy derives from sympathy for the dreamer and admiration of his courage and his refusal to recognize constraints. It also derives from our knowledge that a competitive industrial world forces this dream upon its less gifted members in order to energize them. Possibly the sufferers are partly responsible for not being able to detect how they are tricked.

The problem is one of consciousness, education and perhaps 'native' intelligence. The individual may share responsibility for the mechanism of repression. Part of the audience's anguished tie with Willy Loman arises from its wondering whether he will take (or might have taken) stock of the trickery, thus recognizing reality and repudiating dream.

Miller's drama raises consciousness of the issues. He does not present a purely pessimistic view of his salesman's fate, nor is the play a simple demonstration of the evils of capitalism. The play remains open, asking the perennial questions on which dogmas attempt to foreclose. ('As long as my heart keeps beating', said Miller, 'my head will keep asking questions.')[7]

In the context of Miller's later work Willy Loman's situation is one to be changed. In the American edition of *View from the Bridge* (1956) Miller proclaimed: 'Time is moving; there is a world to make . . . a world in which the human being can live as a naturally political, naturally private, naturally engaged person.' This contradiction between private and public interest is the stuff of drama. It is interesting to see Miller striving to move beyond tragedy, beyond acceptance of the inevitability of conflict, towards the kind of reconciliation of private and public worlds which Brecht's epic theatre posited as a possibility to strive for. In his play *After the Fall* (1964) Miller would attempt to resolve both personal and social problems into a form of optimism. It was not a play Americans were ready for, he later said. Michael Blakemore's notable 1990 National Theatre production confirmed, however, that this play, clearly energized by Miller's fractured relation with Marilyn Monroe and mixing past and present in ways which built on naturalist techniques but carried it beyond, placed him among the rare dramatists whose plays continue to live and be performed.

The plays of Tennessee Williams are very different from those of Miller. His interests lie more in private issues than collective, and he tends to explore them through female characters rather than male. His language has a greater lyricism not unrelated to his respect for D. H. Lawrence. (*You Touched Me*, a powerful Lawrence story, was dramatized by Williams in 1946.) The taut scripts of Miller, on the other hand, are closely related to Ibsen, as his early play *All My Sons* strongly indicates. The two writers, however, work in a similar tradition and they share a common subject: the character in a state of desperation who dreams of escape. Miller felt that *After the Fall* (1964) was about reaching a point where one is tired of a burden and the relief with which you let it fall. One knows where this feeling came from. It was something people did not want to hear, said Miller. Williams, too, has the integrity to say what people do not always want to know.

A Streetcar named Desire came to the Aldwych Theatre, London, in 1949. Vivien Leigh played Blanche Dubois, Renée Asherson was Stella, Bonar Colleano was Stanley and Bernard Braden played Harold Mitchell. Laurence Olivier directed. The play sets up an atmosphere of faded charm: a dim white landing, a tender blue sky, the first dark of a May evening, the warmth of the river, the sound of black entertainers around the corner from the two-storey building we see on stage. Williams seeks to create a richness of sound and life in the old quarter of New Orleans. Its name is Elysian Fields and to get there Blanche Dubois needs to take a streetcar named Desire. Symbolism and allegory already threaten to carry the play beyond the limits of realism.

Blanche Dubois has had a rough time. She has coped with death and loss. Her home, Belle Rive, was 'Death's headquarters'. Now she has lost the house, is losing her looks and has no money. With security gone she falls back on raw needs. The only luxuries remaining are her furs, jewels and a few clothes. In her attempt to control her life she fights to persuade her younger sister, the only person still to know or admire her, to leave her run-down home. Stella, however, has a husband, Stanley, who has physically mastered her and Stella by no means wishes to be free. The social standards of her aristocratic background have come to seem unimportant in comparison with her conjunction with her husband. Blanche is doomed to lose.

Blanche fights for control with whisky and her fading attractions. It is obvious she is on the edge of breakdown. The noises of the town, the emotional violence of the environment, the strange mixture of anger, brutality and tenderness of Stella's marriage, affect her nerves. Blanche begins to see the setting as a metaphor of her own condition. As with Lear or Ophelia, or late Ibsen heroines, the strangeness of the world pushes her over the edge. At the same time the audience distinguishes between a world real for the other characters and not for her. The harsh realism of the male characters destroys the dream she is trying to create. When Mitch turns on the light to look closely at her face, when Stanley discovers what her past has been, Blanche's hold on life disintegrates.

A Mexican woman passes by her window selling roses for the dead. The 'blue' piano plays and Blanche puts on a theatrical display for her internalized ghosts. But Stanley enters, smashes the brittle facade and the set turns transparent with grotesque shadows thrown from the street.

After the rape Blanche's needs express themselves symbolically. She feels dirty. She combats her self-disgust by taking baths lasting all afternoon, or eating clean grapes. Finally she wishes to be sewn in a clean white sack and thrown into the sea. A courteous doctor takes her by the arm and leads her to an asylum where she can dream the rest of her life away.

When *Streetcar* was filmed, the ending, with Stella sobbing as Blanche is led out, but on the edge of making love again to Stanley, was changed. The film industry required a moral condemnation of Stanley for his rape of Blanche. But for Williams, a realistic ending was Stella's siding with her husband. Stanley's sexual dominance would reassert itself. People, 'mostpeople' e. e. cummings would have said, do not move in violent moral condemnation of the people they physically need. Stella remains in thrall and Blanche loses her battle. Blanche, in any case, since she is unable to abandon her sense of past superiority and adapt herself to changed conditions, was fighting to win the wrong battle. Her aristocratic background has created in her an estimate of self-worth which must be abandoned if she is to live in free consciousness of the world. As it is she becomes trapped in a symbolism which compensates her for the status and wealth she has lost.

Thus, Williams has succeeded in writing a play which incorporates symbolic levels into a naturalist psychological treatment. His subject is again the contradictions and paradoxes which lie behind the drive to freedom and control. In the plays which follow, Williams will again and again develop this concern, moving nearer to a theatre which abandons realism for symbolism and allegory, but unable to make the full step beyond conventions of naturalism. It was as well, perhaps, he did not. The power of his plays resides in his gift of portraying people in a natural setting, however much that setting may have forced them mentally to resort to some symbolic escape. Both Williams and Miller show that naturalism, despite the continuing attacks on it during the century, still provided a cornerstone on which major drama could be built.

Finding a Voice 1956–68

Osborne, Pinter, Wesker and D. H. Lawrence

The first performance of John Osborne's *Look Back in Anger* at the Royal Court Theatre on 8 May 1956 was an important event in twentieth century English drama. Beckett's *Waiting for Godot* had attacked conventional expectations as to what drama should be; a series of plays by Tennessee Williams had mingled stage symbolism with a more traditional naturalism to powerful effect, but the enthusiasm and fury aroused by Osborne's play was unique. It was far from revolutionary in form since Osborne used a full box-set and accepted the conventions of naturalist fourth-wall drama. But a new tone of voice, a raw class antagonism, set patriotic nerves on edge and articulated the violent opposition to an 'establishment' which in 1956 expressed its injured patriotism by the invasion of Suez.

Osborne's forms remained relatively traditional. It is true that after his first success he began to experiment with different stage techniques. He was to use music hall routines as a structural element in his second great success *The Entertainer* (1957), in which Olivier played Archie Rice, the fading comedian. In *Luther* (1961) he was to employ some of the methods that Brecht had reintroduced into the theatre, and he employed a Beckett strategy in *Hotel in Amsterdam* (1968) where the time is spent discussing a character who never enters. This last play scarcely used the visual resources of theatre. A static play with vivid dialogue, it could almost have been written for the radio listener.

Osborne became a fine craftsman of the theatre, and some of his plays, such as *A Patriot for Me* (1965), much better crafted than *Look Back in Anger*, have not had full justice done to them. *Look Back in Anger*, however, remains the play which is most revived. The naturalism of language, costume, setting and historical detail has made it seem more dated than the epic or absurdist forms of his contemporaries, Pinter, Beckett, and Arden but the vituperative power of Jimmy Porter's contempt (the word Osborne said he preferred to anger) still comes across, even if the complacency and apathy he attacked has changed in nature.

Osborne mixes the social levels, placing his more recognizable middle-class characters in or against a dingy setting which discomfited the West End audience. This was not completely new: Beckett had already placed his tramps and waifs and strays upon the boards and this was to lead Pinter and Bond, quite as much as Osborne, to extend their range of settings and characters downwards in the social scale. Working-class drama had existed at least since Hauptmann's *The Weavers* (1892) and American theatre had been much less inhibited than English drama in its serious representation of the 'lower orders'. In any case, the people around Osborne's kitchen sink are not so much working class as isolated drop-outs, people who are educated beyond, or have married below, their natural communities. Such characters as Alison, Helena, and Alison's father have been seen before on the English stage. Their interest lies in the conflict between their upbringing and the setting, in a way not dissimilar to Blanche and Stella in Tennessee Williams's play. They descend the social scale and it changes or challenges the values by which they have lived. Osborne found neither a new group of characters, nor an original form. The authentic new note[1] is Jimmy Porter's savagery.

Osborne aroused his London audiences because, unlike Williams and Miller, he was exploring the British, not the American scene and unlike Beckett he was engaged in direct social commentary. Nine years later Edward Bond's *Saved* was to arouse strong opposition to its treatment of working-class violence. Osborne had done much to move the theatre closer to such a subject. Bond's dramatic form, however, with its rhythmical short lines, restricted vocabulary and inarticulate characters, showed a naturalism tempered by the experiments of Beckett and Brecht, whereas Osborne relied on a gift for diatribe. His principal characters, unlike those of Beckett or Pinter, have become articulate (and they articulate perhaps too fully the concerns of play and playwright).

Osborne did not use parable. His early subject matter was neither historical nor mythical nor symbolic. His concern was the contemporary scene and he attacked it head on, helping to clear the way for the working class naturalism of Arnold Wesker and the early realism of Bond. This also led, at the end of the 1960s, to the tardy recognition of D. H. Lawrence's drama.

Osborne's vitriolic targetting of an older, richer and complacent generation brought him great popularity amongst the younger generation resentful of establishment attitudes.[2] This generation, associated with the 1944 Education Act, grammar schools and the provinces ('scum' according to Somerset Maugham) began to assert itself. It hailed the content of Osborne's play and enjoyed his vicious wit. It was apathy and complacency that Osborne hated, the English capacity to ignore the existence of events in the world outside, to enjoy privileges as if they lay in the natural order of things. The older universities, the public schools, the ex-professional soldier, the church, the complacency of those who have never suffered, left-wing intellectuals, critics who created nothing, all were objects of his malevolence. Inevitably, sections of the middle-class, theatre-going public took umbrage. But the play hit what T. C. Worsley called the 'authentic new note of the 1950s, desperate, resentful, savage and at times very funny'.[3]

Osborne's early heroes, Jimmy Porter, Archie Rice and Paul Slickey were derisive about English social values. Critics accused these characters of whining because they had insufficient talent to enter the world they attacked, but Osborne was even more derisive about such a view. It is not that they could not find a place in the world around them, they had no desire to do so: 'The complaint had never been that it wasn't possible to get in [to Literary Society] but that it had never been worth getting into in the first place' Osborne wrote in the *Observer* on 30 October 1960.

Jimmy Porter's talent for diatribe was directed against England, a target guaranteed to engender rage. His critics detected an adolescent idealism which had been betrayed, a basic conservatism which looked nostalgically back to the Edwardian era and found no sense of belonging to replace a vanished past. The sceptic, said A. J. Ayer, 'by insisting on an impossible standard of perfection . . . makes himself secure'. (Osborne quoted this in his *Observer* article.) But the play had struck home and the 'establishment' had found newly articulate enemies.

The play's attitudes could not have carried conviction without a strong basis in some human reality. Jimmy Porter is a powerful, convincing and complex character. Vulnerable, he hates his own vulnerability and dependency. Able to care deeply, he has early been exposed to death and loneliness. His instability derives from painful personal experience of a dying father confiding his failures to him at the age of ten. His verbal assaults on his middle-class spouse and her comfortable background also have a subjective basis. They are the more extreme because he resents a strong and physical attachment to his wife. In this way he is still adolescent, yet in other ways he knows more than the secure and confident people he attacks.

His contempt for complacency and class-superiority, his sense of not belonging because, like Richard Hoggart's scholarship boy,[4] he has been educated beyond his social roots, struck a chord with the new non-public school university students, the red brick, or even as Jimmy Porter puts it, 'white tile' universities, resentful of the dominance of Oxbridge, its old boy network and its indifference to talent elsewhere. Many of these students could not make a life in England and went abroad, or returned home to recover their provincial roots, or finally succeeded, as 'outsiders' (another 'in-word' of the decade, popularized by Colin Wilson's momentarily famous book), in careers in the theatre, film, television or elsewhere. The ambivalent feelings of those who succeeded in this way may be seen at a later stage, represented, for example, in Trevor Griffiths's play *The Party* (1973). These 'outsiders' have written a great deal of subsequently important English drama.

For Jimmy Porter, integration into English society was an act of betrayal (although for many of those rebels he was taken to represent, working within the system proved preferable to running Jimmy's sweets stall). Jimmy Porter was individualistic and apolitical. A more reasoned and mature response, it was argued, would have been to join a political pressure group, or become a writer, or both, which is what the talented generation in the post-Suez period mainly did. Trevor Griffiths, Dennis Potter, Harold Pinter, Edward Bond and Tom Stoppard were all people from outside the literary establishment, who found through their vocation a way of working within, if often against, the dominant culture. Osborne did the same. His most famous character, however, found only private expression.

Jimmy Porter prompts us to question why we acquire an education, and what we use it for. Bond was to say that the more inarticulate the group, the greater the chance that it will express itself through violence. Jimmy is articulate. His violence is verbal, not physical. Unlike the inarticulate characters in Pinter's *The Caretaker* and Bond's *Saved* (1965), Jimmy had found a voice and turned it against his own group. No wonder he caused a scandal.

The dramatization of inarticulate characters is usually associated with Harold Pinter, whose career took off with the success of *The Caretaker* in 1960. Although Pinter owes a great deal to Beckett and his plays are usually labelled as absurdist theatre, they contain careful observations of social behaviour within a box-set which derives from the dominant naturalist tradition. What Pinter has done is wed absurdist and naturalist theatre so that the stage room becomes partly symbolic. Sartre anticipated him in *In Camera* and so, more surreally, did Beckett in *Endgame* where the two windows suggest eyes looking out upon a dead world. In Pinter, too, the set is suggestive of conflicts within the head, yet his treatment of setting and human relations within it has a powerful realism. Since he also deals with power relations in which the command of language is often crucial, it is appropriate to discuss at least one of his plays here.

The Caretaker has three characters, Mick, Aston his brother, and Davies, a tramp whom Aston invites back to his room and offers the job of caretaker. Mick is the owner of the house, Aston the tenant and Davies the guest. Mick is articulate, speaks very rapidly and has a command of different verbal styles which he assumes in order to bewilder the tramp. His aim is to switch Davies's allegiance from Aston to himself by informing him that he, Mick, is the one with power to appoint a caretaker. Davies will then break Aston's attachment to him and Mick can throw him out without damaging the relation between himself and his brother.

There is something manic about Mick, and his brother seems in the past to have resembled him. But Aston, it is suggested, was committed to a mental institution where he underwent electric shock treatment and now speaks and gathers his thoughts very slowly. He is trying to re-establish himself in life. In the process he collects a number of odd items which fill his room and need repair: a gas stove, a buddha, a vacuum cleaner, a lawn-mower.

These symbolize a desire to get going, in particular to cut the grass, to build a shed, to contain the tools and to decorate the house where he is a tenant. It is a process of self-repair in which he may or may not succeed. A sign of progress lies in his desire to acquire a human relation and he adds to his collection of miscellaneous items the tramp, Davies, who proves completely incapable of gratitude, of accepting responsibility, or of giving anything in return for shelter. Mick must get rid of him.

To do so Mick plays games with language, talking of his 'apartment' in a decorator's vocabulary. It is to be a palace in 'afromosia teak veneer'. Aston's language, on the other hand, is slow, honest and direct. He speaks for himself and plays no assumed roles. Davies is inarticulate, an uncomprehending bundle of prejudices and fears. He has no understanding of generosity. His world is disconnected and the jumbled items in the room, even a disconnected gas stove, fill him with fear. Yet in the gaps in his vocabulary, behind his hatred of 'them blacks' down the road, behind his boasting that he has an identity somewhere, and in his creation of the utopia of Sidcup which will confirm it, this pitiful figure becomes pitiable. Like Beckett, Pinter finds in silence and contrasting modes of speech a powerful mode of communication. In the naturalism and strangeness of the dialogue, in the naturalism and strangeness of the box-set, Pinter found a powerful tragicomic form.

He worked out this narrow seam in a series of plays about couples and trios and emotional power relations, expressed in varying ranges of vocabulary, accent and social register. The world of Hackney, where the Jews who had moved out of Stepney had not yet achieved the apotheosis of Golders Green, is strongly present. The characters, Jews and non-Jews, seek some social relation, an identity, a place to belong. Neurosis and schizophrenia lurk around the corner.

The Caretaker remains Pinter's most powerful drama. The 'stream of consciousness' plays he later experimented with, such as *Landscape* and *Silence*, moved from the potency and threat of his earlier work to a nostalgic stasis. *Silence*, for example, includes longer and longer gaps which contain echoes of its earlier dialogue. The process appears to weaken his early achievement of identifying powerful tensions in and behind the disjunctions of human speech.

The question of acquiring one's own language, and with it greater freedom and power, has been picked up in the continuing naturalist form by Willy Russell's highly successful *Educating Rita*, which asks questions of working-class language and education, and seems to conclude 'There's got to be a better song'. Yet it paid tribute to the vigour of lower-class speech, and mocked the artificiality of some of the jargon which a person thirsty for self-development may momentarily embrace before finding an authentic voice. Rita is significant in that she retains a native vitality and assimilates her new vocabularies to her personal needs, retaining her spontaneity and widening her range of response, whilst seeking to keep contact with her roots.

Wesker's famous trilogy of plays: *Chicken Soup with Barley*, *Roots* and *I'm Talking about Jerusalem* (1958–60) has a similar concern. The character who acquires a voice is the young uneducated Beatie in *Roots*, who, when she has been educated beyond her background, wishes to share a new-found freedom of expression with the class from which she has sprung. Beatie, like her Norfolk family, has a very limited verbal range and attempts to break out of it by copying the man she loves. In the end she loses him but finds herself. She also seems about to lose her family. She wins a voice at the expense of further alienation: in those she wishes to carry with her she seems only to create resentment and fear.

The subject is familiar. Charlotte Brontë, George Eliot and Henry James all examine the social and psychological restraints on young, mainly middle-class women seeking greater freedom. Ibsen took up the subject in *A Doll's House* (1879). In the novel, D. H. Lawrence had created powerful lower-class and often female characters seeking self-expression. Thomas Hardy's Tess Durbeyfield and Sue Bridehead anticipated him. In drama, Shaw's Eliza Doolittle announced the verbal liberation of a working-class girl long before Wesker's Beatie. Since the 1950s, however, the seeking of a voice has been a preoccupation of working-class and feminist drama.

The intrusion of abrasive provincial voices into the English cultural scene, into the novel, into television as well as theatre, is responsible for much of its vitality. Language and freedom is a central question which Jimmy Porter, in his alleged misuse of both, placed firmly before us. Wesker, less anarchistically, shows us education in a positive light. It gives us a language and with it, freedom to control our lives. Most of his working-class characters, however, are not interested in developing this weapon. In a vivid rendering of a Norfolk family, Wesker presents an unsentimental, squabbling, down-to-earth working class which is by turns direct, bawdy, fatalistic, greedy, unreflective, defensive and mean, and unable to combat the words of an oppressive social group above it. Wesker holds out little hope for the development of the group. It is the individual who can develop by severing himself or herself from the conventional attitudes of the group he has belonged to.

Wesker writes in a tradition which is still thriving. Nick Darke's play *Apart from George* (National Theatre production 1987), for instance, uses similar methods to explore a rural community. Arguably, however, the most convincing dramatic presentation of English working class life was written by a man who died in 1930.

D. H. Lawrence wrote six plays in the period between 1909 and the outbreak of World War I. They were closely related to the fiction he was publishing at the time, but none of his plays was performed until 1926, and he made no powerful impact as a dramatist until 1968, 38 years after his death. *A Collier's Friday Night*, *The Daughter-in-Law*, and *The Widowing of Mrs Holroyd* were then performed at the Royal Court and revealed that in different conditions, Lawrence could have become a major figure in the English theatre. It is extraordinary that despite the exploration of lower-class life and working-class conditions in the nineteenth-century Russian and French novels of Dostoievski and Zola, and in the English novel since Dickens and Mrs Gaskell, such an exploration in drama as Lawrence's *The Daughter-in-Law* (1912) should have had to wait almost 60 years for a West End production.

The plays performed at the Royal Court were the first to be written, *A Collier's Friday Night* before 1909 and the other two by 1911 when Lawrence sent the script of one of them to Edward Garnett for publication. In his confident way he proclaimed in the accompanying letter his intentions and his models. He was *not* writing the middle-class drama which had followed in the wake of Ibsen's revolution: 'It is time for a reaction against Shaw and Galsworthy and Barker and Irishy (except Synge) people – the rule and measure mathematical folk'. His plays owed a great deal to Ibsen, something to Synge and Chekhov. But the experience was of a Nottinghamshire mining community, not a middle-class family.

The commercial theatre of his period was not interested in Lawrence's concerns. To quote Raymond Williams: 'There had been a time when a new English dramatist was ready to engage with his audience, in a theatre of ordinary feeling raised to intensity and community by the writing of ordinary speech, and when it was the institutions – the links between writer and audience which were absent, during the occupation of the theatre by a different class and form'.[5]

Working-class concerns had been found in 'illegitimate' urban melodrama in the nineteenth century, before it was legitimized as thrilling and semi-comic entertainment for the middle-class West End theatre. Plays which made the working class a serious concern had appeared just before and between the wars. They included the work of the 'Manchester School', Harold Brighouse (1882–1958), Allan Monkhouse (1858–1936) and especially William Houghton (1881–1913) whose *Hindle Wakes* (1912) was a lasting success. *Love on the Dole*, Walter Greenwood's classic novel of working-class life in a northern town during the depression was dramatized in 1934. Richard Llewellyn wrote his famous *How Green was my Valley* about a Welsh mining village. Priestley, too, found audiences where Lawrence did not. But the audience for 'provincial drama' lay mainly in provincial repertory not in the West End.

In 1968, as Williams pointed out, Lawrence's plays had been brilliantly dramatized for television and a broader theatre audience existed. The name of Lawrence also attracted the professional classes and students who were more accustomed to the serious fictional and dramatic presentation of working-class experience, even if few working-class spectators attended the Royal Court. In the late 1960s Lawrence's early plays finally found a deserved place in the theatre.

The Daughter-in-Law is about the restrictions of marriage, of class, of consciousness and of cultural attitudes. The central character is seeking recognition and self-expression within the constraints of her chosen life. The action begins within a collier's kitchen and the first interchange between mother and collier concerns the management's refusal to give the collier sick-pay. The mother must therefore keep her son on ten shillings a week club money. The play begins with a view of men/management relations, not however, entirely from the men's point of view. Joe the collier has hurt his arm by fooling around during a snap-break. The management refuses to take responsibility and Joe's mother sees their point of view. The play does not divide its sympathies according to divisions of social power; managers and men are equally human.

The play then shifts into a discussion of another kind of responsibility – this time for pregnancy. Joe's brother Luther, just six weeks married to another girl, is the father. The girl's mother, Mrs Purdy, is asking for £40 in compensation. Luther's mother, Mrs Gascoigne, who looks after her son's money, refuses and sends Mrs Purdy to Luther's wife, who also has money. The women seem to possess all the strength while the men are feckless. There is, however, no moralizing about social misdemeanour. The dialogue is direct, powerful but not violently antagonistic. All three characters on stage accept a common responsibility and they discuss between them how to discharge it. Who pays the money and should the new wife be told? Joe and his mother disagree. Mrs Purdy needs Mrs Gascoigne's agreement if she is to obtain the money she wants. So long as she gets the money, Mrs Gascoigne can control the manner of payment. The women stick together. The result is a highly convincing competition of wills in which all three characters play for a measure of control. The audience is not allowed strong moral preferences: there is too much that is unknown about the characters' motives and about Mrs Gascoigne's relations with her son and daughter-in-law for that. The audience must wait for the stage entry of these two before it can start to decide.

In the second scene this opportunity is offered, for we cut to the house of Luther and his new wife Minnie. If the first scene is marked by an agreement about cultural values and responses, the second shows a collision. It is familiar to any reader of Lawrence's *Sons and Lovers* (1913) – or his dramatic short story *Fanny and Annie* – as a class division between a collier husband and a wife who has married beneath her.

Luther arrives home 20 minutes late. He is dirty, and ready to eat in his pit-dirt. He disarranges the table. There is a momentary clash of social manners before we sense a deeper relation between husband and wife. Minnie is attracted to something strange, something beyond her control in her husband. This magnetism has overcome the differences of class and discrepancies in social etiquette. A balance in this relationship is going to consist of taking new attitudes in the nicely arranged room where Minnie feels happy and her husband ill-at-ease. When they kiss, Luther in his pit-dirt and Minnie in a white blouse, the social differences are shown as not insuperable.

During their dialogue another serious conflict within the family is revealed. Who should pay the first visit to the other, mother or daughter-in-law? 'Your mother can come here can't she?' Minnie asks, battling to prevent her mother-in-law's continuing control of her husband and – by extension – of herself. From a personal conflict the dramatic tension extends to a family conflict.

The scene then broadens to the social conflict already spoken of in Scene 1 and the conversation shifts to a threatened strike. Revealingly, Minnie is on the side of management. Her husband will not get on, does not care to better himself. Behind her carping, however, is the sense that she needs to carve out a place – as Mrs Purdy later puts it: 'She naggles your heart out maybe, but that's just the wrigglin a place out for herself.' The vivid colloquial phrasing, here as everywhere in the play, alerts us to the kind of human needs which lie behind the social surface. What matters between Minnie and Luther is partly, but not entirely, a matter of social construction. Self-fulfilment lies in relationships which are more than social relations.

Social relations count for a very great deal but not, Lawrence believed, for everything. The mind could stand back from social conditioning, indeed needed to. His experience of his own creativity supported this conviction. And if evidence may be adduced, the fullness of his characters, their double dimensionality, their engagement in a physical, as well as a social relation, may be evidence enough. Certainly the presentation by actors in the theatre of this double relation can be made convincing. A single dimension does well enough for parable plays and comedies whose stereotypes provoke laughter because the audience knows that humanity consists of more than socially conditioned reaction. Lawrence's naturalism presents fuller human beings, fuller than Wesker's, or Osborne's. All his characters struggle with their own duality. Within the naturalist mode Lawrence creates a wide range of vividly responsive people.

The fullness of human response comes through powerfully in the second act of the play in which Luther reveals he will be the father of Bertha's child. The exchange between husband and wife is bitter. Luther is half-drunk, Minnie proud, but half-dependent still. The couple sleep separately, their needs unresolved. Out of conflict some resolution will come. Neither wants to leave the other, but the social reasons for breaking, founded on emotions of dignity and shame, are strong. The conflict within each is one between pride and caring. A release from that pride will allow them to accept mutual need.

In Act III Minnie enters her mother-in-law's house. It is a fortnight later. The men are on strike. They want a fair wage and the new manager has been keeping wages down. Moreover, he has hired men to assure the safety of the pits during the strike. The men resent this in 'their pit'.

The analogy between the men's responsibility to the pit and the wife's responsibility in the home is emphasized. Mrs Gascoigne will not act as blackleg by keeping home for Luther during Minnie's absence. Minnie has gone on strike, just as Joe and Luther have done. The community assumes that the relation between managers and men is equivalent to the relation between husbands and wives. Managers and husbands are responsible but may renege. Workers and wives are dependent but may rebel. Luther is a manager from whom support has been withdrawn. He must be a caretaker at home, like the managers at the pit, until support returns.

Luther must work out four relations – with his manager, with his work-mates, with his mother and with his wife. In the competition of loyalties and the need to escape domination, Luther can either lose or find himself.

The difference between the women and the men is that the men have a form of creative occupation outside the home. Their work is important to them. The woman, especially Minnie who is childless, has no form of freedom or room for creativity (which children would partly or wholly supply). She turns on Luther who is not yet even a butty, with no ambition to move on and out. She is trapped in her husband's life.

Lawrence, however, suggests that even within this imprisonment there is a possibility for the woman. If a full relationship can be established between the husband and wife, a relationship in which the two are not superior, or inferior, or even equal but accept each other as *other*, then the servitude can be resolved into a creative interchange. Luther is a slave to management and to his feelings for his mother, and he is not whole. Minnie wants this wholeness which consists in becoming independent of others' judgement. She does not want Luther dependent on herself. The solution she discovers is to abandon her financial independence, in order that Luther can feel responsible for her and so she spends her £120 to escape the power it gives her. Luther, for his part, at the third act climax, burns the £90 of prints which for him symbolize Minnie's cultural and economic superiority.

Act IV is brief. The men leave the women during the night whilst they seek to prevent the blacklegs attending to the pit. Left alone, the women acknowledge they need the men. Luther returns, injured, and the acknowledged need brings Minnie and Luther together. Whether it will last, the play does not say. Minnie has placed herself in Luther's power. If Luther has the kind of human responsiveness the play suggests can exist, then she may not suffer by it.

The apparent conclusions of Lawrence's play, like the apparent maligning of working-class life in *Roots*, did not please the critics who sought a more positive presentation of working-class values. Lawrence was more positive than Wesker and less sentimental than Osborne. Together with Wesker he respected a disciplined middle class and did not condemn their emphasis on education, although, like Osborne, he hated middle-class philistinism. Lawrence's play supports a real and convincing class tension, which asks how far a personal freedom can be won amid a clash between communities in which each both contributes to and threatens the creativity of the central figures. In the portrayal of this deeply felt tension, and for reasons of sheer craftsmanship and linguistic vitality, Lawrence's plays at the end of the 1960s constitute an important dramatic achievement in the naturalist form. The recognition came late, but it was better late than never. His plays dwell on the familiar problem of finding a place, finding room for the self, finding a voice. If he is different, it is that at an early stage in his career he did not see the solution as moving up and out, so much as, in the case of Minnie, moving down and in. In this way freedom could be gained as well as refused, just as in moving out it could be lost as well as gained. It was in his subsequent fiction that this paradox would be examined.

Brecht's Later Epic Theatre and Its Impact

Apart from absurdist drama and American and English naturalism, the dominant genre in recent English theatre has proved to be the 'epic drama' which Piscator and Brecht had worked to create in the Weimar Republic. Under Nazism after 1933, Brecht's plays, which had become more overtly left-wing as Hitler rose in power, were impossible to stage. Nor were they permissible in Russia. Brecht's theatre was condemned as 'formalist' by Stalin's conservative regime. Brecht travelled to Denmark and Finland, through Russia to America, where he settled and wrote 11 plays between 1937 and 1945, including his considered masterpieces: *Mother Courage, The Life of Galileo, The Good Woman of Setzuan, The Resistible Rise and Fall of Arturo Ui, Herr Puntila and his Man Matti* and *The Caucasian Chalk Circle*. In these allegorical or parable plays, set in the past, or in a far-off country, or both, Brecht asked indirect questions about the contemporary world. He offered a story for interpretation, following the method he had developed in *Mann ist Mann* (1926), *Mahogonny* (1930) and *St Joan of the Stockyards* (begun 1930).

After the war Brecht came back to East Berlin. He kept his West German publisher, Suhrkamp, but intended to stage his new plays under the East German Communist regime, for which he was a source both of pride and embarrassment. Early in 1949 he staged *Mother Courage* at the Deutsches Theater. The company adopted the name Berliner Ensemble and spent much of the next five years on tour, returning to a permanent home in the Theater am Schiffbauerdamm in 1954. He opened in June with a celebrated performance of *The Caucasian Chalk Circle* which he later toured in Paris. In 1956, just before the play was due to tour in London, he died of a heart attack, 'a knock at the window pane' Brecht had predicted. The Ensemble under Brecht's widow Helene Weigel nevertheless brought the play to London, together with *Mother Courage* and *Pauken und Trompeten*. The visit made a lasting impact on British theatre, especially on the writers working at George Devine's Royal Court who included John Arden and Edward Bond. A younger group including David Hare, Howard Brenton, Howard Barker and Caryl Churchill also learned considerably from Brecht, using montage in historical parables and placing less stress on naturalist 'character' than on asking political questions.

Brecht's example has more generally encouraged the use of realistically 'worn' costumes, convincing props and vivid stage tableaux. John Osborne's *Luther* (1961) presented a grouping of peasants with a cart and a dead body in just such a 'gestic' way. Directors of the big national theatres, especially the Royal Shakespeare Company, appropriated visual stage techniques without necessarily embracing the politics. Others copied Brecht's abandonment of naturalist scenery, together with the fresh ways in which he handled historical themes – his fusion of Shakespeare's chronicle forms with the dramatic debates of George Bernard Shaw and other forms such as Greek tragedy.

Brecht needed a big theatre. He did not want a theatre in which a handful of people talked in a room. During the rise of Nazism he had witnessed the spectacle of large masses of people drifting inertly, as Herbert Read had said, like fish into a net. A sense of individual responsibility and a collective awareness of the big public issues were necessary for the right functioning of society. Brecht's theatre could help promote this, but to do so it needed a large cast, a large stage, a big repertory company and plenty of rehearsal time. Brecht wished to show characters in social relationships. If he showed them as isolated, their isolation indicated their social and human needs. Characters were thus set against a broad backdrop of human activity, and shown in situations where they needed to make choices and take responsibility for themselves.

His theatre, he had said in the 1920s, was to resemble a boxing ring in which people threw pennies and cheered on the combatants. Brecht wanted an active theatre, not one in which audiences sat in hushed silence in the dark. Nor did he want the theatrical impact of a Nuremberg Rally or a May Day Procession which were indeed agit-prop drama on an epic scale. He wanted conflicts, problems, personal suffering and public analysis. Again it was a theatre about freedom:

> Our audiences must not only hear how Prometheus was set free, but also train themselves in the pleasure of freeing him. They must be taught to feel in our theatre all the satisfaction and enjoyment felt by the inventor and the discoverer, all the triumph felt by the liberator.[1]

Brecht sought to create an optimistic, combative, even gladatorial state of mind, such as he had admired in Shaw. Theatre must be vital, like the amazing *Woyzeck* by Georg Büchner (1813–37), who was another close ancestor of epic theatre. Brecht worked to move and entertain by stimulating thought, not group feeling. As with Shaw, comedy was his natural element, but it was a comedy sombrely tinged by his war experience and the historical realities of twentieth-century Russia and Germany.

The Caucasian Chalk Circle (1945) is an appropriate play to discuss: it is probably the most popular of Brecht's plays in England, having an element of fairy tale that allows commercial management to discount the political elements. The play, however, begins with a debate between two communes (often cut) about who should cultivate land they both claim. The first commune had been ordered to retreat as Hitler's armies approached. It now wants its valley back for the old purpose of goat breeding. But the neighbouring fruit-growing commune wishes to grow fruit there, for which purpose it argues the land is more suitable. The latter wins the debate and when business is over they celebrate with a meal and a story.

A parable is enacted with, as chorus, a Singer, brought in by a girl tractor driver. 'How long will the story take Arkady?' says the Expert. 'It is actually two stories . . . A few hours,' says the Singer. 'Couldn't you make it shorter?' says the Expert, very confidentially. 'No' says the Singer, for time must be taken over pleasure as well as business. In any case the story is related to their business. That is one reason why it gives pleasure.

The commercial temptation for any producer of this play is to remove the opening and closing debate, and provide attractive decor and fine costume, thereby eliminating the intended moral so as to focus on the story alone. The story, by itself, is very attractive and audiences could be scared away by any invitation to think about politics. This seems a danger particularly in England, and many English productions of Brecht are muted in this way. This does not only apply to *The Caucasian Chalk Circle*: other productions such as The National Theatre's *Schweik in the Second World War* (1984) and even *The Mother* (1988) have lacked a feeling of immediate political relevance. They became relics of a bygone age, of historical rather than current interest. Peter Hall's production of George Orwell's *Animal Farm* (1985) had the same air. Brecht's original productions were all of arresting political relevance. The English productions, for all their technical sophistication and acting brilliance, seemed merely antiquarian. Without an immediate political reason for staging it, and with a pressing need to fill the theatre, the temptation is to engage charismatic stars, such as Topol, in the main roles. Parts such as the peasant girl Grusha, who in Brecht's production was powerfully played by a forthright but plain actress, commonly go to a personable beauty. With the brilliant staging the play demands, such as the vivid mime when Grusha crosses the dangerous bridge to escape the soldiers, a charming evening can be had by all. Emphasis is placed on the excitement of narrative, not on the parable, on the signifier not the signified. The result is similar to reading *Gulliver's Travels* for the story and ignoring the satire.

The plays require contemporary political relevance. Perform them when a parallel is obvious, in an electrically charged setting, such as the Athens of 1975 in which *The Caucasian Chalk Circle* was the first Brecht play to be permitted since the fall a few months earlier of the 'Colonels' Fascist regime. Take a politicized audience picking up contemporary references in the highly cari-catural acting performances and the play takes on a powerful new dimension: in Athens, tortured victims of the late Colonels were in the audience, and spectators knew that many right-wing sympathizers were still in office. Brecht's plays throb with deeper life when the satire is current: they need contemporary reference. Brecht's example also encourages irreverence – rewrite the plays in the light of the present, as Brecht rewrote Shakespeare, rather than perform them as museum pieces or for purely commercial reasons.

The Caucasian Chalk Circle begins by voicing an immediate

concern: 'Over there in those hills we stopped three Nazi tanks. But the apple orchard had already been destroyed'. The war is over. The invaders have been driven back. In Europe, recovery is the immediate need. Choices must be made and time is short. Should the valley yield fruit for the good of the country, or should it yield goat's cheese again as in the past? Does the land 'belong' to those whose home it used to be? The matter is to be settled by the examination of plans for the valley's best use. How is the old to be reconciled with the new? The play relates clearly to many post-war situations of which Greece in 1975 is only one. Where parallels are not evident the enclosing framework of the debate easily becomes dated and the temptation is to cut it.

Brecht's aim was to make traditional forms contemporary. The Singer indeed declares: 'We hope you will find the voice of the old poet also sounds well in the shadow of the Soviet tractors.' He sings and the actors illustrate a parable which begins as a fairy tale: 'Once upon a time/ A time of bloodshed . . . The city of the damned . . . had a governor. His name was George Abashwili.'

Joseph Dugashwili of Georgia, otherwise known as Stalin, is a name the Governor, perhaps accidentally, brings to mind. The fairy-tale treatment clashes with the realities related. The beggars and petitioners who fill the stage recall the effects of the Kharkov famines. There is also a war on. 'Strategic retreats' take place. Brecht does not mention what happened during such retreats in his lifetime: the German retreat from Russia involved the destruction and burning of 628 villages in Byelorussia[2] together with their inhabitants. But Brecht does not point up the horror. His concern is with the future and he asks the question 'What must we do now?' A realism which strove for full representation of the past was not his aim. Allegorical satire was his chosen mode and when he speaks of war and violence the satirical tone lends a gaiety to the seriousness of his concern.

The danger of the allegorical method lies in the inveterate desire of the audience to lose itself in the story. To avoid this, Brecht seeks to call attention to its artificiality by means of the prologue discussion and the use of the Singer, who, though silent during the episodes, is always physically present to remind the audience that the play is an allegory. At the end of each scene his comments distance the audience from events and shift its attention to the future. His narrative also saves dramatic time, establishes the scene and sets the characters in ironic context. Where the audience nevertheless becomes engrossed by the story, Brecht estranges the spectator in other ways. He has his characters, the soldiers for example, behave in an obviously inhuman manner without being conscious of doing so. The audience may laugh, but with some discomfort.

The story is set in a country where the *coup d'état* or palace revolution are common events. The current Governor has enemies as usual, but he convinces himself of his own indestructibility and builds a palace to commemorate his rule. The political pendulum swings and the Singer gravely mocks the mentality of a tin-pot dictator, seemingly unaware of the nature of his power: 'Just look around you, once more, blind man', he says, as the Governor's future approaches.

The effect of Brecht's epic theatre is ironic. Characters behave in different ways in the same situation. Brecht presents contrastive groupings, and splits his stage to illustrate different responses, or sets the central characters against a backdrop, to evoke pity or contempt. The audience may move forward in sympathy, or stand off in disgust, or may experience both responses consecutively. The effect resembles that of a Brueghel or a Lowry painting: the observer moves in to examine a detail, then moves back to admire or survey the whole. The audience watches Brecht's small people move in and out, exit and enter, usually seeking their own ends or their own safety, occasionally usurping the narrator's functions, occasionally taking time to relate or at least communicate with one another amid the hurry.

Brecht creates wide spaces and long stretches of time. Within that framework men and women have choices. They may engage their freedom in contracts – like Simon the soldier and Grusha the peasant girl who promise to wait for one another. In moments of crisis characters may forget their obligations and choose their own safety, like the Governor's wife abandoning her child. They may also find like Grusha, when she marries the Peasant to protect the child, that a situation arises in which they must choose to break another contract freely entered into.

The staging is vividly active, caricatural but strangely real. It evokes the greed of the Governor's wife who, miscalculating the enemy's speed, wants to keep everything and is left with nothing. It dwells on the very different situation of Grusha, left with the choice of looking after or abandoning a child to whom she has no obligation, and choosing the child rather than herself. Brecht works with images of contrasted behaviour, invoking judgement on those who work only for the self. Full identification with Grusha is forestalled by the Singer's comments on Grusha's thought processes, as she is tempted to abandon the child to its doom. Yet if she shuts her ears, he says, to a cry for help, she knows 'she will never hear/ The gentle call of a lover/ Nor the blackbird at dawn'. It is the knowledge of damage she will do to herself which helps her to put the child's safety before her own. In order to keep her self-respect and remain emotionally alive (remaining in this sense free), she sacrifices her freedom of movement, and burdens herself with a life she knows others, including her fiancé Simon, will misinterpret.

In the third scene Grusha tries to regain her freedom by finding parents for the child. Her complex mood, which is one of happiness at being free and of sadness at losing her burden, points up the familiar tension between freedom and responsibility, and lends her character a convincing wholeness, especially when she finally commits herself to the burden.

Brecht's emphasis is thus on personal choice and on what it costs to pursue goodness. The treatment is lyrical, yet distanced, for the audience knows this is a fiction, but it is still a fiction which stands for real situations. The realities are material need and human feeling: money, food and shelter; poverty, hunger and cold. The feelings presented are tensions between the desires of the heart and the requirements of a situation which tempts or forces people to lie, to run away, to abandon responsibility, to exploit others, and to raise the price of scarce goods. The 'heart' on the other hand counsels pity and love. The parable simplifies; the complexities the spectator can imagine.

When Grusha and her adopted child are finally caught, the familiar story is told. The Governor's wife reclaims her child. The case comes before the judge, Azdak, who orders a chalk circle to be drawn around the boy. The mothers must each try to pull the child out of the circle. The child, of course, is given to the mother who lets go, thereby proving she cares most. For the peasants of the two communes, still watching on stage, the moral is clear. Possession of the valley, as of the child, should go to those who work for its best good. If you care for your valley, and for your country, you should be prepared to let it go. Good fostering is more important than natural ownership.

When the play first appeared, Harold Hobson of the *Sunday*

Times found it made its appeal to those beneath a mental age of six. And it is true that the fairy-tale element, with its lack of concern for psychological depth, may encourage a critical viewer to see the play as unrealistic and platitudinous. Brecht dwells on situation not character, on story rather than on psychology. The simple, even childlike use of allegory may appear to patronize spectators who enjoy dialogues between intellectuals. Brecht's methods, however, are close to those of Jonathan Swift and George Orwell. The deliberate discrepancy between the tone of the childlike fable and the realities it parallels is part of the method. If the production seems to invite the spectator to enjoy a simple story, we may also take an adult view of the inveterate tendency – our own, the director's, and even at times the writer's – to forget what lies behind. Conspicuously fictional scenes not only engage but distance the audience and offer it the freedom to compare and choose.

The play's simplicity can be censured either as simplification or obviousness. It is a fairly evident truth to say that occasions exist when the rights of parents and owners should be withdrawn, but the play makes subtler observations. The characters are not all of a simple mentality: sometimes one of them takes time to explain a story, an action or a form of behaviour to another character. In such cases the audience can recognize the conventionality of its own assumptions. When the judge, Azdak, enters the play, he shows the fugitive Grand Duke how a poor man eats: 'Don't look so greedily at your cheese – look at it mournfully – because it's already disappearing . . . like all good things . . .'.

Behind the comedy is an awareness of human needs. We are reminded, along with the Grand Duke, of what it might be to be poor. At the same time, the words provide instruction for the actors. Lazy acting easily falls into clichéd representation and to show unmixed greed is a simplification of the probable response. Hunger, in those who are accustomed to hunger, is mixed with a kind of fatalistic resignation. Brecht was a careful observer, and his techniques invite an actor deliberately to demonstrate the way people behave. He heightens and caricatures 'reality' in order to make us think about it. Azdak's mimicry serves that purpose.

Brecht reiterates obvious things: Azdak identifies the Grand Duke by looking at his hands, just as earlier Grusha's hands tell the travelling gentlewoman she is a peasant girl. Brecht constantly calls attention to the physical basis of existence and his characters thereby gain in vividness whilst retaining their sharp allegorical function. When Grusha finally decides to take up the abandoned child she is both human and also a representative figure. The moral perhaps is that we can only retain our humanity by assuming responsibilities. Grusha makes her appeal from the heart of the long comic tradition where stands the figure of the fool. To be a fool for Christ's sake is the paradox which lies behind Grusha's taking up the child. Azdak, in the second half of the play, is a different kind of fool figure, a poor man dressed in brief authority who confronts Grusha as a judge confronts the accused, and parodies the whole system of law and justice.

Brecht also parodies language use. When he passes judgement upon who should have the child, Azdak has two kinds of language to listen to. The first is standard rhetoric which argues that the child Michael belongs to the mother who has borne him: 'Of all bonds the bonds of blood are the strongest . . . Can one tear a child from its mother . . . ?' The second language is prosaic: 'I brought the child up to be friendly with everyone . . . I taught him to work.' The contrast in dialogue, emphasized by differences in the body language of the two mothers, place the audience in the detached position of judge.

The values Brecht appeals to are those of human concern, forgiveness, commonsense, the capacity to laugh at others and also oneself. He sympathizes with the venial sinner rather than the solemn pretender to virtue and the pious condemner of others. He makes a humanizing appeal to a freer spirit that can laugh at and recognize personal fallibility. In that resides a hope for the future.

Brecht's tone of mocking irreverence has not always been copied by those British writers who borrow epic theatre techniques: the use of song, choral commentary, episodic action, discussion, 'gestic' acting, and contrastive stage groupings on a split stage. His seriousness goes along with a subversive mockery which prevents solemnity, recalling Peter Brook's: 'Theatre should not be solemn'. Brecht's human sympathies and sheer enjoyment of the dramatic process mark his work. A greater harshness in the human presentation, a greater aloofness in the treatment often marks the work of those who follow him.

John Arden (1930–) was probably the first British dramatist to attempt to create a type of epic theatre. He became well known in the years following the visit of the Berliner Ensemble with plays subsidized by the great success of *Look Back in Anger* at the Royal Court. Of the plays he wrote then, *Sergeant Musgrave's Dance* (1959) has been most frequently revived. It had a contemporary political relevance since it is about a group of deserters who return to the native town of a comrade who has been killed in a colonial war, and British troops were fighting Eoka freedom forces in Cyprus at this time. The deserters, led by a religious fanatic, Sergeant 'Black Jack' Musgrave, wish to convert the townspeople to pacifism.

John Arden's concerns, like Brecht's, are social and historical. The situations are representative of forms of social interaction and his characters tend towards the stereotypical. He also uses song and separates his scenes to make 'gestic' statements. Nevertheless he is a more naturalistic writer than Brecht. He mainly uses the fourth-wall convention to project a rapidly moving plot, and his songs are not so much separate from the action as incorporated into it. At the same time, Arden takes a harsher and more distant view of the scene he presents. Identification with his characters is difficult. Unlike Brecht, whose alienation techniques cut across a strong invitation to sympathize, Arden often seems too dispassionate. He offers less conflict, less concern, less surprise, and less motivation to analyse.

Despite this, *Sergeant Musgrove's Dance* is a fine play. It begins by creating a sensation of intense cold, in a Northern town cut off from the rest of Britain by the winter. In this it parallels the chief figure, who is also cold and isolated. The soldiers are four in number, and represent the four suits in the game of cards with which the play opens. Their names are: Sparky, Hurst (hearsed), Attercliffe (at a cliff), and Musgrave (diamonds, clubs, hearts and spades respectively). The first two are younger than the other pair. One of each pair is red (for the more positive feelings) and the other black and they are appropriately distinguished by darker and lighter hair, stronger and weaker physique. They resemble the characters of a morality play and represent, in order of entrance, Gaiety, Violence, Experience and Power. There is also a bargee who joins them and acts as the anarchic Joker and figure of misrule. His name is Joe Bludgeon, a sadist who enjoys anarchy, encourages civil disturbance, and aligns himself with no one unless for his own purposes. The dominant colours are the red of the uniforms, and the white of the snow, together with black, for the contents of the mysterious box they carry with them.

The four outsiders find a parallel in four townspeople who represent not only different social functions but are different aspects of the law: the Mayor (Industry or Law), the Constable (Executive Law and Order), the Innkeeper Mrs Hardcastle (Business and the Law in her hostelry) and the Parson who is also a Magistrate. A further important character, balancing the individualistic bargee, is the unstable Annie, in love with the soldier whose death has brought Black Jack Musgrave back from abroad. In this modern morality play she plays the part of Love. Finally, lying between the forces of order and rebellion, there is a group of as yet uncommitted miners who, in the power game, must be wooed by both sides. Since there is a lock-out in town, Musgrave's task in raising them to revolt would not appear too difficult. As it turns out, Musgrave's methods prove repugnant to the miners; the means he advocates contradict his pacifist ends. The rebellion fails and the power structure remains unchanged. Winter breaks up and Musgrave's rule is over.

The implications of the play are bleak. Arden's dramatic and to some extent moral sympathies seemed at this early stage to lie with an anarchic individualism (but not that of Joe Bludgeon). He built most of his plays round two opposed and mainly unsympathetic groups. In *Live Like Pigs* (1958) it was the gypsies challenging the values of their neighbours on a lower-middle-class council estate. In *The Happy Haven* (1960) a group of anarchic and joyous old folk rise against the doctors and staff in the nursing home. Again in his ambitious updating of Goethe's *Götz von Berlichingen (Ironhand)* (1963), the robber baron, Götz, defends his way of life against the extension of law, the rise of an amoral politician, Weislingen, and the dominance of the new middle-class he represents.

Arden made a powerful attempt to represent complex issues in a broad chronicle and social drama, which was a cross between Brecht's epic drama and a more mainstream naturalism. When Arden and his wife, Margaretta D'Arcy, who co-scripted many of the plays, withdrew from the established theatre at the end of the decade, it would be Ireland's considerable gain. In the fringe and subsidized theatre other writers would benefit from his example and his extension of Brecht's practice.

Artaud, Brook and the Theatre of Cruelty

Apart from epic and absurdist theatre, and the continuing impact of varying forms of naturalism, the 'Theatre of Cruelty' of Antonin Artaud (1896–1948) and the 'Theatre Laboratory' of the Polish director, Jerzy Grotowski (1933–   ), were strong influences in England, especially on the work of the director Peter Brook (1925–   ), in the 1960s. Artaud was also influential on the Living Theatre of Julian Beck (1925–85) and Judith Malina (1926–   ) in America. The phenomenon of the theatrical 'happenings', which emerged from the synaesthetic experiments of Allen Kuprow in Black Mountain College in North Carolina in the 1950s, also derived in part from the ideas of Artaud. Kuprow's original Happening (1959) encouraged many such experiments in the next decade. These, too, led into Brook's work.

Artaud's theories began to have their effect from about 1927 when he established the Theatre Alfred Jarry, producing Strindberg's *Dream Play* and the surrealist drama of his partner Roger Vitrac (1899–1952), who was a leader of the French Dada movement. One of his characteristic experiments was to play the third act of Claudel's *Partage de Midi* as a farce. Artaud's *First Manifesto* was published in 1932 and encouraged a rebellion against 'psychological theatre', by which he meant drama dependent on language, therefore making its appeal not to the senses but to the intellect. Such a theatre he saw as having distanced audiences from vivid spectacle ever since Racine. Where all is verbalized, the spectator grows unaccustomed to theatrical immediacy. Artaud aimed to reverse this process: 'We need a theatre that wakes us up . . . nerves and heart . . .' he said, a theatre 'the burning magnetism of whose images' will provide a 'therapy of the soul'. His *Second Manifesto* in 1933 proclaimed the need to rediscover 'essential passions' through the recovery of ancient myth, old cosmogonies, and the actualizing of heroes and monsters. He wished to attack an audience's whole organism and to effect, though a kind of cruel Dionysiac breakdown, a more profound state of perception. The image with which Artaud chose to identify this process was that of bubonic plague.

Plague, said Artaud, acted upon individuals as a kind of 'contagious delirium' which transformed the sufferer's personality and engendered extreme gestures. In this it resembled the acting process itself. Artaud wanted theatre to concentrate 'the perverse possibilities of the mind', creating 'an abnormal intensity in which the difficult and impossible become normal'. It is not surprising Artaud was attracted to the extremes of Jacobean drama, notably to John Ford's *'Tis Pity She's a Whore* (1633) and Shelley's sub-Jacobean drama *The Cenci* (1819). He sought a theatre which induced an *epidémie salvatrice* ('redemptory epidemic'). Actor and audience were to be gripped by a gratuitous contagion which prompts the discovery of other personalities within the self. This theatre aimed at a breakdown of normality and loss of a sense of personal identity, similar to definitions of the Dionysiac impact of Greek Tragedy in Nietzsche's *Birth of Tragedy* (1872). Artaud sought knowledge in the effect of drugs and the exploration of madness, spending nine years certified insane in the five asylums he attended. Wagner, Adolphe Appia, Edward Gordon Craig and the symbolic drama of Maeterlinck lay behind him, as well as the writings of Nietzsche and Freud. These influences were mingled with his admiration for the use of dance, song and gesture in oriental and, in particular, Balinese theatre.

Artaud's was a theatre of extreme sensation which aimed to effect a cathartic cleansing by combinations of colour, sound and movement, mass spectacle, surprising objects, pounding rhythms, ancient instruments, light changes and ritual costuming and masks. Its enemies found this no basis on which to build a necessary, rational human discourse. But for Artaud: 'It is through the skin that metaphysics must be made to re-enter our minds . . . Without an element of cruelty at the heart of every spectacle the theatre is not possible.' It is paradoxical that a man who wished to reduce the importance of speech in the theatre

should make so many converts by handling language so brilliantly, for the theoretical publications, during his necessary
absence from the stage, greatly extended the influence of his
previous theatrical experiments.

When Artaud returned from the asylum at Rodez in 1946,
homage was paid him in Paris at the Théâtre Sarah Bernhardt.
The breadth of his influence was shown by the presence of Charles
Dullin, Colette Thomas, Roger Blin, Jean Vilar and Jean-Louis
Barrault. Blin was to work closely with Beckett; Barrault, the
celebrated mime and theatre director, together with his actress
wife Madeleine Renaud, became director of the Odéon Théâtre
de France in the 1950s where he mounted many famous productions, including Claudel's early symbolic drama *Tête d'Or* (1890–
1901) in 1959. He was deeply interested in absurdist theatre,
producing *Waiting for Godot* and *Rhinocéros* at the Odéon
in 1959–60. Jean Vilar as Director of the Théâtre National
Populaire became involved in much political drama, performing
in and directing many of the later Brecht plays, including in 1960
the allegory of Hitler as a Chicago gangster, *The Resistible Rise
and Fall of Arturo Ui*. Through such channels, Artaud's search to
undermine the dominance of language and the conventions of
théâtre de boulevard fed into French post-war theatre.

Artaud's influence began to be felt in Britain in the 1960s along
with that of the Polish director, Jerzy Grotowski (1933–) with
whom he had certain things in common. Grotowski, however,
repudiated Artaud's idea of a 'total theatre' in which, as in
Wagner's *Gesamtkunstwerk*, many forms of theatre language are
fused to achieve one powerful effect. Grotowski's was an actor-
centred theatre, as befitted a director saturated in the work of
Stanislavski. Grotowski sought to create a 'poor theatre' which
eliminated all technology and abolished clever lighting and sound
effects, rich costume, make-up and mask. He concentrated on
direct actor/audience involvement, with actors using their vocal
and physical resources to the full. The actors played in the body
of the hall, using only still light sources and occasional props.
They began with a Stanislavskian exploration of character but
moved beyond naturalist techniques towards a stylized, ritual
intensity. At moments of shock or terror, says Grotowski, in
Towards a Poor Theatre, human beings do not behave naturally.
They use 'rhythmically articulated signs' and begin to dance and

sing. 'A sign,' asserted Grotowski, 'not a common gesture, is the elementary integer of expression for us.'[1] This drew Grotowski closer to Artaud. He sought extreme moments in archaic situations involving taboo. The confrontation of these situations enables actors 'to touch an extraordinary intimate layer . . . where the life mask cracks and falls away'.

Grotowski, like Artaud, was seeking liberation. Artaud sought liberation from the bonds of language and from bourgeois and theatrical convention. Grotowski at first sought freedom through personality models: 'There was a time when I wanted to be Stanislavski'. Later 'I was so fascinated by Gandhi I wanted to be him'. But neither was enough, 'If I were to build the self-portrait of my dreams,' he says, 'at the centre would be a liberated life, the original state, freedom.' But it was not the concept of freedom assumed by some 'man of the east' – the yogi's idea that one must liberate oneself from bodily existence. 'I don't feel that. And I would not confuse the word freedom with "freedom of choice" . . . Freedom is associated neither with freedom of choice nor sheer voluntaryism, but with a wave, giving oneself up to this huge wave in accordance with one's desire. And when I speak of desire, it is like water in the desert or a gasp of air to someone drowning.'

Grotowski declares he has gone through several phases of 'seeking to exist'. At first, he sought domination of others, then he sought to establish states of relationship. Then he felt a need to wander, thereby meeting people 'before whom there was neither fear nor shame . . . So I set out towards something, which for me lies beyond art.' He worked with his company for a form of community which he defined as 'paratheatrical' seeking a form of trust in which 'only the most simple of things should take place, what is most elementary and trustful between beings. Sharing and recognition and . . . a transcendence of the barriers of self-interest and fear.'

Grotowski embarked, therefore, on a quasi-religious quest for the sources of drama, since in drama 'the beginning is always present'. He wished to rediscover the spontaneity of children, animals or a force of nature. It was not, however, a simple question of casting art and artificiality aside, so much as working through a highly developed technique, like the Samurai warrior, to recover the spontaneity of a primal state. It was with a community of actors that Grotowski embarked on his pilgrimage.

175

He established his Theatre Laboratorium in Warsaw and toured abroad from 1966. His production, *Akropolis*, made a strong mark on the British scene at the Edinburgh festival in 1968.

In Britain, Peter Brook was a channel for many of the European influences as he sought to incorporate new forms into a theatre he considered in crisis. Commerce was dominant; the audiences' responses were dulled, the actors had lost courage and new playhouses were needed. In an article published in November 1960, 'From Zero to the Infinite', Brook argues a case for the reality of what he calls abstractions: speed, strain, space, frenzy, energy, brutality. These non-measurables have neither size nor weight and yet they are very real – more real, Brook suggests, than the concrete facts of life, such as prices and hours of work. For him, economics need not determine life. Brook felt that human responses were dulled by emphasis on material needs. The theatre should concern itself with the 'abstractions' he cites.

Brook had made his name in the post-war period with productions of Shakespeare, Anouilh, Cocteau and Christopher Fry. In 1962 he was appointed co-director of the Royal Shakespeare Company along with Michel Saint-Denis and Peter Hall. He directed the famous production of *King Lear* with Paul Scofield and the extraordinary *Marat/Sade* by Peter Weiss in the same year. The full title of the latter: *The Persecution and Assassination of Marat as Performed by the Inmates of the Asylum of Charenton under the Direction of the Marquis de Sade* sufficiently suggests the influence of Artaud's Theatre of Cruelty. The dominant impression for most spectators remained the extraordinary behaviour of the choral and individual lunatics which derived from the company's intensive research into abnormal states.

The *Marat/Sade* was followed by another extraordinary production, *US*, a 'documentary' about America's intervention in Vietnam which went on at the Aldwych Theatre in October 1966. The rehearsal period of 15 weeks involved considerable improvisation, and sought to use 'happenings', events and episodes arising suddenly and often violently in a spontaneous and probably unrepeatable manner. Beneath the anarchic surface of his rehearsal methods, Brook was looking for pattern and design. If cruelty was one of the 'abstractions' he thought theatre should portray, he sought some way of fixing it within a dramatic form.

He made great, even cruel demands on his actors, seeking an 'inner reality' within the text, within the actor and within the company. He hoped in this way to tap hidden forms of energy which would communicate the horror of Vietnam more deeply than any newspaper article, television documentary or recitation of statistics of killed and wounded.

However, he also found outer realism important and invited his cast to lay its hands on all the information it could about the war. The recorded speaking voices of the Fulbright Committee hearings provided dramatic material which suggested that the war machine had got out of control. If this was so, Brook felt, the theatre could fulfil a public function. It could explore the situation and possibly enable a solution to be found. With this in view, US became not so much a documentary as an exploration of realities under the social surface. In this production the influences of Artaud and Grotowski mingled with the methods of Stanislavski and the intentions of Brecht.

The actors improvised a mass of chaotic material out of which the play was shaped. (It is easy to see how Mike Leigh's methods[2] developed from assisting Brook during the 1960s.) The assumption was made that the war derived from something within American culture and the preparation period was devoted to its discovery. Actors studied aspects of American life – horror comic material, adverts, excerpts from feature films – and derived from them dramatic images, postures, gestures and forms of behaviour which needed to be worked into a seamless whole 'as paint dries off a brush' in Brook's words.

Alongside the improvisations and happenings, Brechtian exercises were employed to help actors cope with sudden transitions and retain the seamless flow which Brook desired. He also hoped to achieve the Brechtian 'gestus', the sharp, clear, vivid, summarizing image which in the early stages the naturalistically trained actors, according to Albert Hunt, did not provide. Something close to mime, or to the stylized oriental theatre was called for. Interestingly, Edward Bond (1935–), using a kind of amalgam of Brecht, naturalism and Beckett, had already achieved a style which presented violent action with great power. Brook, however, wanted a more caricatural performance, hence the emphasis on American comic strips, political speeches and pop songs. At the same time he encouraged the actors to develop their knowledge of the very different culture of Vietnam.

The cruelty Brook sought to present was not only discoverable in cultural products, but lay, too, within the actor's psyche. The problem was to bring together the inner and outer 'research' so as to discover a dramatic form which would contain and communicate the cruelty. Artaud knew that cruelty could be externalized and had admired the formal dance theatre of Bali just as Brecht had found inspiration for his precise objective acting style in Chinese and Japanese theatre. For a play about the Vietnam war such a style seemed very appropriate. Chaing Lui, a Chinese actor, was brought in to develop a 'new language' out of external and inner stimuli. Jerzy Grotowski also came over from Poland for ten days. Many actors found his rigorous methods, dedicated to making the actor a fully flexible instrument, difficult and painful.

In the course of rehearsals it was decided that self-incineration was a central image. The actors sought to discover the state of utter dedication of Buddhist monks, without ever finding the same power of sacrifice, and the same total control in extreme situations. Nevertheless, such a search released intense energy and awareness of suffering.

When the play reached the public it was accused of bias against the United States. It was also accused of not reaching a conclusion. But no one denied its power. In the famous final episode, a butterfly was apparently burned on stage. (According to its defenders, this was a stage trick which persuaded the audience that the burning of a piece of paper was an abomination.) The play brought home the reality of cruelty, but unfortunately it aroused more anger against Brook than against the Vietnam war. The theatre momentarily became more real than the scene it was representing and the audience, perhaps in relief, was able to protest against the immediate, not the distant. The director was cruel, not the napalm bombers.

Responses to US were, of course, varied. Much of the talk was aesthetic, avoiding the issue of content by assigning the play to a genre – documentary, living theatre, psycho-drama, and so on. The Bishop of Woolwich, on the other hand, identified a religious meaning. He saw US as a mass, a liturgy involving participants in an act of redemption. Like the mass it re-enacts a story. During the mass, the priest officiates as Christ, dispenses the body of Christ and recalls His sacrifice, thus redeeming the congregation from time and place. It is a corporate presentation in which all share responsibility. There is no separating proscenium arch. In *US* a central figure, bedaubed and torn apart, represents the people of Vietnam. Then 'readings', songs, refrains, antiphonal dialogue, preaching, confession, intercession, ritual movement and recurring symbolic action and image bring home the reality of the descent of the dead soldier. But, unlike the mass, there is no resolution, no absolution and no communion, which perhaps allowed it to strike home more sharply. 'When is the church going to commission someone like Peter Brook to show us what it might look like to begin from the secular sacrifice of our time?', asked the Bishop. Brook might have answered that his production made such a commission unnecessary.

Unsympathetic reactions came from the political right. In parliament Sir Knox Cunningham demanded the withdrawal of the Royal Shakespeare Company's subsidy, since the play was 'full of poisonous anti-American propaganda'. Jennie Lee, Under Secretary of State for Education and Science replied: 'It would be a bad day for this country when the arts and the theatre began simply to reflect whatever happened to be the policy of the government, or even the prejudices of the honorary gentleman and myself.' (In *The Times* 4 November 1966.)

On the left Brook also had his critics. For Charles Marowitz, Brook was a romantic liberal. The time had come, Marowitz felt, to take up positions in the theatre. In his view 'A century ago the theatre's task, according to Chekhov, was to ask questions. This has been superseded by a world situation, in which if the theatre is to pull its weight, it must at such times and on such themes begin to supply answers.' Marowitz was right about Brook's sympathy with Chekhov's position. 'When the theatre is healthy it is never the expression of a single point of view' said Brook. 'You can only ask people questions, and open your ears to their answers.' Brook has continued to ask questions. 'What is Brook's greatest strength?' John Heilpern asked one of his actors. 'Hunger' she replied. 'And his greatest flaw?' 'Hunger' she replied again. (*The Observer* 18 January 1976.) For Brook no answer fully suffices. Critics will differ as to how far this is a strength and how far a weakness. To hunger is never to be satisfied.

The impact of the Vietnam war, together with memories of World War II, the nuclear threat and the Russian invasion of Hungary, had much to do with the emphasis on cruelty in the 1960s. In the stage and film productions of Ingmar Bergman, for instance, in *The Silence* (1963), *Persona* (1966) and *Shame* (1967), it was strongly apparent. Bergman worked to discover cruelty deep in the human psyche using naturalistic methods and a brilliant team of actors. In the 1950s he had used Artaud's analogy of plague in his historical parable *The Seventh Seal* (1957). He had also employed dream and flashback effects in *Wild Strawberries* in the same year. In the 1960s Bergman developed his methods, using his small cast of actors in a series of 'chamber films' which indirectly owed much to his study of Strindberg and Shakespeare. The outside world tended to enter in momentary glimpses, like the image of the burning monk in *Persona*, or the tanks flashing past the young boy's eyes in *The Silence* as he watches from the train window.

Brook had directed films but in the theatre the cinematic close-up and momentary flashback were not available to him, even if he could have handled them as brilliantly as Bergman. In *US* he found other methods to bring the theatre closer to political reality.

If the play found ways of demonstrating horror, it also implied the impotence of the left. In a lecture given at Bonn on 4 December 1966, later published as an essay: 'Myth and Reality in the Theatre', Jean-Paul Sartre commented on the production: 'It is true that the war in Vietnam is a crime. It is also true the left is quite incapable of doing anything. Has it anything to do with theatre? . . . This situation is an excellent example of what we can call the crisis of the imaginary in the theatre.' Whether fiction now had a function was a question asked by the German sociologist Adorno after the discovery of the horrors of Auschwitz and by Thomas Mann in *Dr Faustus* (1947) and its sequel, *The Origins of Dr Faustus* (1949). Art was now seemingly impossible. Atrocity brought a feeling of impotence and despair. With the Vietnam war even Ingmar Bergman expressed a loss of belief in the power and purpose of art. In *Persona* (1966) one of his characters – the actress Elizabeth Vogler, played by Liv Ullman – retreats into silence and repudiates her dramatic career when faced with images such as the self-immolation of a Buddhist monk. But Bergman, though he stated the impotence of artists, continued to write out of and about breakdown, about the breakdown of the self, the breakdown of personal and the breakdown of language. He consistently recovered from such a threatening state to make more films and direct more plays.

Brook seems to have been less threatened. He continued his

obsessive search for some universal reality at the heart of theatre, performing with his company at the edges of language, and sometimes in the middle of a desert. Along with Artaud and Grotowski and Bergman he explores extreme states, sinister areas at the edge of normality to which the most powerful works of Shakespeare and Dostoievski, of Greek Tragedy and Ibsen lead us. It is an area which their vocation leads actors to explore and continues to exist as an element of theatre which defies rational discussion. A reading, for instance, of a recent book by Brian Bates, *The Way of the Actor*, which includes an interview with Bergman's leading actress, Liv Ullman, depicts the continuing reality and ungraspability of what these men and women seek. He supplies extraordinary descriptions of actors in workshop conditions manifesting forms of psychic energy which Bates, who is a trained psychologist, cannot define within the limits of science.[3]

The exploration of the psyche and the exploration of the outside world are not fully separable. The psyche is, to a disputed degree, created by material circumstance, material circumstance to a disputed degree created by the 'free' psyche. Artaud's work, and that of Brook, Grotowski and Bergman, though often emphasizing a private, inner world, derives from a fertile if painful interrelation with the world outside. These directors did not take as their starting point the dramatic forms which Bertolt Brecht had developed for dealing with the public realm. They began with more primitive forms and worked more directly from physical sensation. Brecht was more concerned with finding political solutions to social violence. John Arden, like Brecht, saw the problems in a wider social context. He, and the prolific Edward Bond would wed Brecht's methods to a greater naturalism. Arden sought to retain Brecht's intellectual distance. Edward Bond's methods were to mingle Brechtian forms with those of expressionism, absurdism and Artaud's immediate and direct Theatre of Cruelty.

Tom Stoppard

Freedom, play and
Rosencrantz and Guildenstern

A consideration of drama in the 1960s can appropriately end with a comparison of three very different dramatists who came to the fore during the decade. Two of these are Tom Stoppard and Edward Bond, the former strongly concerned with artistic form, freedom and creativity and the latter with political freedom and control. The last is Athol Fugard who explores problems of racial oppression and the search for both individual and social liberty through a more traditional naturalism.

In Edward Bond's early plays the influences of Brecht and Beckett, together with an older naturalism and forms of expressionism, fuse in a new and original theatre with a strong political emphasis. Stoppard also attempts a fusion of forms, experimenting in as large a way as Bond with dramatic conventions, but the influence of absurdist drama, with its anarchic emphasis on logical contradictions and the disparity between language and experience, is much stronger in Stoppard's works. Unlike Bond, Stoppard is drawn towards comedy, taking a delight in theatrical play for its own sake. He probably has an even greater grasp than Bond of the possibilities of theatre form and language.

Stoppard, born in Czechoslovakia in 1937, lived in India during World War II and attended a multi-national American school, before returning to England with his step-father and mother when the war ended. (His natural father was killed in Singapore by the Japanese.) His plays did not at first reveal any strong political concern. His first success, *Rosencrantz and Guildenstern are Dead* (1966), showed a fascination with a general and tragi-comic human situation. At the end of the 1950s the example of Beckett and his 'two guys who don't know why'[1] was very strong, as was the vogue of Harold Pinter, with his potentially more violent pairs and threesomes. The image of two characters caught in uncertain situations intrigued Stoppard and he incorporated Gogo and Didi from *Waiting for Godot* into a new play by fusing them with the characters of Rosencrantz and Guildenstern from *Hamlet*. These two pairs have things in common. Just as Beckett's tramps spend the play waiting for someone called Godot to arrive, the two friends of Hamlet, summoned by Claudius to spy on the prince, spend most of the time waiting for orders. Beckett's characters, however spend long periods alone on stage and the play focuses on their responses. In Shakespeare's play the personal feelings of Rosencrantz and Guildenstern are not explored. They always appear in contexts in which their social inferiority makes them hide feeling beneath a veneer of deference. The actors must express their characters' private lives by momentarily lowering the deferential mask, by tone of voice, ironic expression, posture, giveaway movements and indirect hints. The dialogue they speak is mainly in response to a king who wishes to use them and to Hamlet who is interested in how they are being used. It does not allow the characters to express themselves directly before the audience, whereas in Stoppard's play they can. There, Rosencrantz and Guildenstern resemble Beckett's heroes, discussing their situation and playing games to pass the time as they await a sign from the powers above. They are in the hands of God, fate, destiny, history, society, time, whichever the spectator wishes to stress. In *Hamlet*, in the company of those with power over them, their words are guarded. But in Stoppard's play, since they are alone, they are free to speak.

Stoppard 'steals' other characters from Shakespeare's play – the Travelling Players who, like Rosencrantz and Guildenstern, have patrons to whom they must defer. At court they must fulfil the will of the Prince and entertain the King. It is their misfortune, as Hamlet said of his former Wittenburg friends, to be caught between the conflicting wills of mighty opposites. But Shakespeare does not dwell on their future, his dramatic interest is elsewhere.

Stoppard takes these two groups of supporting characters, whose off-stage lives were irrelevant, and makes the absent life the central focus. He investigates how they think, speak and behave when they are not an immediate function of other people's wills and gives us a wry and sympathetic sense of the inner lives of little men whom heroic drama has never taken seriously. He presents them to us dispossessed of function, experiencing an empty freedom which, like Beckett's tramps, they combat with 'pass-times'. For the Players, of course, the creation of a pastime has become their normal function. They take the responsibility from those who do not want to entertain themselves when they have nothing to do, but Stoppard gives us a sense of their lives beyond this function. Play for them is work and they do not always like it.

This contrast between work and play, function and freedom, contributes to the doubleness and convincing humanity of the characters. Arguably, Stoppard has adapted Stanislavski's recommendation that actors should explore the sub-text of their roles by imagining what their characters do between scenes and before the play begins. This generates a series of private dialogues between the minor but now central characters which alternates with powerful and familiar fragments from the original source. The consequent tension between action and inaction, 'life' and play, poetic and colloquial dialogue, and Shakespearean and modern language also appears as a tension between the public and the private, between the characters' sense of themselves and others' appropriation of them, between their need of social function and a need to be more than an instrument of others' wills. The method is so successful that Rosencrantz, Guildenstern (and the senior Player) achieve that rare and apparent independence of the play framework which lends continuing vitality to performance. They have the secret of the 'living' character – the possession of their own private consciousness.

The first performance of *Rosencrantz and Guildenstern* was given on 24 August 1966 as part of the Edinburgh 'Fringe' Festival. The first professional performance was given on 11 April 1967, by the National Theatre Company at the Old Vic Theatre, with John Stride as Rosencrantz, Edward Petherbridge as Guildenstern, John McEnery as Hamlet and Graham Crowden in the powerful role of the Player. Apart from John Russell Taylor who felt the play was only a clever one-acter spun out to three, the critics were enthusiastic. An exceptional talent had arrived.

Rosencrantz and Guildenstern is about freedom and control. The characters escape into a 'freer' world of play. They also use play to handle threatening events. Stoppard dwells on the responses of his Beckettian anti-heroes and reveals their varying states of mind. By turns bewildered, anguished and stoical, they wait for other people, notably Claudius and Hamlet, to take decisions which affect their lives. They are in the grip of forces stronger than themselves.

The play opens with Rosencrantz and Guildenstern filling in time by spinning coins. From this aimless activity, Guildenstern, who stands in the same relation to his partner as does the philosophizing Didi to the feckless Gogo, tries to formulate the laws within which they live. When he fails to explain why Rosencrantz calls 'Heads!' and wins every time, the loser feels deep anxiety. The unthreatened winner, Rosencrantz, at least temporarily in a position of power, feels no anxiety and no surprise.

Rosencrantz and Guildenstern live in a world without explanations. Like Beckett's tramps they 'don't know why' and they depend on others who know more – i.e. Claudius and Hamlet, who appear from time to time, but when off-stage function like Beckett's absent Godot. Stoppard's central characters know very little. Dramatic irony, which makes its appeal to spectators aware of a character's ignorance, is thus constantly at work, and since it works at the expense of little men, the emphasis of the play is tragi-comic rather than tragic. We as audience know the situation whilst the heroes do not and perhaps do not want to know.

Hamlet's two school friends have been sent for and find themselves in a trap: 'We have not been . . . picked out . . . simply to be abandoned . . . We are entitled to some direction . . . I would have thought', says Guildenstern. Stoppard gives them a direction – a stage direction: the sound of drums announcing the vivid entrance of the Travelling Players. The latter, reminiscent of Pirandello's Six Characters and Pozzo and Lucky in Beckett's play, bring variety to a stage situation threatening to become routine. They are sent in to maintain interest and relieve the characters on stage as well as the audience.

The Players also call attention to the way our need for variety provides a source of income for those prepared to make entertainment their profession. Rosencrantz and Guildenstern are a potential paying audience. The play scrutinizes the nature of play when it has become a professional function. It is ironic about its own processes in a way with which Beckett and Pirandello have made us familiar.

The Players' entrance raises more general questions to which Guildenstern wants an answer. Is it coincidence, chance or fate that they arrive at this particular moment? Obviously it is a coincidence planned by the author but it suggests the existence in the world of chance events. What brings the Players along at this particular moment may be pure accident. At the same time it cannot be said that Stoppard presents a world in which there is no causality. Causality operates in the *Hamlet* scenes. It also operates in the scenes where chance seems most to operate. For example, the Players may be a random collection of individuals assembled by chance meetings, but their decision to stay together to live and work has a causal explanation. They are poor and they can act. Since they can support themselves more easily together than apart, economic cause, at least to some extent, rules their lives. At the same time we are aware that some of them, Alfred at least, would prefer to be doing something else. There is a discrepancy between their needs and their preferences. Their freedom to want something other makes them convincingly human.

The need to live causes the Players to try and induce their two chance spectators to pay for a performance of a more or less dubious nature. Rosencrantz and Guildenstern are invited to choose. Their humanity is assumed. If they can choose between alternatives they are alive, not machines subject to rigorous law. They can choose to pay or not to pay; to look on or get caught up in the action. They can even ask for different kinds of performance. Small choices are possible and communicate that sense of the independence of individual characters which is necessary if the audience is to feel they exist.

But these characters cannot control the overall situation. Rosencrantz and partner have laid their service 'freely' at Claudius's feet. One may imagine what would have happened if they had exercised the right to refuse – and Claudius maintains the courtesy of pretending that they are free to do so. Theirs is the same freedom, one assumes, as soldiers in the army when given an order. The two attendant lords have signed on and are therefore subject to the laws which require they keep their contract.

To this degree the play is mimetic. It suggests the existence of chance and choice and the limitations on choice. It conveys the way in which all men and women are caught up in contractual obligations. It reflects the way people work for as much freedom as they can get by learning the rules of the game and developing superior strategies, linguistic and otherwise. Lack of mastery of the rules and of the appropriate language reduces us to slavery. At the same time the rules are a form of self-defence. To behave slavishly according to the 'book' indicates a fear of freedom, for the rules often serve people more powerful than oneself. They can bolster a false self-esteem and in certain situations must be broken. Hamlet is surrounded by people who follow the 'book'; these include Rosencrantz and Guildenstern. It is Hamlet who actively seeks a way to break the rules, not his erstwhile friends. They only talk of freedom; action is replaced by an intellectual game:

'Is there a choice?
Is there a God?
Foul! No non-sequiturs'

says Rosencrantz. The pair continue to hope they can dominate the situation and control their own future. The method they adopt remains the actor's technique of improvised role-play, a method useful in life as well as art. Thus they try to anticipate Hamlet's thoughts, as if he were an opposing general, or a businessman they wish to outguess. Guildenstern pretends to be Hamlet and they improvise responses. Unfortunately this preparation will not be enough; Hamlet has too much talent and intelligence to be beaten at this game. He thinks too rapidly and his is the mastery of language which establishes control: 'Twenty-seven questions he got out in ten minutes and answered three . . . Half of what he said meant something else and the other half didn't mean anything at all.'

Stoppard's characters fight for liberty. The degree to which they achieve it is greater or lesser according to the resources of the individual – his or her social position, knowledge, mastery of vocabulary, or perhaps an indefinable power of will. The limits on liberty are the physical resources of the body, the resources and acquisitions of the mind, and social position and situation. There are destinies that shape our ends and within the process characters strive for comprehension in order to hew themselves a clearing.

'If one starts being arbitrary it'll just be a shambles. Because if we happened, just happened to discover, or even suspect, that our spontaneity was part of their order, we'd know we were lost'. The spontaneity of which Guildenstern talks seems to be the capacity to play and to dream, even to lie. Thus he shouts 'FIRE' to demonstrate the use of free speech. It remains, however, an arbitrary liberty within a confining situation. Even spontaneity may not be free.

How can they escape? And how can the audience rid itself of its sympathetic frustration at seeing them trapped? One way is to explore the origins of the situation – the reasons why they are there, the pressures upon them and the choices they have previously made. But Stoppard remains as enigmatic as Shakespeare about the characters' origins. The characters live in the present only, without past or future. Where they come from and where they are going is not clear.

For one character this is more of a problem than for the other. Whereas Guildenstern seeks to obey Stanislavski's injunction to discover his off-stage self, his past and his destiny, Rosencrantz does not wish to do so. Guildenstern may, like Beckett's Didi, seek to jog his partner's memory, but Rosencrantz, like Gogo, does not want to remember:

> *Guildenstern*: What's the last thing you remember?
> *Rosencrantz*: I don't wish to be reminded of it.
> *Guildenstern*: We cross our bridges when we come to them and burn them behind us, with nothing to show for our progress except a memory of the smell of smoke.

'Memory', says Eliot, 'you have the key'. Proust would have agreed. Memory is a source of creativity and imaginative liberation. But Stoppard's Rosencrantz and Guildenstern lack a memory and lack a past. They therefore cannot control the present and write the play of their own lives.

The Players, on the other hand, try to control their lives by exercising their function and entertaining an audience. But what if no one comes, or the audience absents itself? When this happens, as when Rosencrantz and Guildenstern desert them, their function is over and identity itself becomes suspect: 'You don't understand the humiliation of it – to be tricked out of the single assumption that makes our existence viable – that somebody is *watching* ...'. For the Players, Rosencrantz and Guildenstern have performed the function of Godot, then departed.

The Player understands that a sense of security depends on trust. Good ensemble playing is built on it and audiences can inspire confidence too. There are no certainties, but there are rules and conventions to be observed. Arbitrary behaviour causes dismay and consternation. Inside the game one is momentarily safe but insecurity reigns outside. The human condition is to alternate between insecurity and security, between being people and being actors – 'the opposite of people' says the Player. The players feel safer within someone else's script. Their game demands that others will pay attention and lend them value. Rosencrantz and Guildenstern, by refusing to watch, have reduced the actors to the status of people in the process of trying to 'write' or at least understand the larger game they are embroiled in.

'Relax. Respond. That's what people do. You can't go through life questioning your situation at every turn ... one acts on assumptions!' In other words, the Player recommends Rosencrantz and Guildenstern become like actors: 'We're trage-dians you see. We follow directions – there is no choice involved'.

Even actors, of course, know that they need freedom from the rigours of dictatorial direction. Actors who are manipulated as marionettes are apt to resent it. The director who commands their every movement is unpopular and loses the energy and vitality which emerges when, within the general frame, actors are allowed a certain freedom to explore. Liberty leads to discovery. It can also lead to chaos and anguish, thus the preference of actors and people for the assigned role. It provides a certain comfort. At least you know who you are supposed to be, as more than one actor has said. The anguish of choice must be balanced against the need for rules and conventions. Stoppard's characters dwell in the tension between two fears and two desires: the fear of freedom and the fear of manipulation, the desire for freedom and the desire to be controlled.

For Claudius, Rosencrantz and Guildenstern have no separate independence. They are to be kept in a corner of his jaw to be first mouthed then swallowed. For the audience their freedom mainly consists of a capacity to question their own limitations. It is a freedom of speech and thought rather than action. In England, where Rosencrantz says they will be free, they will, as Guildenstern says, find themselves under the same sky. Their condition is that of people on a boat. They are 'contained'. 'You don't have to worry about which way to go ... I think I'll spend most of my time on boats . . . One is free on a boat. For a time. Relatively', says Guildenstern. The direction is controlled but within it one can think. The question, of course, is whether one can transform passive thinking into action. Guildenstern, on the voyage, thinks he has lost Claudius's letter to the English king. Chaos threatens. Rosencrantz and Guildenstern must enact Claudius's will or they are lost. 'We must not lose control. Tighten up,' says Guildenstern. To be in control means, for Guildenstern, to enact a function imposed by authority. It is to retain a place within the power structure. To be outside that structure is to lose power, retaining only the consciousness of lack of power. It is to jump overboard. Yet to remain on board is still to be trapped. What is needed is to remain on board, to become conscious of whose will one is performing, and to establish a separate identity and separate control. That is what Hamlet does. He discovers the King's will by opening the letter and substituting another. In Stoppard's play, Rosencrantz and Guildenstern discover the King's will by chance but have insufficient talent, imagination, confidence, training or power to change events. They are less free than Hamlet. They are not convincing performers in the competition of wills which constitutes the dramatic, and to an uncertain degree the historical, process. Thus, when they use their usual technique of improvisation to anticipate the way in which the King of England will receive them, they discover more information than they bargained for. They open the King's letter and are supplied with a choice, which is either to carry out the King's will and allow Hamlet to be killed, or not to deliver the letter. They choose not to have a choice:

'It would be presumptuous of us to interfere with the designs of fate or even of kings', says Guildenstern, using logic to shelve responsibility. 'Don't apply logic', he continues. 'He's done nothing to us' says Rosencrantz. 'Or justice' says Guildenstern, pursuing his line of thought.

Sartre would have said the choice confronting them is the choice which faced the French in 1940: Do we continue serving the Vichy government, or do we serve an active will to oppose? In a Sartrean sense, reality and existence pass the pair by. They continue to float without taking charge of their destiny. They cannot rewrite the ending to Shakespeare's play, but continue like characters in a Buñuel film, travelling an uncomprehended road, playing games which contain the seeds of freedom but failing to realize the potential of the game. Their play remains 'pass-time'.

Hamlet on the other hand uses play to intervene in people's lives whilst the players he employs remain ignorant of the ends to which they are being used. His activity gives lie to Guildenstern's belief that aboard ship they are momentarily free: 'We can breathe, we can relax, we can do what we like and say what we like to whomever we like, without restriction.' 'Within limits' says Rosencrantz.

One might have thought that the pirates' attack and Hamlet's subsequent disappearance on the pirate ship would have taken responsibility from them, but curiously it imprisons them even more. They still need to discharge their social function and without Hamlet they cannot do so. They do not have the resources to cast off or act against their function. For them England is a dead end.

'Our movement is contained within a larger one.' That larger movement is the King's will. And that will again is contained within a larger one – the movement towards Death. It is a movement both containing and contained within Shakespeare's and Stoppard's plays. Death closes in on individual freedom, reminding an audience of the poignancy of a situation all share. Surrounded as they are by glittering or tawdry masks of Court and Theatre, Rosencrantz and Guildenstern represent to us the pathos of ordinariness and mortality. If the play makes us aware of our freedoms, it also reminds us of the unfreedoms which contain our human need for space.

Stoppard's first success is brilliantly theatrical and brilliantly intelligent. Stoppard has perhaps stolen many elements from Beckett and taken over sections of Shakespeare wholesale, but at least he has *stolen* and not borrowed. He has made it his own, which as Brecht said, is what playwrights do.

It is a pity there is no space to discuss Stoppard's continuing contribution to the theatre in the acrobatic *Jumpers* (1972); the amazing incorporation of limericks, sonnets, Wilde's *Importance of Being Earnest* and other verbal and theatrical modes in *Travesties* (1974); the more naturalist and political *Night and Day* (1978); the juggling with Heisenberg's 'uncertainty principle' in *Hapgood* (1987). All these plays reveal an extraordinary theatrical gift which a later book will discuss. Stoppard combines his more general metaphysical interest in questions of freedom and power with a growing political concern and, in *The Real Thing* (1984) for example, develops an awareness of human feeling which is not always attributed to him. It may be, as he himself modestly says, that such a writer as the South African, Athol Fugard, is writing out of a more important situation, but a writer must do what he can with his gifts. Stoppard's are such that when he takes as subject the nature of theatre, or, as in *Travesties*, the processes of writing, he makes acute observations about the nature of creativity and the function of art. In *Rosencrantz and Guildenstern* he carried out a subtle analysis of the nature of freedom and its limits with an energy and verve which is itself a form of freedom.

Stoppard's tone is quite different from that of Bond's *Saved* (1966). In Stoppard a comic gift is in the ascendancy. Yet he, like Bond, is a channel for the different theatrical forms of the century. Bond takes the problem of political and personal violence as his subject. Stoppard, the more anarchic, explores questions of personal and imaginative freedom. Both concerns run through this century's drama and a comparison of two such opposite writers helps to do justice to the variety of the period.

Edward Bond and Ingmar Bergman

Cruelty, freedom and responsibility

If Stoppard made his name in 1966 with a play which combined Shakespeare with Beckett and had no apparent contemporary political relevance, other directors were more immediately concerned with the relation between theatre and contemporary events. The problem of the power of theatre to alleviate such atrocities as were occurring in Vietnam had been voiced in Brook's *US*. Indeed, an actor sitting in the audience had questioned the effect not only of protest theatre but of such extreme gestures as self-incineration:

> Take me. I'm a suitable case. I vote left. I hold progressive opinions about homosexuality and capital punishment. I'm quite well read. I have a university degree. I do my best not to buy South African oranges . . . and what the hell do you think I'll do different from what I did today, just because you burn yourself?

Such a 'suitable case' might not be universal and even if the recognition of a common response shamed a few spectators into disagreement and action, the suffering of others, especially when filtered through the media, was not likely to cause mass changes in behaviour. And if no theatre audience could do anything about Vietnam, what was the use of representing such atrocity on stage? If the theatre was powerless then a dramatist should, like the later Sartre, accept that drama was merely entertainment and choose another field of action.

Pessimism undermines creative energy. *US* would never have

existed without faith in the protest it conveyed and it would not have run long without an active audience response. A pessimist could argue that the energy it released was merely cathartic – a belief as unprovable as the conjecture than no spectator was politicized. In all likelihood it helped to confirm a growing solidarity of opposition and eventually, however minutely, contributed to political change. Certainly the energy which went into it deserved to effect more than an aesthetic purge. Emotional safety-valves, as Brecht's so-called 'anti-Aristotelian' theatre argued, merely stabilize the status quo. The subject of Vietnam required an active, 'kinetic'[1] response, not a 'static' feeling that nothing could be done.

Brecht asked his questions and made his protest within the live theatre, but the rise of new technology during his life and after his death raised ever more pressing questions about whether radical energy was best channelled elsewhere into the newer media with their gigantic audiences, into direct political action, into symbolic and powerful forms of private protest which would receive world-wide publicity. Jan Palacs's self-incineration in Prague, 1968, in protest against the Soviet invasion, came two years after Brook burned his butterfly. This was an extreme 'happening', a form of theatre, which, like the self-immolation of the Buddhist monks, provided an extreme image of protest. It was an act whose cruelty mimicked the effect of the napalm bombing and the Russian tanks. Its representation on film and television made a stronger protest than the theatre could have made. Should not then the theatre remain silent?

The thought had evidently crossed the mind of one major director and writer. Ingmar Bergman, as we have seen in *Persona* (1966), showed us an actress, Elizabeth Vogler, who falls silent in the middle of a performance of *Electra* and thereafter will speak to no one. The theatre for her has become unbearably artificial. She smiles in derision when her nurse turns on a melodramatic radio play, then recoils in horror, in the corner of her hospital room, before the TV image of a burning monk. The horror seems to confirm the greater impact of the newer technology and the actress's silent condemnation of her own profession.

Nevertheless, the film does not argue that silence is the only possibility. Elizabeth Vogler's is a defensive response. It serves her own purposes but hurts others: her son, her husband, her colleagues. Nor does it fully suffice, for her shield is constantly

194

pierced. Impressions enter, not only of horror but also of beauty. From her shelter she studies and is amused by the behaviour of other people. With her actress's training she watches and listens. A gesture or an inflection may help her create or strengthen a role. She appropriates others' lives, using the confidences which Alma, the young nurse, out of generosity or vanity offers her. From such material the artist creates a persona. But however convincing the role Elizabeth Vogler constructs, reality always seeps in. The words of Alma, the images of the television screen, the radio play Alma switches on, the radio concert she changes to, all affect her. The beauty of the music indeed affects her deeply. The world is not all horror, Bergman seems to say, even if art cannot fully console. But silence is not the answer, for the outside world enters whatever his actress does to ward it off.

Bergman, unlike his character, does not remain silent. He shows the actress's response, communicates her private horror to an audience and repudiates her purely private withdrawal. His representation of her refusal to communicate is an act of faith in the value of communication. Elizabeth Vogler is wrong. Her withdrawal, in part, is a theatrical and self-centred gesture. Bergman shows both sides of her response and by commenting on the potential artifice of his character's and his own profession, communicates a sense of the real.

The theatre, like other media, can take root in the minds of people who have, or may acquire, some power of social action, but no one can measure how dramatic images provoke shifts of attitude and induce social change. They mingle in the psyche with many other elements, personal and accidental, which may inhibit us or prompt us to action. Amid an interplay of crowding stimuli the theatrical image, arousing feelings of anger or joy, beauty, or pain, must leave a deep impression if it is to be seen as a dominant cause. If images of cruelty cut especially deep, Artaud may be right to seek in them his particular form of salvation. They are, in any case, as Artaud, Brook and Bergman well knew, central to the dramatic tradition which runs from Oedipus's self-mutilation, to the blinding of Gloucester in *King Lear*, to the nurse's deliberate leaving of broken glass for her patient to step upon in Bergman's *Persona*. Such work is not to be dismissed as purely 'cathartic' or 'Aristotelian'. It is analytical of the nature of cruelty and cuts into the psyche, leaving an unhealed wound.

The problem lies, of course, in the basic and sentimental human desire to embrace pleasure and block out pain; to anaesthetize and subdue the uncomfortable image; to shield the self against words which demand action or subvert our conventional response. It is a human tendency the theatre feeds when it wants to make money and which it attacks when other motives prevail. Osborne attacked British apathy; Beckett mocked traditional expectations of dramatic form; Brecht presented his paradoxes; Brook made his vividly theatrical protest about Vietnam. The new theatre sought desperately to shake the audience's complacency and its understandable and inveterate desire for enjoyment. It knew the resilience and conservatism of institutions and their power to absorb subversive attacks or to exclude them. Sir Robert Renwick announced he went to the theatre only to be entertained and amused. Since he, as chairman of ATV, had taken over 22 Stoll Theatres and Moss Empires in 1965, his views were reflected in the kinds of play selected for production. But sanitized theatre does not entertain everyone and enjoyment often derives from subversion. Such theatre does not exclude entertainment. It may even make a profit for management, if no doubt less predictably.

The commercial system, however, did not encourage new, subversive writing, although backers might take a chance on an established author and star actors. If it makes money a radical play can be assimilated or appropriated – like Joan Littlewood's Brechtian production of the comic opera on the follies of World War I, O What a Lovely War (1963). An established but innovative writer may also command a hushed respect he does not want. One recalls Beckett's puzzled response to a Paris performance of *Endgame*: 'There must be something wrong. They're clapping.' One way of assimilating subversive theatre is to cite it as evidence of the vitality of the culture it attacks. Those who need to feel part of that culture will then applaud it.

Most dramatic work of value since Ibsen has emerged from theatres whose primary purpose was not profit. The English Stage Company at the Royal Court was founded by George Devine in 1956 to counter the dominant commercialism. (In 1954 Ken Tynan identified 27 theatres which offered musicals and light comedy, as against only three new plays worth serious consideration.) The development of recent theatre owes a great deal to Devine and especially to the writers' workshops which grew up around him.

At this point one might also raise one's hat to the Arts Council.

It had been established during the war by Maynard Keynes and by 1956 was subsidizing Devine's theatre. By 1967 its subsidy had gone up to £100,000. The RSC had twice as much (£205,000) in the same year, and the National Theatre from 1963 has been subsidized for up to 50 per cent of every seat sold. In addition the Arts Council was supporting 40 companies outside London to the tune of between £5000 and £50,000. Fifteen theatres were built between 1958 and 1970, all with public money.[2] These new outlets, and the changing student and professional audiences, expanded theatrical opportunities and led directly to the Fringe explosion of 1968 which offered a much wider scene for actors, writers and technicians not only to gain skills and experience but also to express their sense of what was right or wrong with the world.

More recent government policy, of course, has encouraged theatres to replace subsidy by commercial fund-raising, putting great strain on Fringe theatre. But in the 1960s the theatre was expanding. New theatre buildings and new writers made a powerful contribution to the general buoyancy. So, too, did the relaxation of theatre censorship brought about by Edward Bond's *Saved* with the strong support of Sir Laurence Olivier. This play had an indisputable effect on the theatre, and also aimed to bring social realities to the attention of the public. Bond believed in the social function of the theatre and its capacity to effect change.

Edward Bond was born in Holloway in 1935. He belonged to a generation of writers whose childhood spans the war years and whose central theme is cruelty and world violence. It is a concern which is surprisingly less evident in the writings of an older generation of writers, mainly poets, who actually fought in the war. Their sense of the violence of things is summed up by the famous line of Donald Davie (1922–): 'How dare we now be anything but numb'. But Bond's was, and is, a more active and militant reaction, stemming from a childhood spent as an evacuee among strangers and then in London again among doodle-bugs and V2s. His plays express a feeling of class violence as strongly as those of Harold Pinter. They reveal, more naturalistically than Pinter, a knowledge of life at the very bottom of the social scale. Bond became a writer, he claims, because of one evening in the theatre when he saw Donald Wolfit play *Macbeth*. The production fertilized his will and imagination. He describes his reaction thus: 'Well, yes, now I know what I have to do, what it means to be alive.'[3] Shakespeare seemed to speak to him of his own problems: 'about the life I'd been living, the political society around me'. So Bond wrote obsessively and saw all the plays he could. He was particularly interested in what was going on at the Royal Court, which included Beckett and Ionesco whose strange theatre images he attempted to humanize. There was one figure in Ionesco's *The Killer* (1959) whom he wished to 'get inside'. This became the murderer, Scopey, in *The Pope's Wedding* (1962). His next play, examined the theme of cruelty and violence so forcefully that it broke the censorship. It is the famous play, mounted privately three years later at the Royal Court, which the Lord Chancellor banned and which Laurence Olivier argued for.

Saved (1965) is about escape from a narrow environment. All the characters lead restricted lives: they are restricted by their tastes, their habits, their lack of education, by their working and home environment, but above all by the parameter of their thoughts and lack of expressive vocabulary. The men speak in brief phrases, sentences, exclamations, and are preoccupied with sex and violence. The girl Pam, who opens the play, has no resources or hobbies. She eats sweets, watches TV and asserts her identity by claiming possession of objects, such as the *Radio Times*. When she becomes tied down by the birth of her child she refuses all responsibility and founders in resentment and self-pity. She, like the gang of boys in the play, is not able to grow.

The older generation, Pam's parents Mary and Harry, are tied in a silent, hostile marriage, whose failure is linked to the death of a child from bombing during the war. Harry has withdrawn into himself. He keeps himself up, irons his clothes, but finally emerges from his withdrawal to try to establish a relation with the main character, Len, the lodger and Pam's former boyfriend. Len, despite rejection by Pam, is accepted by Mary and Harry. He also takes responsibility for the child which Pam and the child's father, Fred, repudiate.

In its human concerns the play is reminiscent of Brecht's *Caucasian Chalk Circle* in which the girl, Grusha, takes responsibility for an abandoned child, and Simon, her fiancé soldier, eventually takes responsibility for her. A less obvious comparison is Harold Pinter's *The Caretaker* (1960) which was also concerned with questions of responsibility.[4] Brecht and Pinter both illustrate the necessity and the danger of taking responsibility.

Bond's *Saved*, despite the notorious stoning scene and its negative reputation, also treats this subject and indeed presents it more positively than Pinter.

Bond's principal character, Len, is inarticulate but possesses curiosity, sympathy and a sense of others' needs. This he shares with Mary who runs the house, shops, cooks and provides a basis for family living. Her husband, Harry, caters only for his own needs and Pam seems quite unable to take responsibility for her child, other members of the family, or even herself. In the contrasted social group the youthful members of the gang feel a loyalty to each other but they acknowledge nothing beyond that. They have no work they take pride in and they bolster each other in opposition to the social patterns of the world outside. ''Ow's the job?' enquires Len. 'Don't talk about it,' replies Fred. The young need the group but feel no gratitude. They pride themselves on their own parasitism. 'Got any fags? I left mine behind' is the usual refrain.

Len is the exception. He cares about others: 'the child needs a 'ome'. 'You never took yer medicine'. He fixes plugs (like Aston in *The Caretaker*), mends chairs, calms the child: 'Someone's got to pick it up.' By contrast, responsibility drives the others mad. Pam dopes the child with aspirins, and leaves it with its father Fred, who rejects it. The gang are left with a child in a perambulator. They handle the situation by inventing a game which ends with the notorious scene in which the child is stoned to death. There is an inversion of the code of parental responsibility. 'Why don' you clout it Fred? It ain mine . . . Shirker . . . Yer got a do yer duty'. This 'duty' becomes a competitive sport, and by the time the mother returns the damage is done. Characteristically, the mother is not sufficiently aware of the child's existence even to look at it as she pushes the pram off-stage.

The play seems to say that to rebel against the restrictions which the acceptance of responsibility, such as care of a child, places on individual freedom, creates an unfreedom which only inverts the normal code and takes the form of an ultimate fascism, scapegoating the helpless to revenge itself on the outside world.

How far the gang are freely responsible for their actions is a question asked of the audience. We do not see the whole process in which they have been bound, as we see the inside of a family but not the world of work. The members of the gang do have jobs (this was the 1960s), but apart from Fred's acting as boating attendant, their work is not described or represented. One infers their behaviour owes something to the mindlessness of the production line, but this is not shown, and it cannot be assumed that it is the only form of labour to exist. The play implies but does not prove that an industrial 'society' is to be blamed.

Leisure is presented: boating on the lake, fishing, and the jokey game in the park which ends in violence. Fred's work and private enjoyment of his hobby of fishing at first separate him from the gang. When he takes the blame for the child's death and is imprisoned, he avows his need of human contact by asking Pam to write to him in jail. But the discipline is beyond him and he does not write. When he emerges from jail he is fully one of the gang. He has been shut up and is now shut in. Pam can give him nothing and he finds her dependence on him abhorrent.

Pam also is shut in. Sexually and emotionally enslaved, Pam has no thought of breaking free, no awareness of a need to break this dependence, only a wearisome desire to serve. Fred's indifference leads to her illness and bad temper. Len is chosen to suffer the abuse, to take the blame for Fred's rejection of her, perhaps because she had begun to emerge into an active relationship with him before Fred came along.

Fred goes back to the gang whose code he has upheld by not giving them away. The aggressive joking at the expense of the law, of the handicapped and of women continues. Death also figures large: 'Why was the undertaker buried alive?' Laughter and shared racial, sexual and social attitudes protect the group against the threat of seeing others as real. The joking consolidates its inner loyalties and anaesthetizes all other fellow-feeling. Any attempt to escape this imprisoning mentality is labelled 'soft'. Fred, who was in mid-position between Len's humanity and Pete's fascism, has chosen Pete.

When the play cuts back from presenting the group to the private family situation, the silent Harry expresses a desire to keep established patterns. 'Yer fit in now' he says. Len pays his rent and has been accepted. Perhaps loneliness and a need for company have loosened Harry's tongue. Hatred and jealousy had done so in the previous scene (Len has been mending Mary's stocking with her leg inside it, a scene the censor liked as little as the stoning of the baby), but Harry's anger is not turned against Len. On the contrary the threat of Len's going encourages a male fraternity: 'Don't let em push yer out' and even brings Harry to the expression of private feeling: 'I'd like yer to stay' . . . 'if yer can see yer way to'. He thus recognizes Len so far as to recognize his freedom to choose. Harry, however, does not extend such recognition across the gender barrier: 'Don't speak to 'em at all. It saves a lot of misunderstandin''.

Harry is afraid of giving himself away to women, out of fear perhaps of providing ammunition for family rows. He has spent most of the play not speaking. 'Funny we never talked before' says Len. 'They listen all the time' is Harry's reply. 'She's eard us' says Len. 'Best keep away, yer see,' says Harry.

The gender relations which inform the play are interesting. Harry's is an army mentality, which puts the male relation first. The gang treats women as sexual objects, and food and tobacco providers. Mary and Pam are also involved in power relations. They establish ownership of objects in the house, reduce the men at times to the status of objects. Len is the one who asserts a human concern. He accepts ridicule, takes on 'female' work, goes shopping, looks after the child, mends stockings, ignores the joking, seems in fact to be independent of the gang's judgement. His 'goodness', as Bond himself claims, is the central concern of the play. It consists in caring about others and taking responsibility. Len is therefore freer than the gang members. Although he may be trapped in the family environment, he seeks to give. In the final scene he tries again: as each character silently attends to his or her own concerns, Len mends a chair. It is a chair which is not entirely stable by the play's end, but perhaps it will do for the moment.

According to Bond, he does not present men as 'naturally violent' and argues that if they were they would have destroyed each other before now. For him a belief in a violent basis to human nature is a convenient doctrine which allows a power structure to maintain itself and justify its own oppression. Similarly the idea of perpetual torture in hell, says Bond, is a myth perpetuated to serve the institution which purports to save men from such an afterlife. A belief in natural violence is a political strategy. Violence is contingent, not necessary, and occurs in situations which can be identified and prevented. Man's selfhood derives from human bonds and relations, which is the essence of human freedom, not just the condition of it. A threat to it provokes a violent response. Bond's preoccupation with violence derives from a belief that it can be contained, and the theatre can help contain it.

Bond uses Brechtian techniques to distance the violence. The scenes are episodic, taking place on a semi-bare stage, using simple props and much stage activity – eating, drinking and everyday chores like darning, shopping and ironing. These activities have a vivid 'gestic' effect. The placing of characters 'sculpturally', says William Gaskill, is important. The characters 'own' particular parts of the stage, and very precise playing is required. 'The greater the restraint the greater the effect of violence.' He is more naturalistic than Brecht, however, less caricatural and comic, and he does not employ song and extraneous commentary, although, like Brecht again, he leaves the audience with an open question: 'What I hope happens in *Saved* is that an audience better realizes the nature of its society, what the nature of its problem is, and therefore what sort of solutions are needed'.[5] He indeed manages to present scenes of violence in such a way that the audience can scrutinize the violent behaviour with a certain Brechtian objectivity.

From Beckett, in these early plays, he took a spare, rhythmical, colloquial dialogue. He also shares Beckett's gift for creating vivid theatrical images. But he is less static than Beckett. There is more overt conflict, less comedy, more social concern and less vivid symbolism. He is, he says, an optimist determined not to learn from experience. The central image in much of his work is of a character becoming free, by shaking off a dead self. In *Lear* (1971) the central figure must shake off the Gravedigger's Boy who haunts him like a ghost. In the expressionistic *Early Morning* (1968) a Siamese twin must actually shake off the skeleton of his dead brother. As he does so his character emerges and he begins to make sense of the world.

Bond's *Saved* remains a play of historical importance. It was commissioned on the basis of the success of the first play and sent to the Lord Chamberlain for scrutiny. The latter objected to the swearing, to Scenes 9 and 10 (the baby and stocking repairing scenes) and issued a directive that Pam must not unfasten Len's belt in Scene I. William Gaskill decided to put the play on intact at a club performance on 3 November 1965. There was an unpleasant press reaction and Bond wrote in protest. Business later improved but the theatre was fined £50. Bond was surprised audiences had not liked his characters: 'My life was actually very like the one shown in this play. I was very surprised when people were upset about it.'

Saved was the last play to be prosecuted by the Lord Chancellor. It helped provoke the Theatre Act of 1968 which opened up the British theatre to new writers and theatre companies. Its achievement can be deduced from the statistics: it had its first professional English production in 1969, after 33 different productions had been staged abroad. The 1965 Royal Court club performance brought changes which affected the general climate in the theatre perhaps more than any other event of the decade. It is a convenient watershed at which to pause.

Athol Fugard

Naturalism, racism and imaginative play

In a consideration of the theatre up to 1968 it would be wrong not to mention the South African writer who came to prominence in the 1960s and whose deep concern with political and personal forms of freedom reflects a central theme of this book. Athol Fugard's practice also emphasizes that, although the theory and practice of Bertolt Brecht has continued to prove very influential in the writing of social and political drama, Stanislavskian naturalism is an abiding influence. Brecht aimed to 'show' rather than embody reality and his episodic and open-ended drama, although frequently sombre in subject matter, uses comic techniques of stereotypng and caricature, relying on powerful contrastive effects whereby it mocks the conventional images of a consumer society. This has not, however, superseded Stanislavski's emphasis on psychological realism and audience involvement, which finds a powerful exponent in Fugard's work.

The naturalist tradition in the twentieth century has already been defined. Stanislavski continues to influence schools of acting. His 'system' clearly fed into the so-called 'method acting' of the post-war New York Actors' Studio from whence it carried into the films of Elia Kazan. Film, with its material resources, could achieve far more convincing representations of reality, whether working in the studio or on location. But naturalism also persisted in the theatre, especially in America. It was carried forward in varying ways in the drama of Tennessee Williams and Arthur Miller and in the 'kitchen-sink' naturalism of Osborne and Wesker. Later we see Stoppard amusingly parodying

Stanislavski's exercises within his mixed genre of farce, absurdist drama and discussion play. More recently, Mike Leigh and Caryl Churchill have used Stanislavski's techniques of collective improvisation to create plays which are partly naturalistic in style, even if the resulting play structure, as often in Churchill's case, breaks up the 'natural' time sequence, or, as in the case of Mike Leigh, brings the effect closer to caricature. Leigh, however, keeps to a conventional time structure and explores, with close, painful and often hilariously accurate observation, the tensions arising from a collision of middle and working-class mores.

The same, in a more conventional sense could be said of Alan Ayckbourn. His plays have much in common with Labiche, Feydeau and the astringent nineteenth-century French farces which still work powerfully in the theatre. There is in them close awareness of human differences, together with sombre, often neurotic material related to sex, race and class, which continues to trigger laughter. Even though farce is reputedly shallow in characterization, and indeed depends on the reduction of humanity to mechanical behaviour, the Stanislavskian exploration of 'sub-text' is still relevant to the actor who wishes to make them live.

In the forms cited, a psychological concern, especially marked in the American writing, is fused with the presentation of social issues. In the case of Leigh, Ayckbourn and Churchill in their different ways, caricature mingles with a deeper psychological emphasis, indicating a fusion of the Brechtian with the Stanislavskian theatres. Sartre had suggested in his essay 'On Dramatic and Epic Theatre', that the distinction was less great than Brecht had claimed. Brecht's epic theatre, with its emphasis on public pressure rather than private motivation as a cause of action, has exerted a strong influence on recent British writers, but Stanislavski's encouragement of the deep exploration of personal motives has been present in the theatre throughout the century. Dramatic conflict often finds its centre in the anguish of a character compelled to act against his or her own wishes. Dramatic interest is sustained by the spectacle of a character forming itself by choosing what outside pressures to yield to and what to resist. To examine private motives one must examine social pressures, but the explanation of public pressures does not entirely account for the private response. If it did, much of the dramatic interest would disappear. In the twentieth century

Brecht's practice has extended but not superannuated the natural-ist and psychological forms on which Stanislavski built. The plays of Chekhov, Ibsen, Strindberg, and, of course, Shakespeare – have remained fundamental.[1].

The claim of naturalist drama to hold the mirror up to life has, of course, aroused much twentieth-century opposition. It is argued that naturalism projects 'bourgeois' family life as the central unchanging human condition and where naturalism over-laps with *théâtre de boulevard* there is some truth in this. Naturalistic comedy, however, arguably mocks human fixity and fear of change. Where naturalism leans towards the tragic it arguably applauds the struggle against constraints.

It is also as well to define the term 'bourgeois'. Plays may be considered bourgeois in four basic ways: in content, i.e. Ibsen dramatizing the experience of a middle-class family; in form, because the play employs the form a middle-class audience expects; in audience appeal, because it is successful in a theatre which a middle-class audience attends; in attitude, because the writer's views coincide with those of the middle-class.

In practice, plays can be bourgeois in form but not content, as perhaps is the case of Osborne and Wesker; or in content and even form but not attitude, as in Ibsen's attacks on middle-class hypocrisy; or in neither content nor in form but in attitude and effect. Sartre considered Beckett's plays 'bourgeoise' since they say 'No change'. The word needs very careful use.

Sartre uses the term to define a French middle class which sees others as guilty and itself as innocent, but drama has always attacked such hubris. Both Oedipus and Lear shared a tendency to think well of themselves, and Tartuffe was certainly not the first hypocrite. Much naturalist drama was similarly analytical of bourgeois forms of posturing and cannot be accused of sharing it.

If the naturalist movement seemed at first to encourage audiences to enjoy watching their own middle-class image, it did so in order to carry them further in this direction than they may have wished to go. Its plays gained the audience's confidence only to shake it. The radicalism worked from within, subverting the hubristic assumption that human beings can entirely be accounted for by a class concept. No one is fully bourgeois, or working class, or aristocrat (Brecht, in *The Messingkauf Dialogues* agreed) just as no one is fully a monster or a saint. Good naturalist plays pay tribute to the freedom which exists between the categories – the freedom an actor must discover if he is make a character live.

Major drama watches the struggle of men and women not to become a product of historical circumstance. If they allow themselves to become fixed objects, if they lose their freedom and their awareness of the forces attempting to shape them, they become objects of pity or derision. Both laughter and empathy pay homage to the existence of a kind of freedom in the face of the threat of occupation by historical and material pressures operating both within and without.

Drama thus seems to work in areas where there is a threat of dehumanization. This can apply both to those who rule and those who rebel. Characters may lose humanity and treat each other as objects, which is an immediate source of dramatic tension since audiences reject such behaviour. Dramatic sympathy goes out to those who are so treated and rejection or mockery is reserved for those who refuse to acknowledge the freedom of others or themselves. Even the so-called 'bourgeois' audience, which likes to see its own prejudices confirmed, can never be entirely defined in terms of class. When it disapproves those who threaten the social framework it may not be fully wrong. An audience which disapproves the Iagos and Edmunds who treat others as objects, and approves the Emilias who show Iago foolish to take others so for granted, is not necessarily expressing class prejudice. It demonstrates a sympathy with those who acknowledge the rights and independence of others.

Villains, of course, have an anarchic appeal and many things can be said in their favour when they oppose the ideologies of power. But the ethic which judges them is not necessarily based on power relations, and in the conflicts between one power and another some qualitative ethic may make an entrance. Drama from the time of Sophocles and Aeschylus has staked its claim in the territory between the codes which power relations generate, and in an ethic which may have other roots.

Where the drama itself becomes sardonic about values – as in Shakespeare's *Troilus and Cressida* or, in Nietzsche's view, in the plays of Euripides, there is a powerful gain in realism, but also some form of qualitative loss. If the possibility of the existence of high value is ignored or denied, life and art become less rich. Even in *Troilus*, if less than in *Othello*, the mockery of Shakespeare's fools is tempered by poignancy. There are distinctions invited between the qualities of the lives lived and the beliefs held. The drama still lives between the double possibility, whatever the final intellectual case it makes.

Athol Fugard is a dramatist who has a strong and important relation to questions of value and mainly writes from within the mimetic and naturalist tradition. His primary concern is with race relations, and the impact of political situations on the people caught up in it. He lies outside the mainstream of Brechtian 'epic' political drama and does not rely on unusual alienation devices, overlapping dialogue, or elaborate stage design. He employs a standard naturalist set, usually a room where the characters discuss and develop their situation. His method is no more dated than that of Sophocles, or Shakespeare, or Chekhov, or the anonymous writer of *Everyman*, when they present characters grappling with a situation larger than themselves.

Fugard was born in June 1932, in a semi-desert township in the South African Karroo. His father was a crippled shopkeeper and former jazz pianist with an Irish Huguenot background. His mother was from a Voortrekker, pioneering Calvinist family. He had an English-speaking education and he has continued to live in Port Elizabeth, a car manufacturing town of half a million people with black townships, poor whites, few 'liberals' and many large rich houses on the coast.

Fugard won a scholarship to Cape Town University and read widely, especially in literature concerned with racial issues set in the American South or in North Africa. He read Tennessee Williams, William Faulkner and Albert Camus. He travelled through Africa, signed on board a ship, wrote a novel and threw it overboard. In 1956 he married an actress, founded a theatre workshop and began writing plays. Not surprisingly, since the American influence was strong, his drama lies within the naturalist tradition.

His first successes were with *No-Good Friday* and *Nongogo* (1958). They emerged from his work in Johannesburg at the Native Commissioners Court which brought him experience of the effect of the pass laws. *The Blood Knot* came in 1961 after a lean period in Europe and England, and his return to Port Elizabeth. The play ran for 140 performances before going to London and New York, where it made his name and was acclaimed 'Play of the Year' by the *New York Times*. It is a powerful two-hander about two strongly-attached brothers, Morris and Zach, one light-skinned and one dark, living in a shack in a Port Elizabeth shanty town, built close to a stinking factory and a dead stretch of water. The whole drive of the play is towards escape from this appalling place, from the poverty, and by extension the political situation and social attitudes which keep them there. Morris, by virtue of his light skin, lives within a wider arena of social acceptance and has more chance to escape than his brother, but he has given up 'trying for white' and deliberately chooses to restrict his life to live with the dark-skinned Zach. This act can be seen either as altruistic or parasitic, since it is Zach's job which enables them to live. Morris, however, controls their lives. They save money, yet at the same time they need relief from their situation, even if it is only in the bath salts with which Zach soaks his calloused feet. In penury the smallest luxuries are desired and savoured, yet resented for what they cost. They live near the condition where 'Man's life is cheap as beast's', and they long for what King Lear called the 'superflux',[2] hence the bath salts.

Soaking his feet in a rare moment of ease, Zach is reminded of how he lived before his brother persuaded him to save. His money – and freedom – went on drink and women. He lived in the present with no thought of escape, and his 'Golden Moments' came out of a 50 cent bottle, but Morris has insisted that 'Save now, live later' is a better maxim than: 'Pay now, live now'. ('Live now, pay later' does not apply to those who have no credit.) They save for a small farm, but the dreams, the need for golden moments prove too strong. They need human contact, which takes the form of answering an advertisement for a pen pal, who turns out to be a white woman. The act of writing, in however basic a form, seems to offer them an entrance to a wider world. The exchange of letters, however, evolves into a dangerous game of make-believe. They tell the woman elaborate lies which are so convincing she threatens to come and see them. The dream game is up, unless Morris can dress the part and pass for white. The game has now become theatrical and Morris's costume takes all Zach's savings. He even buys luxuries, such as a wallet and cigarette case, in order to share a white woman's life, if only vicariously through his brother. The white woman writes that she is engaged and cannot come and the brothers are left with the properties purchased to sustain a dream. In a final powerful sequence, Morris dresses and enacts the dream of being white,

ATHOL FUGARD

abusing his brother both physically and verbally, thereby emphasizing the dubious and parasitic role he has played. When Morris
comes out of role they are left with the objects which represent a
greater freedom, but remain in a situation from which they have
lost the power to escape.

By using characters who engage in role-play Fugard extends the
apparent limits imposed by a small cast. He symbolically enacts
the relation between black man and white man as human beings
who are ultimately tied together, rather like Beckett's Gogo and
Didi, although one or the other may deny it. On a naturalistic
level, the condition of two blacks, one more light-skinned and
more educated than the other, is vividly presented. Their struggle
to escape and their struggle to tolerate appalling conditions of
servitude are shown to conflict with one another. The conditions
force the pair to seek freedom. Yet Zach abandons his search for
freedom in a bottle by working to save money but the process is
painful and a need for imaginative escape causes them to
indulge in a game which destroys their chance of getting away.

It seems there are two forms of liberty, economic freedom and
freedom of imagination, and each is poor and perhaps of little
value without the other. In the play, imagination is triggered
by poverty. Extreme deprivation erodes physical energy whilst
making it necessary to invent a dream to make it tolerable. The
play is written around this paradox.

At this earlier stage of his work Fugard saw no hope for his
characters or for himself. As Camus in *L'Etranger* had suggested
to him, images of the future were dreams a man could do without.
Living in the present like Camus's Meursault, without hope and
without appeal, was the situation in which Fugard declared he
found himself along with Zach and Morris.

Fugard's positive values thus resided in his emphasis on living
in the present, and *for* the present. Ideologically the plays were
closed to the future and apolitical, yet the spectacle of two black
brothers struggling imaginatively and economically to be at the
centre of their own lives induced in audiences world-wide a deeper
recognition of the human implications of the South African political
situation, and influenced them, perhaps beyond the writer's
intention, in ways essential to the process of political change.

Fugard continued to write two- and three-handers in a naturalistic mode, such as *Hello and Goodbye, People are Living There*
and *Boesman and Lena* before his passport was taken away in

1967. This loss of liberty and the continuing struggle to represent aspects of the human situation in South Africa make a good point at which to pause in this discussion of freedom and the performance of the dramatic form. It is a subject which Fugard himself has pursued more optimistically. We may recall the debate between Hally and Sam the negro in *Master Harold and the Boys* (1982):

'It's a bloody awful world', says the young Hally, 'one day someone is going to get up and give history a kick up the backside . . .'

'Like who?' says Sam. For Hally it seems to be the task of some 'Great Reformer' but neither Sam nor Hally knows where one can be found.

'So we just go on waiting' says Sam.

Sam is not educated. He does not know Hally's mathematics, but he understands people. 'How many times have I told you that examinations don't measure intelligence?' asks Hally. 'I would say about as many times as you failed one of them', Sam replies.

Sam does not know the words that Hally knows, but he picks them up and savours them the moment they are explained. They discuss these potential 'Great Reformers', men of *magnitude*; Sam loves the word and seeks to attribute it to men he most admires. Hally opts for Darwin, who has revealed the truth about the 'Struggle for Existence' (Hally has shown it Sam in 'black and white'). Sam dislikes Darwin since he bases evolution on the scattering of random seeds and opts for Abraham Lincoln. Hally suggests Wilberforce, who freed the blacks in 1833 (but caused the Boers to trek even further from Cape Colony to keep their masters' privileges). He then suggests Tolstoy, an artist who opted for social reform over art. Sam suggests Jesus, then Sir Alexander Fleming, for freedom from sickness is of significance as well as freedom from social oppression. In this way an apparently restricted local situation opens up major philosophical questions. Can figures of 'magnitude' effect historical change without small people in support? Is belief in great men a substitute for personal action? And who brings most to mankind, the politician, the artist, the religious visionary, the scientist, or the medical researcher? In this play Fugard moves towards a positive open structure which invites the audiences to provide answers.

Master Harold and the Boys will be further discussed in a book

211

which can afford it more space. For the moment, suffice it to say that Fugard's work emphasizes the continuing importance of the naturalist movement and the importance both within and outside it, of questions of freedom and form which have been central to this book.

Freedom, Form and Performance

This book has been concerned with the evolution of particular dramatic forms in the twentieth century. It has had to leave out a great deal in the attempt to provide a general framework within which to locate such forms while commenting in some detail on selected plays and productions.

In examining forms and categories such as farce, melodrama, naturalist, symbolist, expressionist, epic and chronicle, absurd, cruel and political theatre, I have tried not to forget how they overlap with each other within and across the general genres of tragedy, comedy and tragi-comedy. Polonius's words about the Players expert in 'tragical, comical, historical, pastoral' drama point ironically to Shakespeare's own procedures. They also hint suggestively at the influential mixed drama of the twentieth century.

Naturalism is a style frequently castigated. Nevertheless, I have taken it to be the most important movement of the century, running through Ibsen and Chekhov not only to Arthur Miller and Athol Fugard but into the procedures of film and television. Other dramatic forms have developed in opposition to what has been seen as a limited realism but naturalism has achieved more than narrow definitions of it have assumed. Despite its focus on private processes with small casts in single rooms, it has opened doors on the outer world, creating a broad sense of space and time. Surface realism can lead towards the inner world of dream whilst containing and tempering its unreality. As an ironic reverberator it is a crucial component of major mixed drama.

The forms reacting against naturalism have sought to express realities that naturalism finds difficult to handle, whether in the depths of the psyche (expressionism), or in the world of politics (epic theatre) or in some transcendency (verse and symbolist drama). However, an element of naturalism, the representation of the lives of particular human beings, is essential to drama, even that which represents gods or animals, biblical characters and moral abstractions. In early drama, the superhuman and the less-than-human is made so by comparison with the human. From the individualization of heroes and members of the Greek chorus, to Mrs Noah in the mystery cycles and Gogo and Didi in *Waiting for Godot*, characters are humanized, played for real. However extraordinary or absurd the dramatic situation, an audience needs to sense a kinship with the humans who play and suffer. Since tragedy in the twentieth century is no longer only a matter for heroes and kings, or even merchants and artists, but includes salesmen and tramps, this broader naturalism has increased its relevance across the social scale. Within the inhuman situations of farce as well as tragedy the indestructible 'little people', like the destructible great, offer a recognizable and necessary fellowship.

The symbolic interpretation of drama, encouraged by the procedures of the symbolist movement, became an attractive critical pastime 50 years ago and still affects the way we read, watch and stage a play. But drama cannot remain purely symbolic. Some directors and designers may consider their actors to be marionettes and visual symbols, but on the stage, actors inveterately work to bring their characters alive. If they remain symbol or abstraction, the performance is dead. There is indeed a tension here which goes to the heart both of dramatic writing and audience response. A character, such as King Lear, sees himself in symbolic terms, or others persuade him to see himself so: 'They told me I was everything'. Then, in the course of the play he recovers a narrower sense of the self: 'I am a foolish fond old man . . .'. His daughters, on the other hand, treated at first naturalistically, are almost transformed to symbolic status. They become saintly or vulpine but always remain within the ironic framework of the play's psychological realism.

In academic circles (but not in the theatre) much energy has been given to arguing against the dramatic emphasis on 'individual' private experience. It is pointed out that dramatic characters, like people, are 'subjects' i.e. sites of competing ideologies and economic pressures, not complete or whole. That this may be so, however, emphasizes how central to drama is the search for wholeness, integrity and liberty. In this search, writers and characters, actors and audience, seek to define and realize themselves.

The contradictions within the psyche, socially or genetically engendered, are important, but so, too, is the desire for individual wholeness. Drama often arises from a desire to heal the fractures in the self which are both a source of creativity and a threat. When the writer's mind fragments into different voices, those voices acquire a body of their own. Pirandello illustrates, and the *Notebooks* of Dostoievski confirm, the process. These characters take on a human, not an abstract form and in telling their story the writer attempts to resolve, at least momentarily, the competition between them.

Freud's model of the dream process, based in part on the study of drama and literature, on Sophocles and Shakespeare, Ibsen and Dostoievski, supports this version of creative freedom. For him the stories told in dreams attempt to heal latent anxieties. Characters appear, disguised by the processes of transference and condensation – the metaphors and metonyms of the 'dreamwork'. Freud was interested in the way fragments of the manifest dream revealed the latent promptings, the characters and events of the past. Jung, for his part, focused attention on the dreamwork and the characters of the transformed story. Each was interested in freeing his patients of the manias, obsessions and fixities, of the characters and events which threatened their autonomy and caused the dream. The symbolic must be placed in time and reality. The 'natural' must be set against the nightmare.

The writing of drama is, of course, far less spontaneous than a dream, though a dream may lie at the centre. Writers may dream, but they must then perform the work of the analyst too. The core material changes under the pressures of convention and the demands of the craft. The needs of an audience to catch the last train, the requirements of a theatre company to be fully and interestingly occupied, the exigencies of a theatre space and a theatre manager, these come into play and mingle with forms of self-discovery and elements still not drawn to consciousness. Perhaps above all, interaction with others clarifies the original stimulus. Indeed, this may well be part of the healing process. The writer may find an autonomy and a momentary serenity in abandoning self-preoccupation and listening, like Pirandello, to voices which come from without as well as within. The form which emerges is partly one the voices demand, within which they can express things the writer did not know, or did not know he knew.

Introspection necessarily leads outwards into awareness of a personal past, into the self's relation with the current world, and with the world which is indifferent to the self. The self is not autonomous in the sense that it is totally independent. Autonomy is an achieved but not fixed balance between self and world which gains by observation and analysis as well as by introspection and dream. Dramatists find their own voice in a common language, and by interaction with family, friends, colleagues, enemies, and the actors and directors who interpret the words. The forms they find arise from analysis of past languages and conventions, as also from the economic and social pressures of the present, which impose conditions always partly, but I would argue in the case of important work not fully, dictating the nature of what is transmitted. In these transactions between the personal and the impersonal a form of freedom may be found.

Drama thrives on contrast and conflict, contradiction and paradox, material over which the author strives for control. It presents a competition of wills within and between private individuals, and also between the individual and social groupings of various kinds. Characters put on the masks of family, clan, nation and institution, conflicting with other characters who are similarly masked. When Hamlet confronts Claudius, each presents a mask to the other, behind which the spectator sees their struggle for autonomy. In the gaps between character and mask, an apparently independent consciousness comes into being. Here the play acquires 'reality' (and the author perhaps his satisfaction). Those critics, historians and philosophers who lack the gift of presenting or creating a reality in human rather than abstract terms, tend to forget Chekhov's implied stricture on his tyro dramatist Konstantin: 'Not one living character . . .'. In drama, the abstract forces which threaten us must be given body.

This qualified autonomy of author and character is one of the forms of freedom I have tried to define. Other and related types are exhibited in play by children when they seek to preserve a space where they can dissolve the threats of the adult world, or test the extent of their power. This is a space Ingmar Bergman's child in *The Silence* enters into, as do the clowns and fools of the dramas he directs (and who also appear in his film). The autonomy of the actor is not dissimilar. Whatever the motive, in the freedom of play a joy arises which derives from the creation in the imagination of a momentary free world which has never existed before. This momentary autonomy is shared with authors and directors. It brings to mind Bergman's statement that when he begins a film it is like taking the toys out of the toy cupboard. 'It is exactly the same feeling,' he said.

An audience shares this sense of freedom when it abandons self to participate in the lives of fictive characters. It is a freedom which can spring a trap, for the pain or embarrassment of identification may require a restoration to self. In the double process of coming close, then standing back, another kind of liberation may take place – that of discarding a former self and repudiating an attitude taken by a character or an author. Ultimately, the refusal to be captured is what Brecht envisaged – a sturdy independence deriving in the first place from an ability to surrender freely.

Whatever the motives a dramatist has for writing, the form which he creates contains and controls the actors who interpret it. Actors are tied by the script, limited by body, voice and sex in ways which force them to invent verbal and visual disguise. The author is less exposed but his wider freedom may be more painful. It can cost heavily to resolve image, idea and memory into something concrete – a necessity compelled by his vocation and his pride, if not only by the need to earn. Paradoxically, the actor is freed by being tied, but he must first impose himself on what ties him, working in relation with others who are attempting to do the same. The script is material with which he must enter into balance, just as the more complex script of our everyday lives threatens our mastery, or demands a retrospective rewrite.

It is not surprising that many workers in the theatre find their values within the nature of the work they do: in the freedom which is necessary for successful writing and production. They repudiate forms of thinking which threaten creativity, making their claim out of the theatrical process itself, knowing in the transactions between actors, or between actors and directors, directors and text, actors and audience, that there are mental states which bring life as others death.

217

Before the 1989/90 production of *Peer Gynt* at the National Theatre, the director, Declan Donellan, repeated time-honoured advice to his players: the actor's undertaking with the audience is to reinvent the play spontaneously at each performance as if for the first time. 'Only two things really matter: the depth of your belief and the freedom of your imagination. Our work in rehearsal is to build a framework that will release them, to find the rules that will set you free.' Michel Saint-Denis said something similar: 'Acting is like holding a bird in the hand: if you close your hand too tightly, the bird will be killed; if you open it too much the bird will fly away'.

Donellan was presumably not talking of the social parameters within which he built his frameworks for actors. Nor was Saint-Denis thinking that totalitarian, and to a lesser degree commercial, frameworks can throttle the bird before the actor has the chance to hold it. Each was speaking of a form of truth and a form of reality which they could use as a standard and a guide.

Such frameworks are necessary both in acting and writing. Within or through them drama organizes varying voices and competing faiths. It invites an audience to choose its values, to judge between the ways characters live their lives. It also invites an audience to judge the limits of human capacity to know the forces which control their lives. Drama shows the process of living as one of continuous destruction and reconstruction of frameworks of belief. But like all human beings, the author is not an absolute authority. His work is not all-seeing. The works which see deepest, like *Hamlet*, present as many problems as solutions, and the audience and interpreters are free, within limits, to readjust its statements.

Recent criticism derides the impetuous claim that literature and art express values which are independent of historical process. The case is not provable nor is it easy to assert in the face of recent studies of cultural and social forms. On the other hand, to claim that the dramatic forms I have tried to describe are entirely dependent on historical changes and power relations is also a matter of assertion. It assumes that consciousness and the historical process can be fully accounted for. But it is also possible that certain feelings of human responsibility and solidarity, although often arising out of fear and a desire to protect our own and our group's security, cannot entirely be accounted for in terms of power. A difference of kind may exist between feelings based on self and feelings which do not see the self as centre. In the capacity of individuals to detach themselves from themselves, whether in successive drafts of a book or in rehearsing a role, in living a life or claiming a better life for others, a broader consciousness and a qualitative ethic may exist. If Ibsen, Brecht and Fugard combat commercial or fascist power structures they make an appeal on behalf of a richness which suggests their work has high value. Here we are in regions where people stake their claims and find their energies. Here also, we become dangerously solemn.

If at this point we step back from our assertions, we may admit that the dramatic form is a better medium than the prose essay for exploring the paradoxes of value and power. It protects one against inevitable simplifications and one can always deny – as Brecht did before the anti-American activities committee – that a character's opinion is one's own. Yet argument and counter-argument continually demand a resolution. It is a need which prompts the writing of drama and a need to which it makes its appeal.

In the 200 years since the *Declaration of the Rights of Man and Citizen* (27 August 1789), the right of liberty has been asserted more strongly than that of equality and fraternity. Mill, in *On Liberty* (1859), claimed that 'the struggle between Liberty and Authority is the most conspicuous feature of the portions of history with which we are most familiar, particularly in that of Greece, Rome and England'. He quotes von Humboldt to the effect that 'two things are necessary to human development, because necessary to render people unlike one another, namely freedom and variety of situations'. Hence the importance of giving scope to new opinions and suppressing the fear which derives from finding one's own values and customs threatened. Fear is the great consolidator of faith, hence the wisdom of leavening our faiths with scepticism.

Drama provides this scepticism. It provokes anxiety by challenging convention. It also challenges the fear that causes audiences to hold to conventions, whether of style or opinion. Valuable dramatic work challenges our fears, keeps us aware of challenges to our frameworks, keeps us alive.

The dramatic form from Aeschylus to Brecht has also provided a model of the way events relate and people interact, in processes of chance, fate and choice. It shares a preoccupation with the nature of history and freedom which has been a feature of political writing in very different writers, from de Tocqueville to Mill, through to Collingwood and Raymond Williams. The last, in his attempt to wed an individual liberalism to Marx's dialectical materialism, defined the concept of determination as 'the most difficult problem in Marxism': 'A critical and revolutionary doctrine was changed . . . into the very forms of passivity and reification against which an alternative sense of determination had set out to operate.' He notes the facility with which certain minds harden ideas into facts. The dramatist resists this tendency. A human possibility operates at the heart of the causal process.

No human choice, of course, is fully free. Any choice is challenged by other choices. Life is a competition of wills within an inherited situation. Some wills are strong, some weak; some minds recognize their situations, other minds do not. The dominant wills are not always the clearest minds, for wills can be strengthened by fastening onto a false doctrine as well as a truth. Engels wrote in a famous letter to Bloch: 'What each individual wills is obstructed by everybody else and what emerges is something no one willed.' What one hopes for in this process is that the wills which dominate should have human as well as technical skills – insights and sympathies and a sense of the autonomy of others which affect their choices. That choices may be made – may have to be made – which deny humanity, drama also testifies to.

Drama embodies the struggle against material and impersonal forces, which can destroy both from without and within. In tragedy and comedy, in different ways, the kinship which develops between an audience and the character who struggles asserts the existence of a common humanity. This kinship, which may take the form of part-identification with a character, a group, or a nation which may be other than one's own, operates in the writer, director, actor, and reader as well as in the spectator, and is a form of learning. To project oneself into another's experience, into another situation, into another's imaginings, is a great release and, although the playing of a role may be a compensation for a lack of certainty about the self it can also be a great aid to defining and extending the limits of the self.

In that release from self, as any actor knows, it is important not to lose oneself entirely or the world goes black and the lines disappear. The self must perch on the shoulder saying: 'the people you are speaking to are over there, get into the light so that they can see your face, emphasize this word or that if you wish to communicate with them'. Control is necessary for freedom, and freedom lies in the knowledge of communication and the awareness of response. The experience of the dramatic art provides in intense form the kinds of sympathy necessary in life. It is a form of training and exchange.

Auden says that 'poetry makes nothing happen'. This may be truer of poetry than drama, although we may be greedy to ask for more than the experience of either. But Auden's statement is unprovable. If poetry makes things happen within us, then it affects, for better or worse and in minute ways, what happens outside us. Drama certainly makes things happen to people who engage in it and may in this way contribute to the living of those around them.

When drama speaks of our world and the need to control and change it, we do well to watch, listen and possibly to act. Or if art, like dreams, enchains us on a magic island, we can still, like Shakespeare and Prospero, in the final words of what seems a final play, ask for release. In Peter Brook's 1991 Paris production of *The Tempest*, Jean-Claude Carrière was especially concerned that in his French translation the word 'free' should remain the last word.

It is a better word than most but it contains its ironies. There is never a last word. Edward Bond speculated in his play *Bingo* about the life Shakespeare led in retirement after the play: free to understand, to deplore but not to change the new social order. We, too, might wonder what Prospero found back in the 'reality' of Milan. If we imagine the further story of Prospero, or better, if we conduct a Stanislavski 'improv' to examine and enjoy the further doings of Stephano and Trinculo or Caliban and Ariel, it could release energies and lead to insights which critical analysis inhibits. Touchstone and Stanislavski were agreed there was 'much virtue in "if".' We are free to explore what they meant.

Notes

(Pages 5–12)

1. The 'fit-up' was a temporary theatre offering a diet of popular plays at low prices.
2. Chekhov's own description. See Karlinski, *Letters of Anton Chekhov*.
3. A phrase employed by Enid Welsford in her standard book on *The Fool*.
4. In Bergson's *Laughter* (*Le Rire* (1900)).
5. See Hegel's *Aesthetics*.
6. Kant and Herbert Spenser are associated with the theory of laughter known as 'Incongruity Theory'. Spenser's development of Kant's insight is to be found in 'The Physiology of Laughter' in *Essays on Education and Kindred Subjects*, 1910.
7. The film was drawn from Lew Wallace's novel: *Ben Hur: A Tale of the Christ* (1880). There have been three versions: Olcott 1907, the epoch-making Fred Niblo epic of 1927 and William Wyler's film of 1959.

(Pages 13–25)

1. See M. Baker, *The Rise of the Victorian Actor* for more details.
2. A section of Zola's 'Naturalism in the Theatre' is available in E. Bentley (ed.) *Theory of the Modern Stage*.
3. See J. W. McFarlane, *Ibsen Penguin Critical Anthology* and M. Meyer's *Ibsen* for this and much other useful background material.
4. See Meyer's *Ibsen*.
5. The cast was in some doubt as to the appropriateness of the gesture and Juliet Stevenson did not consistently adhere to it.

(Pages 26–35)

1. S. T. Coleridge, *Biographia Literaria*, Chapter 13.
2. E. Zola, 'Naturalism in the Theatre'.
3. See G. B. Shaw, Appendix to *The Quintessence of Ibsenism*.
4. The Meininger Company, founded by the Duke of Meiningen (1826–1914), was, in the rigour of its practice, a major influence on

the development of naturalism. Its methods were admired during the European tours it engaged in after 1874. Antoine saw the company in Brussels.

5. Eugene Scribe (1791–1861), the ingenious French author of over 400 plays.
6. See Stanislavski, *An Actor Prepares.*
7. See also Stanislavski, *My Life in Art.*
8. See the correspondence in Karlinski's edition of Chekhov's letters.
9. See *Chekhov par lui-meme* in the Seuil series for this quotation and other background material.
10. In W. James, *Principles of Psychology*, 1890. Chapter entitled 'Self'.

(Pages 36–43)

1. T. S. Eliot, in G. Cambon, ed., *Pirandello: a collection of critical essays.*

(Pages 44–54)

1. Odilon Redon (1840–1916) French symbolist painter.
2. Aurelien Lugné-Poë (1869–1940) reacted against Antoine with whom he worked in the Théâtre Libre. Member of the famous Parisian 'Cartel' with Baty, Jouvet and Dullin in the inter-war years.
3. See also L. Miller's *The Noble Drama of W. B. Yeats.*
4. Ibid. In an earlier letter to Olivia Shakespear (7 April 1895) Yeats says Maeterlinck 'touched the nerves when he should touch the heart'.
5. See 'Two aspects of language and two types of aphasic disturbance' in *Fundamentals of Language*, The Hague, 1956. D. Lodge in *The Modes of Modern Writing* expands Jacobsen's theory.
6. For a discussion of the relation between Joyce and Dujardin see L. Edel, *The Modern Psychological Novel.*
7. E. Auerbach, *Mimesis.*
8. For an insight into Strindberg's state of mind at this period see his *Inferno.*

(Pages 65–76)

1. 'Incongruity theory'. Kant's theory that laughter was due to the sudden release of tension was developed by Herbert Spencer in 'The Physiology of Laughter'.
2. See A. Norman Jeffares and A. S. Knowland, *A Commentary on the Collected Plays of W. B. Yeats* for Yeats's own observations, drawn from a wide variety of sources.

3. Yeats speaks of *Cathleen ni Houlihan* and his debt to Lady Gregory in the preface to *The Unicorn and the Stars and other plays* (1908).
4. In a note to the play in 1907. See L. Miller, *The Noble Drama of W. B Yeats.*

(Pages 77–90)

1. E. Zola, arguing against romantic theatre in 'Naturalism in the Theatre' asserted that there was more poetry in his brand of realism than 'in all the worm-eaten palaces of Europe . . .'.
2. At the famous premiere of *Guy Domville* (1895). See Leon Edel's biography of Henry James.
3. 'Certain Noble Plays of Japan' in *Essays and Introductions* (1961).
4. Later published in the above.
5. See Tyrone Guthrie's *A Life in the Theatre.*
6. Preface to *Purgatory*, see A. Norman Jeffares, *A Commentary on the Collected Plays of W. B. Yeats.*
7. Recorded under the title: *Homage to T. S. Eliot*, it includes Groucho Marx reading one of the 'Practical Cat' poems.
8. T. S. Eliot, *Music and Poetry.*
9. Ibid.
10. See *Curtains* (1961) or *Tynan on Theatre.*
11. In *Origins of Tragedy.*

(Pages 91–103)

1. Mariano Fortuny (1871–1949) invented a 'skydome', enclosing the stage, which gave the effect of dispersed natural light. Unfortunately it limited the flexibility of the stage by reducing the number of entrances.
2. In 1908 a committee was set up to examine whether a National Theatre in honour of William Shakespeare could be founded by 1916. Garrick first mooted the idea in the eighteenth century.
3. Hughes is best known as the author of *In Hazard, High Wind in Jamaica* and *Fox in the Attic.*
4. Neue Sachlichkeit, usually dated from about 1925. See J. Willett, *The New Sobriety* and his other work on the Weimar period.
5. See Saint-Denis, *Training for the Theatre.*
6. Ibid.
7. Gossip may malign Sir John Gielgud.
8. Described in Piscator's *The Political Theatre* ed. H. Rorrison.
9. Ibid.
10. See the index references in *Brecht on Theatre*, trs J. Willett. The Gestus is the 'gist' of a scene, expressed vividly in word or gesture.

NOTES

11. Much else is omitted – much eastern European drama including the 30 plays of Stanislaw Witkievicz (1885– 1939), the Polish expressionist dramatist whose work anticipated Beckett and absurdist theatre. Like Toller he committed suicide just before the outbreak of World War II.

(Pages 104–112)

1. I take it Polonius's words both mock the fixers of categories and constitute an ironic comment on Shakespeare's own practice of mixing the genres.
2. G. B. Shaw, Preface to *Saint Joan*.

(Pages 113–124)

1. *Un Théâtre de Situations* (1973), translated as *Sartre on Theatre*, contains Sartre's main essays on drama. A fascinating summary of Sartre's career may be found in 'Sartre par Sartre', *Le Nouvel Observateur* (26 January 1970). A further bibliography can be found in R. Lorris, *Sartre Dramaturge*.
2. See Sartre's essay: 'Forgers of Myths' contained in the above.
3. As in *The Resistible Rise and Fall of Arturo Ui*.
4. This is asserted in Sartre's autobiography: *Words (Les Mots* [1964]).
5. *Sartre on Theatre*.
6. See *Words*.
7. Ibid.
8. Sartre is speaking of Heinrich, the unfree priest in *Lucifer and the Lord*.
9. Sartre, 'On Epic and Dramatic Theatre'.
10. Ibid.

(Pages 125–136)

1. *Sartre on Theatre*.
2. Frazer was identified by Leslie Hotson, in a search through parish records, as the man who killed Christopher Marlowe.
3. This play is more fully discussed in the Chapter on Pirandello.
4. See the Chapter on Yeats and Eliot.

(Pages 137–147)

1. Details are published in W. Armstrong, *Experimental Drama*.
2. A remark taken from Arthur Koestler's self-description in *Arrow in the Blue*.
3. In E. Bentley, *What is Theatre?*
4. *Tynan on Theatre*.

225

NOTES

5. The reference to the last line of Eliot's 'Love Song of J. Alfred Prufrock' is deliberate.
6. Engels, letter to Bloch.
7. TV interview with A. Yentob repeated 1990.

(Pages 148–160)

1. Professor C. Watts reminds me that James Dean's *Rebel Without a Cause* (1955) anticipated Osborne's Jimmy Porter by one year.
2. Later the feminist movement would see the play as violently chauvinist.
3. See K. Allsop, *The Angry Decade.*
4. See the chapter thus entitled in Hoggart's *Uses of Literacy.*
5. R. Williams in the introduction to the Penguin edition of Lawrence's plays.

(Pages 161–171)

1. *Brecht on Theatre* ed. J. Willett.
2. Figure taken from a Soviet war film, released after the Gorbachev liberalization.

(Pages 172–181)

1. In Grotowski: *Towards a Poor Theatre.*
2. See the comments on Mike Leigh in the Chapter on Athol Fugard.
3. One actor experienced a form of separation from the body. Another developed a blue aura, visible to Bates, around his head and shoulders.

(Pages 182–192)

1. S. Trussler, *New Theatre Voices in the Seventies.*
2. Ibid.

(Pages 193–203)

1. The terms 'stasis' and 'kinesis' are discussed by James Joyce's character Stephen Dedalus in *Portrait of the Artist as a Young Man.*
2. For further detail and discussion see Alan Sinfield's *Society and Literature 1945–70.*
3. Interview with Bond in S. Trussler's (ed) *New Theatre Voices in the Seventies.*
4. *The Caretaker* is discussed in the Chapter 'Finding a Voice'.
5. Preface to *Saved.*

NOTES

(Pages 204–212)

1. Contemporary French writers still produce plays based on naturalist models. *L'Ourse blanche* (1990) by D. Besnehard is very reminiscent of Strindberg. *Zone Libre* (1990) by J-C Grumberg is more reminiscent of Chekhov.
2. See *King Lear* Act II iv 266–9; Act III iv 34–5.

Bibliography

ACKROYD, R., *T. S. Eliot*, Hamilton, 1984.

ALLSOP, K., *The Angry Decade*, Owen, 1958.

ANSORGE, P., *Disrupting the Spectacle*, Pitman, 1975.

ANTOINE, A., *Mes Souvenirs sur le Théâtre Libre*, Fayard, 1921.

APPIA, A., *Music and the Art of the Theatre*, Miami UP, 1962.

ARCHER, W., *Masks or Faces*, intro. by L. Strasberg, Hill & Wang, 1957.

ARISTOTLE, *Poetics* trs. L. Potts, Cambridge University Press, 1953.

ARMSTRONG, W., *Experimental Drama*, Bell, 1963.

ARNHEIM, R., *Film as Art*, University of California Press, 1957.

ARTAUD, A., *The Theatre and its Double*, trs. V. Corti, Calder, 1970.

AUERBACH, E., *Mimesis and the Reproduction of Reality in Western Literature*, Doubleday, 1953.

BABLET, B. D., *The Theatre of Edward Gordon Craig*, Eyre Methuen, 1981.

BAKER, M., *The Rise of the Victorian Actor*, Croom Helm, 1978.

BARKWORTH, P., *About Acting*, Secker and Warburg, 1980.

BARRAULT, J-L, *Reflections on the Theatre*, Hyperion, 1979.

BARTHES, R., *Image, Music, Text*, trs. S. Heath, Fontana, 1977.

BARTRAM, G. & WAINE, A. E. eds., *Brecht in Perspective*, Longman, 1982.

BATES, B., *The Way of the Actor*, Century, 1986.

BEAUVOIR, S. de, *Memoirs of a Dutiful Daughter*, Deutsch, 1959.

BECKETT, S., *The Complete Dramatic Works*, Faber, 1986.

BENJAMIN, W., *Illuminations*, Cape, 1970.

BENTLEY, E. R., *The Theory of the Modern Stage*, Penguin, 1968.

BENTLEY, E. R., *What is Theatre?*, Methuen, 1969.

BERGMAN, I., *Bergman on Bergman*, Secker and Warburg, 1981.

BERGMAN, I., *The Magic Lantern*.

BERGSON, H., *Laughter*, Macmillan, 1911.

BIDDLE, B. and THOMAS, E., *Role Theory*, J. Wiley NY, 1966.

BIGSBY, C. W. E., *Confrontation and Commitment: a study of contemporary American drama 1959–66*, MacGibbon and Kee, 1967.

BINER, P., *The Living Theatre*, trs. R. Meister, Avon, NY, 1972.

BOOTH, M. ed., *Hiss the Villain: Six Melodramas*, Eyre and Spottiswoode, 1964.

BOOTH, M., *English Melodrama*, Jenkins, 1965.

BRADBY, D., *Modern French Drama 1940–80*, Cambridge, 1984.

BRADBY, D. and MCCORMICK J., *People's Theatre*, Croom Helm, 1978.

BIBLIOGRAPHY

BRANDT, G. W., (ed.), *British Television Drama*, Cambridge University Press, 1981.

BRAUN, E. ed., *Meyerhold on Theatre*, Methuen, 1969.

BRECHT, B., *Brecht on Theatre* trs J. Willett, Methuen, 1964.

BRECHT, B., *Messingkauf Dialogues*, trs J. Willett, Methuen, 1965.

BROOK, P., *The Empty Space*, McGibbon and Kee, 1968.

BROWN, J. R., *Theatre Language*, Penguin, 1972.

CALLOW, S., *Being an Actor*, Methuen, 1984.

CAMBON, G. ed., *Pirandello: a collection of critical essays*, Prentice-Hall, 1967.

CARLSON, M., *Theories of the Theatre*, Cornell, 1984.

CHINOY, H. & JENKINS, L. eds., *Women in American Theatre*, Crown, 1981.

CLURMAN, H.. *The Fervent Years*, Hill and Wang, 1957.

COLE, T., ed., *Playwrights on Playwriting*, Macgibbon, 1961.

COLE, T. and CHINOY, H. eds., *Directors on Directing*, Peter Owen, 1966.

COLE, T. and CHINOY, H. eds., *Actors on Acting*, Crown, 1974.

COLERIDGE, S. T., *Biographia Literaria*, Dent, 1906.

COPEAU, J., *Cahiers du Vieux Colombier*, Paris 1920–1.

COURTNEY, R., *Play, Drama and Thought*, Cassell, 1974.

CRAIG, E. G., *On the Art of the Theatre*, Heinemann, 1958.

CRAIG, S. ed., *Dreams and Deconstructions*, Amber Lane Press, 1980.

DAVIS, J. M., *Farce*, Methuen, 1978.

EISENSTEIN, S., *The Film Sense*, Faber, 1986.

ELAM, K., *Semiotics of Theatre and Drama*, Methuen, 1980.

ELIOT, T. S., 'Rhetoric and Poetic Drama' and 'A Dialogue on Dramatic Poetry' in *Selected Essays*, Faber, 1951.

ELIOT, T. S., *Poetry and Drama*, Faber, 1951.

ELLIS-FERMOR, U., *The Irish Dramatic Movement*, Methuen, 2nd ed., 1954.

ELLIS-FERMOR, *Frontiers of Drama*, 2nd ed., Methuen, 1954.

ELLMAN, R., *Oscar Wilde*, Hamish Hamilton, 1987.

ESSLIN, M., *The Theatre of the Absurd*, Penguin, 1980.

ESSLIN, M., *Brecht: a choice of evils*, Heinemann, 1965.

ESSLIN, M., *Antonin Artaud*, Calder, 1976.

FERNALD, J., *Sense of Direction: the director and his actors*, Secker, 1968.

FINDLATER, R., *Banned*, MacGibbon & Kee, 1967.

FO, D. & RAME, F., *Theatre Workshop at Riverside Studios*, Red Notes, 1983.

FREUD, S., *Jokes and their Relation to the Unconscious*, Penguin, 1976.

FREUD, S., *The Interpretation of Dreams* and *Some Character Types Met With in Psychoanalysis* in *Complete Works*, Routledge, 1960.

FRYE, N., *Anatomy of Criticism*, Princeton, 1957.

FURST, L. R. and SKRINE, P. N., *Naturalism*, Methuen, 1971.

BIBLIOGRAPHY

GEDULD, H. M., ed., *Film Makers on Film Making*, Penguin, 1967.
GOFFMANN, E., *The Presentation of the Self in Everyday Life*, Allen Lane, 1969.
GROTOWSKI, J., *Towards a Poor Theatre*, Methuen, 1969.
HARTNOLL, P., *Oxford Companion to the Theatre*, 4th ed., 1983.
HEGEL, G. W. F., *Aesthetics*, Clarendon, 1975.
HEGEL, G. W. F., *On Tragedy*, ed. H. and A. Paolucci, Harper, 1975.
HENN, T. R., *The Harvest of Tragedy*, Methuen, 1956.
HETHMON, R. H., ed., *Strasberg at the Actors' Studio*, Cape, 1966.
HIRST, D. I., *Dario Fo and Franca Rame*, Macmillan 1989.
HIRST, D. I., *Tragi-comedy*, Methuen, 1964.
HODGSON, T., *Batsford Dictionary of Drama*, 1988.
HODGSON, J. ed., *The Uses of Drama*, Methuen, 1972.
HOLROYD, M., *Bernard Shaw*, Chatto, 1989.
HUIZINGA, J., *Homo Ludens: a study of the play element in culture*, Routledge, 1949.
IONESCO, E., *Notes and Counternotes*, Calder, 1965.
ITZIN, C., *Stages in the Revolution*, Methuen, 1980.
JACKSON, J. A., *Role*, Cambridge University Press, 1972.
JAMES, H., *The Scenic Art*, Hart-Davis, 1949.
JOSEPH, S., *Theatre in the Round*, Barrie & Rockliffe, 1967.
JOSEPH, S. *New Theatre Forms*, Pitman, 1968.
KAMINSKI, S. S. N. and HILL, J. F., eds. *Ingmar Bergman: Essays in Criticism*, Oxford University Press, 1975.
KAPROW, A., *Assemblages, Environments and Happenings*, NY, 1965.
KARLINSKI, S. ed. *Letters of Anton Chekhov*, Bodley Head, 1973.
KAVANAGH, P., *The Irish Theatre*, Blom, NY, 1969.
KEYSAAR, H., *Feminist Theatre*, Macmillan, 1984.
KIERKEGAARD, S., *The Concept of Irony*, Collins, 1966.
KIERKEGAARD, S., *Crisis in the Life of an Actress and other essays on drama*, Collins, 1967.
KOESTLER, A., *The Act of Creation*, Hutchinson, 1964.
KOMISSARZHEVSKI, T., *The Actor's Creative Work and Stanislavski's system*.
KOTT, J., *Shakespeare our Contemporary*, Methuen, 1967.
KOZNITSEV, G., *Shakespeare: time and conscience*, Dobson, 1967.
KUMIEGA, J., *The Theatre of Grotowski*, Methuen, 1985.
KUNDERA, M. *The Joke*, Penguin, 1970.
LABAN, R., *The Mastery of Movement*, revised by L. Ullman, Macdonald and Evans, 1960.
LAUTER, P. ed., *Theories of Comedy*, Doubleday, 1964.
LECOQ, J., 'Le mouvement et le théâtre', in ATAC – information 13, December, 1967.
LEHMANN, A. G., *The Symbolist Aesthetic in France 1885–95*, Oxford University Press, 1968.

BIBLIOGRAPHY

LEWES, G. H., *On Actors & the Art of Acting*, Greenwood, 1968.

LUKACS, G., 'The Sociology of Modern Drama', trs. L. Baxendall, in *The Tulane Drama Review*, 1965.

MCFARLANE, J. W., *Ibsen: A Critical Anthology*, Penguin, 1970.

MCFARLANE, J. W., *Ibsen; the temper of Norwegian literature*, Oxford University Press, 1960.

MACGOWAN, K., *Continental Stagecraft*, Blom, NY, 1964.

MCGRATH, J., *A Good Night Out*, Methuen, 1981.

MAETERLINCK, M., 'Le Théâtre', in *La Jeune Belgique*, 9, 1890.

MAROWITZ, C., *Prospero's Staff*, Indiana University Press, 1986.

MARTIN BROWNE, E., *The Making of T. S. Eliot's Plays*, Cambridge University Press, 1969.

MILLER, A., *Collected Plays*, Secker, 1981.

NIETZSCHE, F., *The Birth of Tragedy*, Doubleday, 1956.

NORTHAM, J., *Ibsen: a critical study*, Cambridge University Press, 1973.

OLIVIER, L., *On Acting*, Weidenfeld, 1986.

ORME, M., J. T. *Grein; the Story of a Pioneer, (1862–1935)*, Murray, 1936.

OSBORNE, J. *The Meininger Court Theatre (1866–90)*, Cambridge University Press, 1988.

PAVIS, P., *Language of the Stage*, Performing Arts, 1982.

PIRANDELLO, L., *Naked Masks: Five Plays*, ed. E. R. Bentley, Dutton, 1952.

PISCATOR, E., *The Political Theatre*, ed. H. Rorrison, Methuen, 1980.

PLATO, *The Republic*, 2nd ed., Penguin, 1974.

PRUNER, F., *Le Théâtre Libre d'Antoine*, Lettres Modernes, 1958.

PUDOVKIN, V. I., *Film Acting*, Newnes, 1935.

ROBINSON, I., *Ireland's Abbey Theatre*, Sidgwick, 1951.

ROWELL, G., *The Victorian Theatre: a survey*, Oxford University Press, 1956.

SAINT-DENIS, M., *Training for the Theatre*, Heinemann, 1982.

SAINT-DENIS, M., *Theatre: the rediscovery of style*, Heinemann, 1960.

SARTRE, J-P., *Sartre on Theatre*, Quartet, 1976.

SHANK, T., *American Alternative Theatre*, Macmillan, 1982.

SHAW, G. B., *Our Theatres in the Nineties*, 3 vols, Constable 1932.

SHAW, G. B. *The Quintessence of Ibsenism*, 1891, Prefaces, 1934.

SHER, A., *Year of the King*, Chatto, 1986.

SINFIELD, A., *Society and Literature 1945–70*, Methuen, 1983.

SPOLIN, V., *Improvisation for the Theatre*, Pitman, 1963.

STANISLAVSKI, K. S., *An Actor Prepares*, Bles 1937.

STANISLAVSKI, K. S., *Building a Character*, 1950.

STANISLAVSKI, K. S., *Creating a Role*, Bles, 1963.

STRINDBERG, A., *The Role of Chance in Artistic Creation*.

STYAN, J. L., *The Dark Comedy*, 2nd ed. Cambridge University Press, 1968.

BIBLIOGRAPHY

STYAN, J. L., *Chekhov in Performance*, Cambridge University Press, 1971.
STYAN, J. L., *Drama Stage and Audience*, Cambridge University Press, 1975.
SYMONS, A., *The Symbolist Movement in Literature*, 1899.
TAYLOR, J. R., *The Angry Theatre*, Methuen, 1969.
TAYLOR, J. R., *The Second Wave*, Methuen, 1971.
TODOROV, T., 'The Origin of Genres' in *New Literary History*, Autumn, 1976.
TROYAT, H., *Chekhov*, Dutton, 1986.
TRUSSLER, S. ed., *Theatre Voices of the Fifties and Sixties*, Methuen, 1965.
TRUSSLER, S., *New Theatre Voices of the Seventies*, Methuen, 1971.
TYNAN, K., *Curtains*, Longman, 1961.
TYNAN, K., *Tynan on Theatre*, Penguin, 1964.
WAGNER, B. J., *Dorothy Heathcote: drama as a learning medium*, Hutchinson, 1979.
WALTON, J. M., *Craig on Theatre*, Methuen, 1983.
WANDOR, M., *Understudies*, Methuen, 1981.
WARDLE, I., *The Theatres of George Devine*, Methuen, 1978.
WELSFORD, E., *The Fool*, Faber, 1935.
WHITING, J., *The Art of the Dramatist*, London Magazine Eds, 1970.
WILLEFORD, W., *The Fool and his Sceptre*, Arnold, 1969.
WILLETT, J., *The Theatre of Erwin Piscator*, Methuen, 1978.
WILLETT, J., *The New Sobriety* (1917–33), Thames and Hudson, 1978.
WILLIAMS, D., comp., *Peter Brook: a theatrical casebook*, Methuen, 1988.
WILLIAMS, R., *Modern Tragedy*, Chatto, 1966.
WILLIAMS, R., *Drama from Ibsen to Brecht*, Chatto, 1968.
WILLIAMS, R., *The Long Revolution*, Penguin, 1965, pp. 271–300.
YEATS, W. B., *Autobiographies*, Macmillan, 1955.
YEATS, W. B., *Essays and Introductions*, Macmillan, 1961.
ZOLA, E., 'Le naturalisme au théâtre', in *Oeuvres Complètes* ed. H. Mittérand, Paris, 1968.

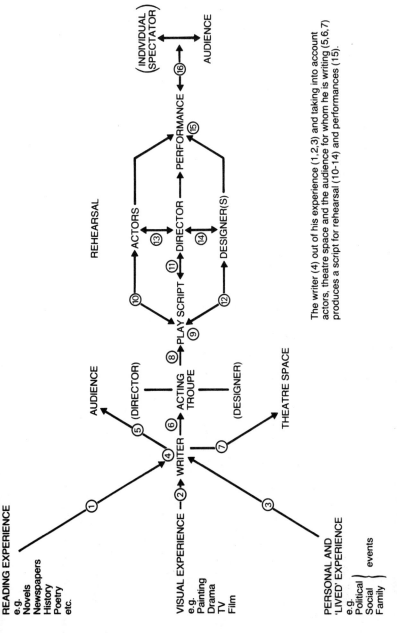

The writer (4) out of his experience (1,2,3) and taking into account actors, theatre space and the audience for whom he is writing (5,6,7) produces a script for rehearsal (10–14) and performances (15).

Diagram A Simplified diagram of the dramatic process

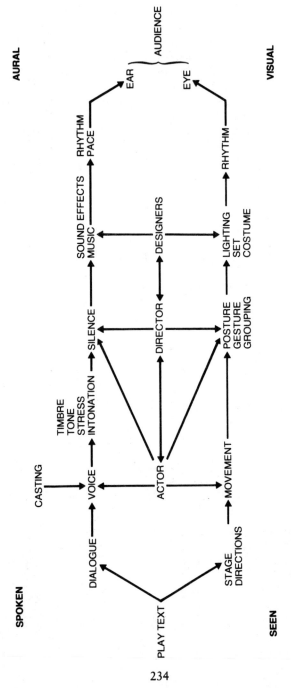

Diagram B Simplified diagram of theatre language

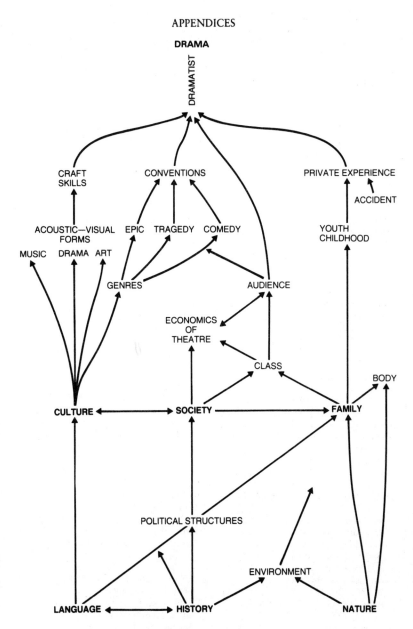

DRAMA

DRAMATIST

CRAFT
SKILLS

CONVENTIONS

PRIVATE EXPERIENCE

ACCIDENT

ACOUSTIC—VISUAL
FORMS

EPIC   TRAGEDY   COMEDY

YOUTH
CHILDHOOD

MUSIC   DRAMA   ART

GENRES

AUDIENCE

ECONOMICS
OF
THEATRE

CLASS

BODY

CULTURE

SOCIETY

FAMILY

POLITICAL STRUCTURES

ENVIRONMENT

LANGUAGE

HISTORY

NATURE

'The artist is like the trunk of a tree.' **Paul Klee**
A simplified pattern diagram of 'roots' which feed into the dramatist
and his work. There has been much debate over the relative importance
of 'language', 'history' and 'nature' in the process.

Diagram C   The roots of drama

Index

In addition to the usual list of authors and works, this index lists references to dramatic techniques and the dominant ideas of the book.

INDEX